Grace Revealed

Grace Revealed

The Message of Paul's Letter to the Romans—
Then And Now

Robert P. Vande Kappelle

WIPF & STOCK · Eugene, Oregon

GRACE REVEALED
The Message of Paul's Letter to the Romans—Then And Now

Copyright © 2017 Robert P. Vande Kappelle. All rights reserved. Except for brief quotations in critical publications or reviews, no part of this book may be reproduced in any manner without prior written permission from the publisher. Write: Permissions, Wipf and Stock Publishers, 199 W. 8th Ave., Suite 3, Eugene, OR 97401.

Wipf & Stock
An Imprint of Wipf and Stock Publishers
199 W. 8th Ave., Suite 3
Eugene, OR 97401

www.wipfandstock.com

PAPERBACK ISBN: 978-1-5326-3090-3
HARDCOVER ISBN: 978-1-5326-3092-7
EBOOK ISBN: 978-1-5326-3091-0

Manufactured in the U.S.A.   APRIL 28, 2017

New Revised Standard Version Bible, copyright 1989, Division of Christian Education of the National Council of the Churches of Christ in the United States of America. Used by permission. All rights reserved.

To Georgia Metsger
a "second-half-of-life" Christian
and
the leaders and members of her study groups:
Helen Benson, Jess Costa, Ray Lengvarsky, Rev. Albert Valentine
and other participants in the churches and communities of western
Pennsylvania

"constantly remembering your work of faith
and labor of love and steadfastness of hope"
—1 Thessalonians 1:3

Contents

Preface | ix

Acknowledgments | xv

Session 1 Introduction and Overview | **1**
  Essay 1: The Reliability of Acts as a Source for Paul's Life and Ministry · 17

Session 2 Reading Romans | **21**
  Essay 2: Paul's Gospel of Grace · 37

Session 3 Grace and Paul's Apostolic Work (Romans 1:1–17; 15:14—16:27) | **42**
  Essay 3: Understanding Paul's View of Justification by Faith · 53

Part I All for Grace: The Unity of Gentiles and Jews | 61

Session 4 The Universal Need of Grace (Romans 1:18—3:20) | **63**
  Essay 4: Understanding Paul's View of Divine Wrath and Judgment · 76

Session 5 The Gift of Grace (Romans 3:21—4:23) | **81**
  Essay 5: Understanding Paul's View of Sin and Salvation · 89

Session 6 The Work of Grace (Romans 4:23—5:21) | **94**
  Essay 6: Understanding Paul's View of the Cross · 106

Session 7 Law, Sin, and Grace (Romans 6:1—7:25) | **111**
  Essay 7: Understanding Paul's View of the Law · 123

Session 8 Spirit and Grace (Romans 8:1–39) | **130**
          Essay 8: Understanding Paul's View
             of "Inaugurated" Eschatology · 140

Part II Grace for All: The Unity of Jews and Christians | **147**

Session 9 Grace in History (Romans 9–10) | **149**
          Essay 9: Understanding Paul's View
             of Divine Righteousness · 164

Session 10 Grace for All (Romans 11:1–36) | **168**
          Essay 10: Understanding Paul's View of Election · 177

Part III All from Grace: The Unity of Jewish Christians and Gentile Christians | **183**

Session 11 Grace and the Community
(Romans 12:1—13:14) | **185**
          Essay 11: Understanding Paul's View of Spiritual Gifts · 195

Session 12 Grace and the Neighbor (Romans 14:1—15:13) | **199**
          Essay 12: Equality: Paul's Vision for Life on Earth · 206

Appendix A: Chronology of Biblical Events | **211**

Appendix B: Guidelines for Leading a Group Bible Study | **214**

Appendix C: The Essentials: Twelve Takeaways From Our Study of Romans | **222**

Bibliography | **225**

Subject and Name Index | **227**

Preface

MY LOVE AFFAIR WITH scripture began at the age of four, lasted through a forty-year career in the field of biblical studies, and has not wavered since. Having completed *Securing Life*, a survey of the Bible that introduces readers to the study of scripture and its enduring message, I return to an earlier focus, adding a fourth volume to my "Then and Now" series on books of the Bible: *Hope Revealed* (on the Book of Revelation, 2013); *Truth Revealed* (on the Gospel of John, 2014), and *Wisdom Revealed* (on the Biblical Wisdom Literature, 2014). The concept "Then and Now" is taken from Matthew's Sermon on the Mount, particularly the antithetical sayings in 5:21–48, where the author introduces paradoxical teachings of Jesus with the repeated formula: "You have heard that it was it was said . . . but I say to you." The contrast is between the old and the new, between the meaning then and now; in sum, between what was believed formerly and what is needed today—for growth, transformation, witness, and mission.

Like earlier volumes, *Grace Revealed* contains commentary plus questions and other aids for individual and group study. It adds a segment on teaching pedagogy (see guidelines for discussion leaders in appendix B) and suggested activities for small groups (found at the end of each chapter). The intent behind the "Then and Now" designation is to create a setting whereby modern students of the Bible, like their first-century forebears, are able to read books of the Bible (in this case the letter to the Romans) as addressed specifically to them, with all the passion, mystery, and apprehension of the original audience, but also, like twenty-first-century Christians, with the desire to understand and apply the biblical message to current issues and concerns. [This latter undertaking is addressed in the essays that conclude each chapter.]

PREFACE

Is it possible to accomplish either task, let alone both simultaneously? Both tasks seem impossible, and one could easily marshal evidence against attaining either goal. Both, however, belong together, and to isolate one from the other promises dire consequences. When individuals, groups, or sects stress the former in isolation from the latter, they might end up looking Amish or like a Gentile version of "Jews for Jesus." Both groups embrace traditionalism, but neither approximates first-century Christianity. The early believers lived in a time of transition, before the church had become an institution, fully doctrinal and creedal. The first Christians were open to newness and change; they were charismatic, led by the Spirit rather than by councils, edicts, pronouncements, and doctrinal statements; they didn't have everything figured out; their Christology, eschatology, and soteriology were in flux, but they were committed to the lordship of Christ, focused on following his example. They looked backward so they could look forward, to the consummation of all things in God's new creation, based on newness, not oldness, on a sense that their lives were part of a great drama that moved toward the creation of "the new heaven and the new earth" (Rev. 21:1), and firm in their belief that such a new creation had already begun. Whatever they envisioned about the coming of God's kingdom, they understood that it was already present, and that it was present on earth—here and now.

The essential message of the New Testament is this: The kingdom of God, though not of this world, has been manifest in this world through the life, death, and resurrection of Christ. Although God's kingdom is a higher order than any political reality or human ideal, it influences and penetrates the kingdoms of this world—not as a tangent touches a circle, but as a vertical line intersects a horizontal plane. The enduring task of the church, understood in part by those early believers, is to bear witness to this "vertical dimension" of history and, in so doing, to seek to leaven and redeem society in the name of Christ. Their attitude toward society was not one of "detachment" but one of "transfiguration," involving a rhythm of withdrawal and return through worship and action, faith and good works. Their openness to the mystery and power of God's presence in their midst must be ours as well.

Is it possible for Christians to live and think like that today? I submit it is not only possible, but essential. However, to do so requires humility and submission. As today's followers of Jesus become less dogmatic, doctrinaire, and intolerant, and yield themselves, their belongings, and their

PREFACE

ecclesiastical institutions to God's transformative grace, they will find their new purpose and identity. Today's church will become the people of God when Christians hear afresh the ancient words of scripture and resolve to love their neighbors—and that includes people of other religions, races, cultures, and sexual persuasions—as themselves (see Rom.13:8–10). Herein is the fulfillment of the law (God's will and purpose for humanity) and herein the relation between first- and twenty-first-century Christians of which we speak: the latter can accomplish even greater things than the former, when they apply anew and afresh the words of scripture. It is my conviction that as twenty-first-century Christians learn to read scripture with first-century eyes, we will impact our world as first-century Christians did theirs, for as Jesus told his followers: Those who believe in me will do the works that I do and, in fact, will accomplish even greater things (John 14:12).

As you embark on this ongoing journey of faith through the study of Romans, my hope is that as you ask, it will be given; as you seek, you will find; as you knock, the door will be opened (Matt. 7:7–8).

Distinctive Features

My goal in this book is to produce a commentary on Romans that addresses the interests and needs of a general Christian audience, providing guidelines for understanding the message of this ancient work and its application to twenty-first century readers. *Grace Revealed* is not an exegetical commentary, for it does not offer verse-by-verse analysis of the text. Neither is it a textual study, in which a scholar makes a case for a preferred reading. Instead it offers perspective on specific topics that arise as one follows the narrative, always with an eye on the big picture, namely, grace for daily living.

Various methodologies are adopted in this study, including:

- Combining deductive and inductive techniques to elicit engagement with the text.
- Questioning biblical literalism and related traditional hermeneutical approaches to scripture (see the discussion in chapter 2).
- Reinterpreting traditional theological paradigms and terms (see, for example, the discussion on the "heaven and hell" paradigm in chapter 2, the "wrath" of God in essay 4, and sin and salvation in essay 5).

- Distinguishing between ancient and current understanding of biblical concepts (see, for example, the discussion on election in essay 10 and spiritual gifts in essay 11).
- Limiting the discussion of Paul's theology and message to his seven undisputed letters.
- Emphasizing the Hebraic rather than the Greco-Roman background for understanding Paul and New Testament Christianity.
- Questioning the usefulness of Acts as a reliable guide to Paul's life and ministry (see essay 1).

Grace Revealed divides the study of Romans into twelve sessions, two introductory sessions and ten on the text itself. My goal is to proceed from text to understanding and from understanding to application. To that end, sessions 3–12 include the following features:

1. summary of the passage
2. homework assignment
3. key verse or verses
4. technical words and concepts
5. main theme
6. learning objectives
7. outline of the passage
8. flow of the argument (narrative section)
9. textual analysis (includes interactive material)
10. essay on a Pauline topic
11. suggested group activity

Teachers and leaders should note that various important resources for group study appear at the back of *Grace Revealed*, including a chronology of biblical events, guidelines for leading adult Bible studies, and a list of essential ideas or takeaways.

Having conducted seminars on Romans with students at Washington & Jefferson College during a forty-year teaching career, I am attentive to the literary form, the context, and the spiritual message of Romans. For the purposes of this study, it is important to address four tasks:

PREFACE

- the outline of the passage;
- the key verse or verses in each passage;
- the movement of Paul's argument (avoiding peripheral matters);
- difficult concepts or ideas as they arise.

Group leaders are encouraged to add or substitute their own priorities or methodologies.

Acknowledgments

WHEN BUCKMINSTER FULLER CREATED the "Knowledge Doubling Curve," he noted that until 1900 human knowledge doubled approximately every century. By the end of World War II knowledge was said to double every twenty-five years. Human knowledge today is said to be doubling every thirteen months, with IBM recently predicting that the evolution of the Internet will lead to the doubling of knowledge every twelve hours.

While the Knowledge Doubling Curve may not apply equally to all types of knowledge, it is nevertheless true that biblical studies have experienced vast change in recent decades, both in methodology and perspective, to the extent that texts on the Bible and on theology—including translations of the Bible—are being revised and updated every few years. This means that scholarly books published thirty, twenty, or even ten years ago need to be read critically, if at all.

Some books, however, whether from antiquity or of more recent vintage, seem to gain relevance with time. The Bible is such a classic, and thanks to recent versions and translations, continues to speak "out of the depths." The ancient words of Qoheleth, the anonymous author of Ecclesiastes, offer a perspective that, countering the Knowledge Doubling Curve, manifests another: "there is nothing new under the sun" (Eccl. 1:9). When these words apply to scholarship, they acknowledge indebtedness to the past. While the present ethos of quest and discovery has led to the transformation of pedagogy in all fields of study, such ethos itself is dependent upon the contributions of the past.

In this study I stand on the shoulders of twelve predecessors, whose ideas have shaped my understanding of Paul in general and of Romans in particular: F. F. Bruce, James S. Stewart, James Moffatt, C. K. Barrett, Paul

ACKNOWLEDGMENTS

Achtemeier, Ben Witherington III, Krister Stendahl, J. Christiaan Beker, Robin Griffith-Jones, N. T. Wright, Marcus J. Borg, and John Dominic Crossan. Their scholarship represents a wide spectrum of views and interpretations, and it is this multiplicity of perspectives—their divergence—that has pulled, prodded, and stretched my understanding of scripture, rekindling my understanding of Paul and his relevance for twenty-first century thinking and living. *Grace Revealed* builds unapologetically on their contributions. My dependence is most transparent in the essays that conclude each chapter.

Because my target audience is lay people unfamiliar with the latest scholarly contributions or debates, my intention is practical. While scholarship is important, its role here is that of a midwife renewing faith and practice.

Over the years I have learned much from students in my seminars on Romans, due in large measure to the participatory format used in those classes. At the end of each term I experienced a renewed love for the subject matter, a new understanding of the message of Romans, and a greater appreciation for the genius of Paul. Writing *Grace Revealed* has renewed my love for scripture, challenged previous conclusions and interpretations, and convinced me that Romans, properly understood, speaks as profoundly to the present as it did to the past.

I dedicate this book to Georgia Metsger and to the leaders and members of her study groups at the Gladden United Presbyterian Church, especially Helen Benson, Jess Costa, Ray Lengvarsky, and Rev. Albert Valentine. A "second-half-of-life Christian," Georgia has helped revitalize her family, church, and friends through Bible study and has inspired me to continue writing. Her friendship and selfless service have resulted in transformed lives and renewed efforts to honor God through faith and devotion.

This commentary could not have been written without the ongoing support and encouragement of my wife Susan. Her demeanor and comportment personify gracious living.

Session One

Introduction and Overview

Summary: Session 1 provides background to Romans, including an outline of the letter and an analogy from football to understand the letter's message. Readers are introduced to the author (the apostle Paul), including his former identity as a pharisaic Jew, his conversion and resultant religious identity as a follower of Jesus Christ, his impact upon Christianity, and an overview and evaluation of his literary output. The concluding essay examines the reliability of the book of Acts as a source for Paul's life and ministry.

Assignment: Read the Preface and Introduction of *Grace Revealed*. [There is no homework from Romans for this session. The assignment for Session 2 asks you to read Romans in its entirety, so the sooner you start, the better.] Answer the following questions, writing the answers in your journal. [If you are in a study group, be prepared to share your views with others in the class.] (a) Briefly explain your understanding of Paul's "gospel" (including his view of God, Jesus, human sin, God's plan for salvation, and God's plan for creation). (b) After you complete the first part of the assignment, write a letter to yourself answering the question: What does God's good news mean to me? (in other words, what is your understanding of God's gospel?).

Technical Terms and Concepts: Pharisees, Sadducees, Sanhedrin, individual eschatology, Messiah, Christology, soteriology, Torah, Gentiles, *paraenesis*, pseudepigraphic, apologetic purpose, apostle, the Twelve

Learning Objectives
After completing this Bible Study, participants will:

INTRODUCTION AND OVERVIEW

1. Demonstrate an understanding of the epistle to the Romans and its message in the original setting
2. Apply a variety of approaches and interpretations to the book
3. Understand, appreciate, and carry out acceptable and effective biblical exegesis (reading "out of the text" its intended meaning)
4. Explain how the book relates to the rest of the Bible and to biblical themes
5. Be able to distinguish between ancient and current interpretations of biblical concepts and thereby to apply the message of Romans to the modern age

At the heart of Christianity and at the center of the New Testament lies the epistle to the Romans, one of the most controversial and perhaps the most groundbreaking letter ever written. When this letter arrived in Rome, hardly anyone read it, certainly no one of influence. There was much to read in Rome—imperial decrees, exquisite poetry, and finely crafted moral philosophy—and much of it was world-class. And yet in short time this letter left those other writings in the dust.

The letter to the Romans takes the life, death, and resurrection of Jesus of Nazareth and thinks through its implications for Gentiles, Jews, and Christians. The author is Paul, an early convert from Judaism and the greatest early figure in the development and spread of Christianity. Romans contains his most cogent and compelling presentation of Christian faith and practice. The author takes logic and argument, poetry and imagination, scripture and prayer, history and experience, and weaves them into a letter that has become the premier document of Christian theology.

In Romans, Paul deals with problems as contemporary as today's headlines: divisions and sectarianism in society; fixation with violence; discrimination, prejudice, and inequality; social injustice; the fate and future of the Jewish people; the role of the individual in the total sweep of history; the responsibilities of citizens to their government; and the morality of actions in which adults engage, sexual and otherwise. After all, Paul is writing to Christians in Rome, and therefore to the political, military, and economic capital of his world, and he could no more avoid such problems than could a Christian today writing to Christians in Washington, D.C.

INTRODUCTION AND OVERVIEW

Paul's Pedigree

From his letters we know that Paul's Jewish name was Saul and that he was born and reared at Tarsus, an important city in the Roman province of Cilicia, in southeastern Asia Minor (present day Turkey). Though Paul was brought up in the strict observance of the Hebrew faith and traditions, his father having been a Pharisee, at an early age Paul went to Jerusalem, where he received religious instruction from the famous Jewish teacher Gamaliel. At Gamaliel's academy he became versed not only in the teachings of the Old Testament, but in the subtleties of rabbinical interpretation. Whether in that setting or elsewhere, Paul acquired a zeal for the traditions of Judaism, bringing him eventually into bitter conflict with the followers of Jesus Christ. Later, looking back on the advantages in which at one time he had taken pride, he described his lineage thus: "circumcised on the eighth day, a member of the people of Israel, of the tribe of Benjamin, a Hebrew born of Hebrews, as to the law, a Pharisee, as to zeal, a persecutor of the church, as to righteousness under the law, blameless" (Phil. 3:6). That's quite a pedigree!

As a Pharisee, he belonged to one of the most prestigious sects in Judaism. Together with the Sadducees, an educated elite who exercised a widespread influence in politics, economics, and religion, they constituted the Sanhedrin, the great council of Jerusalem composed of seventy persons, presided over by the high priest. It was before such a body that Jesus was tried (Matt. 26:59; John 11:47), Peter and John were interrogated (Acts 4:5-7, 15; 5:27, 34), and, toward the end of his ministry, Paul made his defense (Acts 20:30).

Whereas the proportion of Pharisees to the total Jewish population was relatively small (the number of adult male Jews who belonged to the sect of the Pharisees at this time seems to have been around six thousand), they were quite popular with the Jewish masses. While the origin of the Pharisees is uncertain, it is surmised that they came into existence in the second century BC, during the time of the Maccabean uprising. They seem to have come from a group called the Hasidim ("pious or strict ones"), the name possibly derived from the term *porash* or *perisha*, meaning "separated ones." In distinguishing the Pharisees from the Sadducees, the Jewish historian Josephus (AD 37-100) enumerated four doctrines held by the former and denied by the latter:

1. Scripture: The Pharisees recognized as the supreme authority in religion the written Hebrew scriptures as well as the oral tradition (the

accumulated body of pronouncements of Jewish teachers from the time of Ezra), whereas the Sadducees accepted the Torah alone as authoritative, discounting the authority of the prophetic literature, the Writings, and the oral tradition.

2. Determinism: The Pharisees held a doctrine of divine foreordination or predestination, and considered it consistent with human free will, whereas the Sadducees denied that history was divinely controlled, insisting on individual freedom to direct one's life and thus history itself.

3. Individual Eschatology: The Pharisees believed in the immortality of the soul as well as the resurrection of the body. They held that humans are rewarded or punished in the afterlife, whereas the Sadducees rejected these views, affirming that "souls die with the bodies" and that divine rewards and punishments are confined to the fortunes of this life.

4. Spirit Beings: The Pharisees had highly developed views of angels and demons, whereas the Sadducees denied their existence (see Acts 23:6–8).

Though these doctrinal differences distinguished Pharisees from Sadducees, the essence of Pharisaism was its promotion of Jewish piety through prayer, fasting, tithing, giving alms, and otherwise living in conformity to the laws and ordinances of Judaism. Despite their depiction in the New Testament as legalistic, on the whole Pharisees viewed Judaism as a living and evolving religion. Combining conservative and progressive elements, this group alone, of the chief religious Jewish sects, survived the destruction of Jerusalem in AD 70, becoming the basis upon which rabbinic Judaism would be based.

In addition to their piety, the Pharisees prepared the way for Christianity by taking the Old Testament concept of the Messiah and working it into the common Jewish consciousness. Interestingly, it was through the Pharisaic wing, primarily as espoused by Paul, that many distinctive Christians doctrines emerged, including divine inspiration of scripture (2 Tim. 3:16), election and predestination of believers (Rom. 8:28–30; Eph. 1:4–5), bodily resurrection of the dead (1 Cor. 15), and belief in spirit beings. The two most controversial issues, however, which led to Paul's departure from Judaism and to the eventual schism between Judaism and Christianity, were Christological (the person of Jesus) and soteriological (the means of salvation). The Pharisees, stressing the primacy of Torah, limited God's grace to those who keep the commandments.

INTRODUCTION AND OVERVIEW

Paul's Conversion

By his own admission, Paul's first connection with the emerging Christian movement was as a persecutor (1 Cor. 15:9; Gal. 1:13). According to the testimony of Acts, Paul associated himself with the accusers of a faithful Christian named Stephen, guarding the garments of the witnesses as, in conformity with the ancient law, they threw the first stones at his execution (Acts 7:58—8:1). Then he took part enthusiastically in the campaign of repression against believers in Damascus, intending to make them renounce their faith or face trial and punishment.

If Stephen saw the logic of the situation more clearly than the apostles, Paul saw it more clearly than the Pharisees. In the eyes of Stephen and Paul alike, the new order and the old were incompatible. Whereas Stephen might have argued, "The new has come; therefore the old must go," Paul for his part argued, "The old must stay; therefore the new must go." Only on one condition could Paul accept that the customs delivered by Moses might be changed. There was an ancient Jewish tradition, possibly predating Paul, that taught that when Messiah came, he would change the customs or even abrogate the law. But for Paul to believe that Jesus of Nazareth was the expected Messiah was out of the question. It is unlikely that Paul's conception of the status, career, and teaching of the Messiah conformed to that of Jesus. Furthermore, Jesus had been crucified; such a concept contradicted the meaning of the pronouncement in Deuteronomy 21:23 that "anyone that is hung on a tree is under God's curse." Since crucifixion was a Roman form of hanging, although a prolonged and more extreme version, it stood to reason that Jesus could not be the Messiah. The Messiah, by definition, was uniquely endowed with the divine blessing ("The Spirit of the Lord shall rest on him," Isa. 11:2), whereas the divine curse explicitly rested on one who was crucified. To the Jews, the very idea of a crucified Messiah was blasphemous (1 Cor. 1:23). Furthermore, it was believed by the Jews that the coming of the messianic age could be delayed by apostasy within the nation. Thus, as Moses took strong action in Numbers 25 when he hanged chiefs and slayed those who worshipped false gods, so Paul believed that in persecuting Christians he was following a righteous path

With astonishing suddenness, the persecutor of the church became the apostle of Jesus Christ. He was in mid-course as a zealot for the law, bent on exterminating the plague which threatened the life of Israel, when, in his own words, "Christ Jesus made me his own" (Phil. 3:12). What caused this transformation? His own repeated explanation is that he saw the crucified Christ now exalted as the risen Lord: "Have I not seen Jesus our Lord?" he asks when his apostolic credentials are questioned (1 Cor. 9:1), referring to that same occasion later in the same letter where, after listing earlier appearances of Christ in resurrection, he adds, "Last of all, as to one untimely born, he appeared also to me" (1 Cor. 15:8). When, in 2 Corinthians 4:6, he says that "God . . . has shone in our hearts to give the light of the knowledge of the glory of God in the face of Jesus Christ," his language implies a reminiscence of his conversion, described in Acts as having occurred on the way to Damascus, when about midday "a light from heaven flashed around him" and he fell to the ground, hearing a voice say: "Saul, Saul, why do you persecute me?" When Paul asked who was speaking he heard the reply: "I am Jesus, whom you are persecuting" (Acts 9:3-5). This experience of Jesus had a profound and lasting effect on Paul. Blinded temporarily by the preternatural light that shone at creation when God said "Let there be light," Paul witnessed Jesus, the likeness of the glory of the God unveiled at last to him.

No single event, apart from the Christ-event itself, has proved so determinant for the course of Christian history as the conversion and commissioning of Paul. It is so for the author of Acts, who provides three accounts of the conversion (Acts 9:1-22; 22:6-16; 26:12-18). "With no conscious preparation, Paul found himself instantaneously compelled to acknowledge that Jesus of Nazareth, the crucified one, was alive after his passion, vindicated and exalted by God, and was now conscripting him into his service."[1]

Paul's conversion represents a radical shift in his thinking about Jesus and the church. At his conversion Paul learned two things about Jesus: that he was not dead, but alive, and that Jesus was not cursed, but blessed by God. Hence the cross, rather than discrediting Jesus as an imposter, is truly God's provision for humanity and the fulfillment of the promise that through Abraham all nations and peoples would be blessed (Gal. 3:6-9). Jesus was indeed the expected Messiah, but also the "Son of God." This discovery became the subject of his preaching in Damascus (Acts 9:20). As a Christian, he still believed in only one God, but he became convinced that God could only be fully known through Jesus (2 Cor. 4:6). At his conversion he also learned that Christians are not heretics, but God's people. He discovered that in persecuting Christians he had been persecuting Christ (Acts 9:5). That correlation would lead him to one of his most profound

---

1. Bruce, *Apostle of the Heart Set Free*, 75.

insights, that the church was neither a building nor a sect but the "body of Christ" (1 Cor. 12:27). Theologically, the church was a microcosm of the transformation that God's new order would bring for the whole world. To be in the church was to have a foretaste of life in God's kingdom. Socially, the church in the Roman Empire was an alternative society, based on the new freedom and fellowship that Jesus had announced: freedom to love God and to love and serve others (Mark 12:29–31). It must have taken Paul some time to process his new understanding about Jesus and the church, but as far as he was concerned, it was in Damascus that the essential core of his faith as a Christian was first revealed to him.

The Impact of Paul

One of the heroic figures in the life of the early church, the apostle Paul emerged from being an arch-persecutor of Christians into an unrelenting missionary of the gospel. The impact of Paul upon the church was both widespread and permanent. His influence was fourfold:

- the first great theologian of the church;
- the first full-time missionary to the Gentiles;
- the founder of numerous congregations in Asia Minor, Greece, and Macedonia;
- the author (actual or alleged) of a group of letters that now comprise one-fourth of the bulk of the New Testament.

Paul is sometimes called the second founder of Christianity. As the first great theologian of the church, he was both a practical theologian—in that he addressed specific needs arising in the church—and a task theologian. To him belonged the unique task of developing or disclosing a theology for the Gentile church, indicating how Gentiles would be brought into full participation in the fellowship of Christ, what Paul would refer to as "the body of Christ" (Rom. 12:5; 1 Cor. 12:13, 27; Col. 1:18; cf. Eph. 4:4) and "the Israel of God" (Gal. 6:16; cf. Rom. 11:25–26).

The first full-time missionary to the Gentiles, Paul helped bridge the gap as the church became less Jewish and more Gentile in its makeup. Jesus had performed a revolution in religion, recognizing in Judaism a rich spiritual treasure, resulting in a distinct system of worship, a religious way of life, and a high ethical outlook. Yet that treasure was not available to everyone, for Judaism was an ethnic and deeply exclusive faith. Jesus believed himself to be not simply a teacher of truth but the Messiah, through whom God's eternal purpose for Israel and the nations would be fulfilled. This meant that Jesus undertook the task of liberating the spiritual treasure of Israel's faith for humanity. However, his ministry was almost exclusively to Jews, and his faithfulness to God led him to the cross. The work of Christ became entrusted to his followers, who would be empowered by the Holy Spirit to continue the mission Jesus had begun. It is in Paul and his work that we see the task being accomplished. Paul took the work of Christ and set it free from possession by any one ethnic group, sect, or clique. In so doing, Paul remains the classic exponent of the idea of freedom in Christ and of the universality of God's plan for all humanity (see Rom. 3:29–30; Gal. 3:14; 5:1; cf. Eph. 3:6).

Paul also founded new congregations during his missionary travels, providing exhortation, encouragement, and support through letters and personal visits. He helped heal doctrinal and moral difficulties in his churches, providing a form of moral instruction known as *paraenesis* (see, for example, 1 Thess. 4:1–12), such as one might expect to see in the philosophical letters of his day. His letters to the church of Corinth deal with numerous practical issues they were facing, helping later Christians more fully understand the nature of the Christian life.

While not all of his letters remain, by the end of the first century they became preserved through a collection that marks the church's initial Christian canon (see 2 Pet. 3:15–16). As part of scripture they became the most famous and influential set of letters ever written, impacting every major Christian thinker and practically every major revival. Central in the conversion of Augustine and Luther, they held a critical place in their life and teachings. During the Reformation, Calvin patterned his famous *Institutes of the Christian Religion* on Paul's letter to the Romans.

The Paul we encounter in the letters is not a systematic theologian. Quite the opposite. He wrote his letters not to give a compendium of Christian doctrine, but rather to offer practical guidance. He came to herald Christ, not to rationalize him. He came to bring, not a system, but the living Christ. That was his apostle's call, his sole vocation and concern. He was a teacher first and a writer second. His religious position was hammered out, not in the study, but on the mission field. Even a letter as elaborate as Romans should not be construed as a theological treatise designed to set forth Paul's confession of Christian faith, for Romans, like all Paul's letters, is ultimately "not abstract but personal, not metaphysical but experimental."[2] What flows through the head originated in the heart.

Not surprisingly, Paul's phraseology is fluid, not rigid and his terminology—faith, law, spirit—is complex and polyvalent (multi-layered in meaning). Faith can mean "belief" but also "trust;" Mosaic law can be "holy" but also a curse; and spirit, used to denote a person's inner life, can also mean the Spirit of Christ. Paul's readers must remain cautious about constructing theology from fragmentary ideas and restrained in demanding precision from a writer who thinks, as Paul often did, in pictures. As history shows, solitary proof texts create theological mayhem. For example, when Paul mentions predestination, as he does directly in Romans 8:29–30 and indirectly in 9:22–23, it is in the context of God's sovereign freedom and will to save, and we must be careful not to press the metaphor, as Augustine and Calvin and others have done, entangling it with ideas of reprobation and damnation.

When we read Paul's letters, we need to remember that he was not aware when he wrote that his writings would become scripture. He was not mindful that future generations would scrutinize his letters and seek to fit together every thought they contained. He had no idea, when he dictated his letters to an assistant, as was his custom, that centuries later Christians would be building theologies on thoughts and words uttered so precariously. At times his ideas rush so swiftly that they outstrip the flow of his words, and in those places the reader must leap over gaps so as to catch up on his thought. Time and again Paul starts a sentence that he does not complete, for a new thought strikes him and he turns aside to deal with that. His letters are sometimes filled with such lapses that when he returns to the original subject, he has forgotten the start of the sentence. Furthermore, as was the custom of dictation in antiquity, Paul must have given his assistants editorial power to write or complete final drafts of his letters, which explains the strange note found among the greetings at the end of Romans: "I, Tertius, the writer of this letter, greet you in the Lord" (Rom. 16:22).

While Paul had no idea he was writing scripture, there is no denying that he considered his writings to be invested with special authority, and furthermore, that he expected his readers generally to recognize this as factual (1 Cor. 2:16; 7:17; 14:37–38; cf. 2 Thess. 3:14).

---

2. Stewart, *Man in Christ*, 25.

INTRODUCTION AND OVERVIEW

The Pauline Corpus: Which Letters Did Paul Write?

Thirteen of the twenty-seven books of the New Testament are letters attributed to Paul, who helped shape Christian belief, practice, and ethics and was instrumental in the spread of Christianity across the Mediterranean world. Not all were actually written by Paul, but they bear his name. If we add the book of Acts, in which Paul is the main character in sixteen of its twenty-eight chapters, it can be said that half of the New Testament is about Paul. Scholars disagree over which letters were actually written by Paul, suggesting at least three categories: authentic, disputed, and pseudepigraphic. As a way of dealing with this classification, the following views of Pauline authorship have been proposed:

- *Radical Paul* (seven authentic letters): 1 Thessalonians, 1 and 2 Corinthians, Philippians, Galatians, Romans, Philemon
- *Conservative Paul* (three disputed letters; if not Pauline, they are Deutero-Pauline, that is, written by an admirer of Paul): 2 Thessalonians, Colossians, Ephesians
- *Reactionary Paul* (three letters, written by an anti-Paulinist, in order to make Christianity appear compatible with Roman values): 1 and 2 Timothy, Titus.

Paul's authentic letters typically follow epistolary correspondence common in the Greek-speaking world of the first century. Most of these letters are addressed to Christian communities in the northern Mediterranean world, churches Paul visited during his three missionary journeys. The author gives thanks for the people's faithfulness, chastises them for their failings, exhorts them to live as disciples of Jesus Christ, and clarifies his understanding of the meaning of the Christian gospel. Philemon is addressed to a friend of Paul. Three of the letters attributed to Paul but actually written to deradicalize Paul are 1 and 2 Timothy and Titus. Called the Pastoral Letters because of their concern with leadership in the Christian churches, their target audience is other Christian missionaries.

Paul's authentic letters typically follow a customary epistolary pattern, beginning with introductory greetings, followed by the main body of the letter, and ending with concluding remarks, including a word of farewell, a feature that Paul regularly expanded with an expression of blessing and prayer for his readers. The middle section often consists of two parts: doctrinal teaching (sometimes in response to questions raised by his audience), followed by practical teaching or advice concerning the Christian lifestyle. The first part has been labeled "the indicative," because it focuses on what God has done on our behalf, and the practical segment "the imperative," because it focuses on our response to God's initiative. At first glance, this pattern appears in Romans, for Paul opens with greetings, including a reference to himself as author and to his Roman recipients, and states his purpose for writing. The conclusion of Romans contains a farewell, a further statement concerning his purpose for writing, and a personal message to friends. Until recently, the majority of commentators approached Romans that way, viewing 1:17—11:36 as doctrinal and 12:1—15:13 as practical. Now, many biblical scholars question the legitimacy of this approach, finding a mixture of practical and theological concerns throughout Romans.

Like other New Testament documents, the Pauline letters are not arranged chronologically, that is, in the order in which they were written, but rather according to two criteria: length and audience. The first nine letters, written to churches, precede the last four, written to individuals; Romans, the longest letter written to a community, appears first, and Philemon, the shortest letter written to an individual, appears last. The resulting place of Romans is appropriate, not only because it is the longest of Paul's letters, but because it is his most deliberate and reflective letter, and its influence on Christian theology the greatest.

While there is some disagreement among scholars concerning the dating of Paul's genuine (undisputed) letters, the consensus is that 1 Thessalonians came first, making it the earliest written book in the New Testament (c. AD 50), and Romans came last (c. AD 58). If 1 Thessalonians was written during Paul's second missionary journey, the remaining letters seem to have been composed during Paul's third missionary journey, between AD 54 and 58. With the exception of Romans, penned from Corinth and Paul's final extant letter, the remaining letters were composed during his three-year stay in Ephesus, including Philippians and Philemon, written during Paul's Ephesian imprisonment.

The Impact of Romans

The importance of Romans for Christian tradition is incalculable. Each generation of believers has found inspiration, relevance, and transforming power in this letter. In the fifth century, when the Roman empire was floundering and the foundations of that civilization were crumbling, Augustine famously took up Romans when he heard a voice commanding him to "Take and read," and he became convicted, then converted, after reading Romans 13:14. Augustine learned from Romans how to construct a view of human nature and of the state that can survive the breakdown of civilization. In the sixteenth century, at a time when the church exalted itself too highly in its own understanding, Martin Luther and John Calvin learned from Romans how to structure a church in ways that allowed the gracious lordship of God in Jesus Christ to come to clearer expression. Calvin based his systematic theology upon the framework of Romans, identifying this letter as nothing less than the entry point for understanding all of scripture. During the nineteenth century and twentieth centuries, when faith and culture were too uncritically combined, so that the development of human culture and the purposes of God were assumed to be identical, Karl Barth, the era's most outstanding Christian theologian, resisted fascism in general and Nazism in particular when few others were doing so. His theological career was based upon his early study of Romans, resulting in his groundbreaking commentary on that letter, one of the most generative and controversial texts of the twentieth century.

One cannot study scripture without confronting Paul. Fully one quarter of the New Testament is made up of writings bearing his name. One touches the roots of one's Christian faith when one deals with Paul, and nowhere more so than in Romans. To read Romans is to confront one's faith at its source.

Yet this epistle can prove to be as puzzling as any book in the Bible. The letter's dense style and theological nature have provoked enormous controversy and a wide range of interpretation. While some parts remain enigmatic, attentive readers will be pleased to find how much of the book makes sense. Romans, after all, was intended for "lay" men and women in the church, that is, for practicing Christians, and that is the approach this commentary will take. In the spirit of making the message of Paul's letter to the Romans accessible to modern readers, I provide the following whimsical analogy, taken from the game of American football. If you find it useful, consider constructing your own version, or perhaps a better analogy.

INTRODUCTION AND OVERVIEW

Are You Ready for Some Football? Going Deep with Paul's Letter to the Romans

For a long time, baseball was considered America's game, but sometime around the late 1970s baseball was eclipsed by football as America's game. As Mary McGrory, the late Pulitzer-Prize-winning columnist wrote: "Baseball is what we used to be; football is what we have become."

Americans love their football, and what better way to expand our understanding of scripture than by using concepts from this strategic sport to contemporize the meaning of Paul's letter to the Romans, the Bible's most cogent presentation of Christian faith and practice.

Using the outline and storyline of Romans to describe the highlights of our imaginary Super Bowl LXXVII, we might envision the following scenario. Two teams have won the playoffs and are now poised to play in the championship game (known as the Game of Life) for the Newness of Life trophy (see Rom. 6:4). Here's what's at stake:

Victory=eternal life (see Rom. 6:22–23)

Defeat=death (see Rom. 6:21, 23)

Winning Game Plan: "obedience of faith" (see Rom. 1:5; 16:26) and "grace at work" (see Rom. 3:24–26; 5:1–2, 15–17, 20–21; 6:14; 11:6)

The Game of Life

Team Faith (see Rom. 1:16; 3:22, 25–26, 28–31), representing the *LOG (Law of God) Conference* (see Rom. 7:22, 25)

Team Coach: Spirit (see Rom. 8:4–17, 26–27)

Team Owner: Jesus (see Rom. 1:1–7; 5:1–2, 8, 15, 18–21; 8:1; 10:4)

Starting Quarterback: Grace (divine faithfulness, also known as "mercy"; see Rom. 9:16, 23; 11:30–32; 15:9)

Team Flesh (see Rom. 7:14–20; 8:5–8), representing the *LOS (Law of Sin) Conference* (see Rom. 7:23, 25)

Team Coach: Self (see Rom. 7:5, 14–25; 8:5–8, 13)

INTRODUCTION AND OVERVIEW

Team Owner: Satan (see Rom. 16:20)

Starting Quarterback: Law (human effort, also known as "works"; see Rom. 4:4–6; 11:6)

Commissioner of the Game of Life: God Almighty (see Rom. 1:18–32; 2:11; 3:19, 11:29–36; 12:2; 13:1–8, 10–12; 16:26–27)

Game Highlights

[1:1–7] Team Faith introductions: opening words by the sportscaster, Paul of Tarsus, formerly known as Saul the Terminator

[1:8–15] Pregame warmup

[1:16–17] Pregame show: the winning strategy

[1:18–32] Pregame show: the losing strategy

[2:1–11] Coin Toss (Team Spirit wins and defers to Team Flesh)

[2:12–16] Team Flesh offensive players introduced

[2:17—3:18] Team Flesh defensive players introduced

[3:19–20] Opening drive for Team Flesh ends in a fumble

[3:21–31] Opening drive for Team Faith ends in a touchdown: *Score 7–0*

[4:1–25] Sideline interview with former Team Faith greats:

    Former running back Abraham (still holds the running yardage record)

    Former receiver David (still holds the receiving yardage record)

[5:1–21] First Quarter Highlights and Second Quarter Preview

[6:1] Team Flesh drive ends in an interception

[6:2–23] Team Faith drive ends in a touchdown: *Score 14–0*

[7:1–12] Team Flesh drive ends in a touchdown (see 7:11); extra point fails (see 7:12): *Score 14–6*

[7:13–20] Team Faith falters in the Red Zone and fails to score

[7:21–25] Team Flesh drive falters at midfield

[8:1] Team Flesh punts

INTRODUCTION AND OVERVIEW

[8:2–39] A sustained drive by Team Faith before the half ends in a touchdown: *Score 21–6*

[9:1—11:36] Halftime Show: a review of the history of the game of life, including previous playoffs and the recent season

[12:1—15:13] Second-half play, highlighting Team Faith's performance.

Three drives are featured, each ending in a touchdown:

[12:1–21] (touchdown recorded in 12:20–21) *Score 28–6*

[13:1–14] (touchdown recorded in 13:14) *Score 35–6*

[14:1—15:13] (two touchdowns scored, see 14:13 and 15:1–2) *Final Score 49–6*

[15:14–33] Post Game Show

[16:1–23] Closing ceremonies; interviews with fans, coaches, and players

[16:24] Closing words by the sportscast commentator

Outline to Romans

Scholars of the Bible encourage students to outline books and passages they read, both to understand and retain the message as well as to promote involvement with the text. Outlines to Romans are rarely neutral in nature, for they generally incorporate doctrinal, philosophical, or practical concerns. Such outlines can be found in most commentaries on Romans, as well as online. The following outline underscores the centrality of grace. It is my construction and the one I follow in this commentary.

I. Grace and Paul's Apostolic Work	1:1–15; 15:14—16:27
A. In Paul	1:1–7; 15:14–33
B. In Christians at Rome	1:8–15; 16:1–27
C. The Power of Grace	1:16–17
II. All for Grace: The Unity of Gentiles and Jews	1:18—8:39
A. The Need of Grace	1:18—3:20
1. By Gentiles	1:18—2:16
a. Ungodly Gentiles	1:18–32
b. Godly Gentiles	2:1–16
2. By Jews	2:17—3:8

3. By All	3:9–20
B. The Gift of Grace	3:21—4:22
1. The Faithfulness of Christ	3:21–31
2. The Faithfulness of Abraham	4:1–22
C. The Work of Grace	4:23—8:39
1. In Human Nature	4:23—8:17
a. New Life in Christ	4:23—5:21
b. Law, Sin, and Grace	6:1—7:25
(1) Sin and Grace	6:1–14
(2) Law and Grace	6:15—7:6
(3) Law and Sin	7:7–25
c. Spirit and Grace	8:1–17
2. In Cosmic Nature	8:18–39
III. Grace for All: The Unity of Jews and Christians	9:1—11:36
A. Grace in History	9:1—11:36
1. Israel's Rejection	9:1—11:10
2. Gentile Acceptance	11:11–24
3. Israel's Acceptance	11:25–36
IV. All from Grace: The Unity of Jewish and Gentile Christians	12:1—15:13
A. Grace in Society	12:1—15:13
1. Grace and the Community	12:1–21
2. Grace and the State	13:1–14
3. Grace and the Neighbor	14:1—15:13
a. Upholding the Weak	14:1–12
b. Setting a Good Example	14:13–23
c. Serving One Another	15:1–13

INTRODUCTION AND OVERVIEW

Essay 1: The Reliability of the Book of Acts as a Source for Paul's Life and Ministry

In addition to Paul's authentic letters, another source for Paul's ministry and life is the book of Acts, written by the same author who wrote the gospel of Luke. As mentioned above, Paul is one of Luke's heroes, and over half of the book of Acts is about Paul. The literary form of Acts is very different from that of the letters, for it is a narrative, and as such it focuses more on Paul's activity than on his message. It tells us about Paul's conversion, his three missionary journeys, his arrest in Jerusalem and appearances before various officials, and about Paul's winter journey to Rome as a prisoner intent to make his appeal before the imperial court. Because Acts does not report Paul's death, some scholars date Acts to the early 60s, arguing that it must have been written while Paul was still alive. This argument presumes that the purpose of Acts was to provide a record of Paul's life and ministry, but that is clearly not the case. As the author states in Acts 1:8, the plan of Acts is to narrate the account of the spread of the gospel from Jerusalem to Rome. And so Acts ends appropriately with Paul preaching the gospel in the capital of the empire. For the author to have ended with, "And then Rome executed him," would have contravened Luke's apologetic purpose and placed in jeopardy the future of the Christian movement.

There is significant scholarly disagreement about the degree to which the portrait of Paul in Acts is consistently reliable. While there is some overlap between Acts and the letters of Paul, Acts is not always consistent with the letters, making it difficult to assess the historical accuracy of Acts when there is no overlap. Furthermore, scholarly study of Acts leads us to believe that the book was most likely written near the end of the first century, some twenty-five to thirty years after Paul's death. In addition, the author of the two-volume work known as the gospel of Luke and the Acts of the Apostles is not the same "Luke" mentioned by Paul in Philemon 24 or by post-Pauline writers in Colossians 4:14 ("the beloved physician") and 2 Timothy 4:11. There is no persuasive evidence that the author of the two-volume work was familiar with any of the Pauline letters. This "Luke" is writing much later than Paul, for a different audience and with a different intent.

Because many individuals reared in Christianity are taught to take the stories about Paul in Acts literally, it might be helpful here to identify some questionable details from Luke's account.³ The following items are representative of the broader discussion.

1. Paul's *upbringing*. While both Acts and Paul's letters mention Paul's pedigree as a zealous Jew (Rom. 11:1; 2 Cor. 11:22; Gal. 1:14; Phil. 3:5–6; see Acts 22:3; 23:6; 26:5), only Acts provides important information about Tarsus as Paul's birthplace (21:39; 22:3), and only Acts describes Paul's educational status by having him brought up in Jerusalem at the feet of Gamaliel (22:3). The latter claim needs to be examined more closely, however, for the evidence suggests that Paul received his higher education at Damascus rather than Jerusalem. If Gamaliel were his teacher in Jerusalem, Paul seems not to have followed his advice on how to handle dissident Christian Jews. Gamaliel proposed to "keep away from these men and let them alone" (Acts 5:38), whereas Paul persecuted them.

2. Paul's *political (socioeconomic) status*. Whereas Luke insists that Paul was a Roman citizen (Acts 22:25–29; 23:27), Paul himself never mentions that status and seems even to negate it. "Three times," he claims, "I was beaten with rods" (2 Cor. 11:25)—a Roman punishment forbidden to be used on Roman citizens. If Paul was a citizen, he never used that privilege for his own advantage.

3. Paul's *identity as persecutor* of Christian Jews. While Acts and Paul's letters agree that Paul had once persecuted followers of Jesus (Gal. 1:13–14; Phil. 3:6; 1 Cor. 15:9; see Acts 22:3–4), Luke mentions that Paul traveled from Jerusalem to Damascus with high-priestly authority to bring back dissident Jewish Christians for punishment (Acts 9:1–2; 22:4–5; 26:9–12). Such an assertion, according to Borg and Crossan, was impossible, since the Jerusalem high priests lacked any power to dispense capital punishment or exercise trans-border authority. Paul's version in Galatians (Gal. 1:11–17) suggests that he might have been living in Damascus when he persecuted Jewish Christians, but he says nothing about high-priestly authorized travels to Damascus or about bringing Christians back to Jerusalem in chains.

4. Paul's *conversion*. Both Acts and Paul's letters emphasize Paul's conversion, but whereas Luke says Paul only *heard* Christ, Paul insists he *saw* Christ (1 Cor. 9:1; 15:8–9; see Acts 9:4; 22:6; 26:14). The difference is

---

3. The material in this essay is adapted from Borg and Crossan, *First Paul*. For a fuller discussion of the topic, consult pages 59–92 of their work. My intent in this segment is simply to present issues, not debate or resolve them. In the past, literal readings of the biblical text suppressed creativity and led to dogmatic thinking. Exposing students of the Bible to critical readings of the text produces independent thinking and encourages less arrogant pursuit of truth.

significant, not only for Paul, but for our understanding of Paul's call and ministry. It is his sight of Jesus that puts him on a par with the Twelve, an eyewitness—and hence an apostle—of the risen Christ.

5. Paul's *apostleship*. According to Paul, he was an apostle called and sent directly by God—just as the Twelve (generally a term for the original disciples of Jesus)—but according to Luke, Paul had no such status or authority. Whereas Paul claimed to have been sent by personal revelation made directly by God or Christ (Rom. 1:1; 1 Cor. 1:1; 2 Cor. 1:1; Gal. 1:1), Luke's account seems to counter such claims. Although Luke does call Paul an apostle on occasion, in his estimation Paul was only an apostle sent by the community at Antioch (see Acts 13:3) and was therefore subordinate to the apostles at Jerusalem. On the whole, when Luke refers to "the apostles" in Acts, he means "the twelve apostles" named in 1:13 and 26. They are a closed group Jesus called at the start of his public ministry, and into that group Paul could never enter. Paul's claim in 1 Corinthians 15:9, where he calls himself "the least of the apostles," seems to suggest that he considered himself one of the original eyewitnesses of the resurrected Lord, hence one of the Twelve, in the sense of Acts 1:21–26.

6. Paul *missionary strategy*. In Acts we read that Paul's missionary strategy focuses on going into synagogues to convert Jews. That, of course, had been his method during the first missionary journey, led by Paul's colleague Barnabas. Paul tells us nothing directly about this mission, although Luke records it in detail in Acts 13–14. It began at Antioch, with Paul clearly subordinate to Barnabas (see 13:2). On that same mission the crowds, awed by Paul's healing miracle, hail the missionaries as gods. Barnabas they called Zeus and Paul they called Hermes, the latter clearly subordinate to the former. At the end of this mission there was a major apostolic agreement in Jerusalem (the Jerusalem Council of AD 49; see Acts 15:1–35 and Gal. 2:1–10) and a major apostolic disagreement in Antioch (see Gal. 2:11–14), but Luke only speaks of agreement at both Jerusalem and Antioch in Acts 15. The debate at Jerusalem was whether Gentile males who converted to Christianity had to be circumcised, whereas the debate at Antioch was whether a mixed community of Jewish and Gentile Christians should observe kosher rules in their common Eucharistic meals. The result at Jerusalem was a division of labor, with Paul and Barnabas going to the Gentiles and the other apostles going to the Jews (Gal. 2:9). The result at Antioch was a serious breach between Paul and the other apostles and even Barnabas left Paul, who proceeded westward on his own independent

mission. In his account of his mission, Paul always insists that he was divinely called for and to the "Gentiles" (Gal. 2:7–9). If, therefore, Paul went to convert Jews in the synagogue, he was disobeying his missionary mandate from God and contradicting his own calling. We can conclude that when he visited a new city, Paul's strategy was not to go to the synagogue to convert Jews to Christian Judaism, but rather to target Gentile synagogue adherents (the "God-fearers" or "God worshippers"), of whom there were many (in some cases, as many as 50 percent of the attendees at synagogues in Asia Minor were Gentile sympathizers). Throughout Acts Luke uses two different Greek verbs to describe these Gentile synagogue adherents: (1) "those fearing God" (see 10:2, 22, 35; 13:26, 26) and (2) "worshippers of God" (see 13:43, 50; 16:14; 17:4, 17; 18:7). This understanding of Paul's missionary strategy will profoundly impact our reading of Romans.

Questions to Ponder

1. In your own words, explain how Paul's conversion impacted his thinking about God, Jesus, Christians, and God's plan for humanity.
2. In your estimation, which of Paul's contributions had the most lasting impact? Explain your answer.
3. If you could meet Paul and ask him three questions, what would they be? What question would you ask first? Why?
4. Consider constructing your own outline of Romans.
5. What are your takeaways from this session?

Session Two

Ways to Read Romans

Summary: Session 2 explores reading and interpreting scripture. Whether one reads for information, personal formation, or personal transformation, the focus should be on growing spiritually. Since all reading involves interpretation, students of the Bible are cautioned to avoid two pitfalls: reading the Bible literally and reducing biblical language to the fall-redemption framework. Instead, readers are encouraged to use the historical-metaphorical approach, which emphasizes familiarity with the original meaning of biblical and theological terms. This session presents four ways to read and understand Romans: theologically (as a systematic exposition of Paul's faith and beliefs), historically (as an exposition of Paul's theology of history), apologetically (as a defense of Paul's apostolic ministry and call), and therapeutically (as a summons to personal transformation). Readers are encouraged to distinguish between "Paul" and "Paulinism," that is, between his faith and teaching and the elaborate speculative theological systems into which his successors have forced his message. The concluding essay examines the centrality of grace in the New Testament, distinguishing between "cheap" and "costly" grace.

Assignment: Read Session 2 of *Grace Revealed* and Romans in its entirety. Answer the following question, writing the answer in your journal. [If you are part of a study group, be prepared to share your views with others in the class.] Should Romans be read primarily for its doctrinal teaching (what it tells us about our faith), its historical value (what it tells us about the first-century Christians and their context), its apologetic value (what it tells us about Paul and his ministry), or for its spiritual value (what it tells us about our values and priorities and how we are to live as twenty-first-century Christians)? Support your answer.

Technical Terms and Concepts: first- and-second-half-of-life-spirituality, metaphorical, hermeneutical, literalism, fall/redemption paradigm, fundamentalism, historical-metaphorical approach, creation spirituality, diatribe, justification by faith, inaugurated eschatology, Paulinism, Jerusalem Council, Judaizers, Apostolic Decree, Levitical, Mosaic law, legalism, cheap grace, costly grace

Learning Objectives

In this session participants will examine:

1. Three ways to read scripture: for information, formation, and transformation
2. The difference between reading scripture literally (the fundamentalist approach) and historical-metaphorically, and why the latter is preferred
3. The difference between the "fall and redemption" paradigm (original sin) and creation spirituality (original blessing), and why the latter is preferred
4. Four ways to read Romans: theologically, historically, apologetically, and therapeutically
5. The nature and place of grace in the New Testament

Reading Scripture: Three Approaches

People read the Bible for many reasons: literarily (as great literature), philosophically (as a guide for moral and reflective thought), theologically (as a compendium of truth), or devotionally (as a resource for meditation and a source of comfort). Despite the Bible's widespread scriptural use, most devout people read it only occasionally, and superficially. How people read it is perhaps more important than why they read it. For those who wish to engage with scripture seriously and in depth, I recommend that you find a method of study that works for you, whether individually or with others, and commit to it. Of many valid ways of reading scripture, the following are recommended:

- Reading for *information*—to learn as much as possible about the setting of the authors and their primary audience in order to discover the original meaning of a particular passage of scripture and its potential application.
- Reading for *formation*—to establish your identity, values, and beliefs in order to live meaningfully, joyously, and securely; this approach to scripture provides perspective for first-half-of-life tasks, for doing your "survival dance."
- Reading for *transformation*—to provide resources for developing soulcentrically, aligning more deeply with one's powers of nurturing and creating, presence and wonder; this approach to scripture provides perspective for second-half-of-life tasks, for doing one's "sacred dance."

Of course, it is quite possible for these approaches to overlap, due to the complexity of our intellectual, theological, and spiritual needs. It is equally possible that biblical passages convey messages appropriate to our varied abilities and needs. Scripture is multivalent, meaning that it's message allows for multiple interpretations. While one text might strike terror in the heart of an unrepentant person, the same passage might exhort devout believers to greater faithfulness and even greater freedom. When you read Romans, particularly in a group setting, keep in mind the possibility that biblical passages contain multiple messages, depending on one's needs, temperament, and spiritual journey. Scripture, like a good smorgasbord, provides healthy options for different appetites. And you don't always have to eat the same food; sometimes a change of diet can be helpful.

As Paul showed in 1 Corinthians, the important thing is to keep growing spiritually. Paul's concern with the Corinthians was that they were in a state of spiritual immaturity, unable to eat solid food. It takes time—and conscious effort—to grow spiritually, from egocentrism (first-half-of-life spirituality) to soulcentrism (second-half-of-life spirituality). For Paul, how people hear and read scripture (eat spiritually) reflects their spiritual maturity.

Grace Revealed is grounded in the conviction that humans have the capacity to transcend conventional understanding of scripture, exhibiting a genuine and wholesome faith that is dynamic rather than static, future-oriented rather than past-oriented, and affirmed rather than passively acquired.

Interpreting Scripture:
The Historical-Metaphorical Method

Literature invites interpretation; significant literature demands it. This is particularly true of scripture, its truth claims fraught with meaning and therefore open to investigation. There is no such thing as a noninterpretive reading of the Bible. Reading the stories of creation or the stories of Jesus' birth literally involves an interpretive decision equally as much as does the decision to read them metaphorically. When we speak of meaning in relation to a biblical text, five levels come to mind: (1) what the Spirit of God intended and intends; (2) what the human author intended (this concern should be important to all readers, conservative, moderate, and liberal alike); (3) how biblical scholars and theologians interpret a particular passage or verse (their views, both ancient and modern, are readily available in commentaries, handbooks, Study Bibles, and other interpretive aids. Those interested in breadth of insight should consult works from across the denominational and theological spectrum); (4) how leaders in one's church or denomination interpret a particular passage or verse; and finally, (5) what the text means to you. This final level, while indispensable, should not be arrived at quickly. Without the corrective of the other levels, this approach to the Bible can result in as many meanings as it has readers. This postmodern approach, based on the belief that "the meaning of a text is what it means to me," lacks hermeneutical validity.

We who read the Bible need assistance, a method to help us discern how to hear and value its various voices. When we read scripture, we encounter historical, linguistic, social, and cultural gaps between the ancient and modern worlds, barriers we must overcome if we are to understanding the original meaning of the text. In addition, each of us approaches the text with some preunderstanding of the subject. Those who read the Bible only from the perspective of their immediate personal circumstances, who forget that the passage was originally written for someone else, can easily misunderstand what the text says.

Biblical terms such as "sin" and "salvation" are familiar to Christians. Loaded and multilayered in meaning, they have been central to Christian vocabulary from the beginning. Yet both are easily misunderstood. The misunderstandings flow from two major causes: the first is the literalization of language in the modern period, and the second is the interpretation of Christian language within a common framework called "Fall and

Redemption theology" or the "heaven and hell paradigm." Both approaches seriously diminish and distort the meaning of Christianity.

Biblical literalism typically accompanies an understanding of the Bible as the inerrant and infallible revelation of God. About half of American Protestants belong to churches that teach this view of revelation. Like Christians in general, they affirm the Bible is the "Word of God" and inspired by the Holy Spirit. But they draw on a way of reading the Bible that distinguishes them from other Protestants and from Catholic and Orthodox Christians as well as from the first Christians. Here is the logic they use: "A perfect God would not inspire an imperfect Bible. The inspiration of the Bible gives it a divine guarantee of being true—literally, factually, and absolutely. If the Bible says something happened, it happened. If it says something is wrong, it's wrong."[1] The impact of biblical literalism on Christianity is immense. Christians who think that the Bible is inerrant and to be interpreted literally have contributed—consciously or unconsciously—to many harmful ideologies, including racism, sexism, nationalism, and exclusivism, simply because the Bible contains passages that display such attitudes. Furthermore, this way of reading scripture has convinced some Christians that science and religion are fundamentally irreconcilable.

Because many Christians think that biblical inerrancy and its literal-factual-absolute interpretation are traditional and orthodox, it is important to dispel this error. This understanding of the Bible and Christian language is quite recent, going back to the Enlightenment, when religious authority came into conflict with the birth of modern science and scientific ways of knowing. To counter modern scientific and philosophical thought, many Christians adopt a *fundamentalist approach*, identifying religious truth with factuality.

Mainstream biblical scholarship provides an alternative way to understand Christian language that is richer and fuller and does not create the intellectual stumbling blocks generated by literalism. This way of reading scripture, known as the *historical-metaphorical approach*, emphasizes setting biblical and theological terms in their original context. It asks what these concepts meant for the ancient communities that used them, what they meant *"then."* What, for example, did "sin" and "salvation" mean for ancient Israel? For Paul? For the first Christians? This approach asks what words like "Lord," "Son of God," and "Savior" meant before they were applied to Jesus, and therefore what they might have meant to Paul and to the

---

1. Borg, *Speaking Christian*, 21–22.

first Christians. To recognize that biblical language and Christian theology are relative and not absolute has a negative meaning to Christians who fear that such an approach leads to a loss of faith. But the word "relative" also has a positive connotation, for it enables us to ask new questions and to gain new insights. Instead of asking "What does the Bible say?", as if that settles everything, we are led to ask, "Given what their words meant for them then, what might their meaning be for us now?" For Christians who affirm biblical inerrancy and literalism, letting go can be frightening and unsettling, for it means letting go of certainties. For many others, it has been an experience of liberation.

The second adjective in the historical-metaphorical approach takes seriously that religious language often has a more-than-literal, more-than-factual, more-than-historical meaning. This is its metaphorical meaning. Metaphor is about "the surplus of meaning" that language conveys. Metaphorical meaning is not inferior to literal-factual meaning, but superior; not "less than," but "more than." The justification for a metaphorical approach is found in the Bible, for much of its language is overtly metaphorical. To speak of God as a rock, for example, is to speak metaphorically; likewise, to speak of God's anger. Something more or something else is certainly intended. To speak of what theologians call God or God's will, or of what philosophers call absolutes or "ultimate concerns," requires human language, which is ultimately inadequate.

In his seminal work *Original Blessing*, Dominican scholar Matthew Fox calls for a paradigm shift in religious thinking about human origins and the nature and destiny of human beings, from the fall/redemption paradigm to creation spirituality. Fox argues that the fall/redemption paradigm, based upon the doctrine of original sin, developed during medieval times and is essentially foreign to scripture. This tradition, dualistic and patriarchal, considers all nature "fallen" and does not seek God in nature. This tradition does not teach believers about creativity, justice-making, and social transformation, or about the God of play, pleasure, and delight. This tradition has proven unfriendly to artists, prophets, science, and women.

Creation spirituality, on the other hand, begins with original blessing, embodying the biblical emphasis on the goodness of creation. Fall and Redemption theology begins with original sin and ends with redemption. Creation theology begins with original blessing and flows to all subsequent blessings, including those we share with our loved ones and those we affirm in creativity, compassion, birthing, and justice-making; all are prefigured in the grace of creation. Creation spirituality does not ignore sin, but views it differently. Boredom, depression, arrogance, violence, addictive behavior—these occur when we get cut off from the sense of grace and blessing. Original sin is not "original" or primary in time or in biblical theology but derived. Evil is conceived as neither original nor eternal, but rather as something good gone bad.

Hope for humanity and the future of our planet must be based on a proper understanding of the doctrine of creation, one that is not antithetical to science but rather is the subject of the scientist's search, the source of the prophet's vision, and the subject of the mystic's commitment. According to Fox, the universe loves us every day, and the creator loves us through creation.

Reading Romans: Four Approaches

Paul's letter to the Romans, his masterpiece, is unique among his writings in that it is the only letter he wrote to a church that he did not himself establish, thereby appearing less situational than his other letters. Other than Romans, Paul wrote letters as an apostle and leader responding to situations of crisis that developed in churches he had founded. In those other letters Paul wrote to protect, correct, or strengthen some aspect of the gospel in the life of a particular congregation that was at risk. Romans appears to be an exception to this pattern. It does not seem to arise from an occasion that has been forced on him. There is no prolonged defense of himself, as in Galatians or 1 and 2 Corinthians, and no clear counterattack on those who oppose his work.

In the vast sweep of its subject matter, Romans surveys the will of God for all humanity, from Adam to the close of history. Its style, rich and varied, fluctuates from measured arguments to imaginary dialogues (known in antiquity as a "diatribe"), with resolutions rich in poetry. Its structure, equally majestic, has been likened to a mountain range marked by peaks of great splendor. Romans represents a letter of extraordinary complexity, problematic for its original audience and equally challenging for modern interpreters. Almost every paragraph has given rise to a scholarly book, and each climactic passage to dozens. The letter, properly understood, requires the joint effort of mind, heart, and imagination. To fully understand its purpose, at least four readings are needed, the first *theological* (the letter represents a summary of Paul's faith), the second *historical* (the letter represents Paul's theology of history), the third *apologetic* (the letter represents a defense of Paul's gospel and apostolic calling), and the fourth *therapeutic* (the letter represents a summons to personal transformation).

While the first approach has been the most commonly used, the second has emerged to rival the first; the third continues largely neglected and the fourth often overlooked. Because all characterize Paul's intent, this commentary will incorporate each methodology.

Theology: The First Way to Read Romans

This way to read Romans, as a summary of Paul's faith, is the traditional and most popular way. Those who follow this approach find the doctrinal theme announced at the beginning of the letter ("the righteousness of God is revealed through faith," 1:17), developed in succeeding chapters, and then applied to various problems and situations. Following his theme, Paul starts his theological section by addressing the human problem, the universality of sin (1:18—3:20). Paul envisioned the proximity of the Day of the Lord, the day of God's judgment. All humans, without exception, fall short of God's standards and face the wrath of God. But God has revealed a way by which sin can be defeated, through the death of Jesus. The cross is God's means of reconciling humans to himself, through faith in Christ. Faith is the only means by which sinners may be reconciled to God, that is, restored to proper relationship with God. Those who believe in Christ are justified (are made righteous). By trusting in Christ, sinners enter the realm of Christ's power and protection and are no longer under the reign of sin that the law condemns. God's plan is to glorify all believers in the end. The letter concludes with a practical section that demonstrates the results of righteousness in everyday life.

The structure of Romans, viewed theologically, has been likened to that of a mountain range, marked by peaks of tremendous grandeur. The first peak of distinction is said to appear in 3:21-22, with the announcement of the great theme of "justification by faith in Christ." Here we have God's solution to the universality of human sin. Chapter 5 begins the transition to the next section, the salvation (reconciling grace) God is bringing those who trust in God through Christ and his atoning death (5:1-11). Paul then contrasts two ways of life: life in Adam, which leads to death, and life in Christ, which leads to eternal life (5:15-21; 6:22-23). Paul explores these two ways of life in chapters 6 and 7, followed by a chapter of triumph:

"There is therefore now no condemnation for those who are in Christ Jesus. For the law of the Spirit of life in Christ Jesus has set you free from the law of sin and of death" (8:1–2). We begin to think, as chapters 5–8 draw to a close, that the letter has run its course. The mountain peak at 8:28–39, at the center of the range, towers above the hills and valleys on either side. Nevertheless, one final peak awaits. Paul starts his next section, chapters 9–11, with quite a different tone: "I have great sorrow and unceasing anguish in my heart" (9:2). Three chapters on God's sovereign plan for Jews and Gentiles lead to one final peak (11:25–36), the clearest climax of all. The letter closes with instructions about payment of taxes, eating various foods, and the dangers of disunity. This summary highlights the theological approach to Romans.

The problem with the doctrinal approach is that one must identify a doctrine or theme that applies to the letter in its entirety, and that has proven to be difficult. For example, those who consider soteriology (sin and salvation) central to Paul's argument emphasize "justification by faith" as the letter's main concern, viewing chapters 1–4 as the key to Romans. Those who find sanctification (regeneration) central to Paul's argument generally emphasize "life in the Spirit" or "being in Christ" as the letter's main concern, viewing chapters 5–8 as the core of Romans. If "inaugurated eschatology" is central to Paul, particularly how Christ has come to make all things new, then perhaps Romans 8 might be the key to Romans. Those who find "ecclesiology" or "the church's mission" central to Paul's theology, particularly God's inclusive plan for Jews and Gentiles, consider Romans 9–11 as key. Those who consider "Christian service, practical morality, or communal ethics" central to Paul's theology generally focus on Romans 12–16. Approaching Romans this way creates more problems than it solves, for it fails to deal adequately with the totality of Romans, subjectively dismissing remaining texts as secondary or parenthetical. How one reads Romans usually reflects how one understands Paul's theology and his contribution to the Christian faith. And how one understands Paul's theology impacts how one reads Romans.

While it is true that Paul's letters touch on a great many theological topics, individual and corporate, it is important to distinguish between "Paul" and "Paulinism," that is, between his faith and teaching and the elaborate speculative theological systems into which his successors have forced his message. While Paul's letters clearly exhibit a reflective element, whether regarding the nature of sin and salvation, the meaning of the cross and resurrection, the place of Torah and Israel in God's plan, or the role of ethics and the sacraments in the life of the church, Paul is never concerned with these as isolated topics, but only as they related to a way of life focused on the lordship of Christ. His encounter with the risen Christ at Damascus set the tone for his faith; from then on experience was primary, reflection secondary.

When Paul composed his great "Hymn to Love" in 1 Corinthians 13, he began by distinguishing between vital faith in Jesus Christ, as it had gripped his own experience, and various forms of religion that would impinge upon Christianity ever since:

- "If I speak in the tongues of mortals and of angels"—that is religion as *emotionalism*;
- "If I have prophetic powers, and understand all mysteries, and all knowledge"—that is religion as speculation, as *intellectualism*;
- "If I have all faith, so as to remove mountains"—that is religion as *fanaticism*;
- "If I give away all my possessions"—that is religion as *humanitarianism*;
- "If I hand over my body so that I may boast"—that is religion as *asceticism*.

Paul repudiates these religious approaches as one-sided, inadequate representations of the gospel, yet historians and theologians have frequently depicted him as the embodiment of the very things against which he strove. History has given us Paul the ecstatic visionary, Paul the speculative theologian, Paul the organizer and ecclesiastic, Paul the humanitarian moralist, Paul the mystic, Paul the ascetic. Of these portraits, the most unfortunate has been the second: Paul the dogmatist, the doctrinaire thinker, the systematic theologian. Paul's worst enemy through the centuries has not been Paul, as many of his detractors have claimed, but Paulinism.[2]

Historical Theology: The Second Way to Read Romans

An alternative approach, a variant of the first, addresses the problem of disobedience, sin, and salvation corporately, rather than individually, and historically, finding the basic logic of Paul's argument drawn from the

2. Stewart, *Man in Christ*, 1–2; for further discussion on this topic, see Stewart's presentation on pages 1–31.

way history is guided by God. If, for example, the Jews were God's chosen people, with whom God communicated uniquely, that relationship would have to be taken into account in any understanding of how God presently communicates both with the Jews and with non-Jews. If the majority of God's chosen people rejected Jesus as Messiah, that too will be of great importance for understanding both the way God deals with disobedience and the way God keeps his promises. In other words, if Paul's argument in Romans is structured historically, then the place of the Jews in that history will be significant in Romans and will influence how one makes sense of the epistle.

In a recent study, Marcus Borg and John Crossan contend that the subject of Romans is God's passionate desire to heal a world divided along ethnic, cultural, and religious lines. Taken this way, the letter concerns the unification of the three great divisions in Paul's world: Gentiles and Jews (1:16—8:39); Jews and Christians (9:1—11:36); and Christian Jews and Christian Gentiles (12:1—15:21).[3] Considering how the divided human world can become once again the divine world, Paul begins with the widest focus and then successively narrows his parameter. History viewed individually highlights the blessings of individuals' reconciliation with God. History viewed corporately highlights the blessings of such reconciliation for nations and groups, religiously, racially, socially, economically, sexually, and so forth. God's passion for reconciliation—whether of rich and poor, conservatives and liberals, gays and straight, whites and people of color, citizens and refugees, religious and non-religious people, drug-free and drug dependent folks, educated and under-educated, privileged and marginalized, Jews and Gentiles, Christians and Muslims, Israelis and Palestinians, people in the First World with counterparts in the Third World, Democrats and Republicans, Libertarians and Socialists, and everyone in between—must become our passion.

Apologetics: The Third Way to Read Romans

Despite the letter's sustained argumentation and relatively calm exposition, Paul was not as immune to circumstances when he wrote to Rome as we might think at first. To understand how this is so, we must explore an issue that dogged Paul throughout his career, namely, the charge of libertinism or

---

3. Borg and Crossan, *First Paul*, 158. The authors develop this concept on pages 159–81.

moral laxity. The question was not so much whether Paul lived immorally, but whether his Gentile converts were falling short of divinely instituted standards.

The whole issue of the growing number of Gentile converts, including Paul's approach to Gentiles, disturbed not only the leaders of the Jerusalem church, but many of the Jews whose synagogues Paul visited during his travels. The issue had been addressed at the Jerusalem Council. According to Luke's version in Acts 15, the council had been summoned to decide whether circumcision was necessary for the salvation of male converts. Some Jewish Christians (dubbed "Judaizers") were proclaiming that male converts couldn't be saved (that is, couldn't live in faithful covenant with God) unless they were also circumcised, since the Torah required circumcision of all Jewish males. Was God's covenant no longer in effect? Had God's laws been abolished? In effect, the Judaizers' argument seemed to demand that Gentiles first become Jews before becoming Christians. After much debate, the consensus was that Gentile believers not be burdened with keeping all the requirement of the Torah, particularly that of circumcision. The council ended with the Apostolic Decree, which laid down four conditions for Gentile membership in the church (see Acts 15:29). Three related to food: The Gentiles must abstain from food sacrificed to idols (this was particularly offensive to the Jews as a sign of idolatry) and from food improperly killed in either of two ways (slaughtered by strangulation or without draining out the blood). The fourth forbid improper sexual relations (immorality). These four conditions are closely related to the four Levitical commands that are said to be binding on Jews as well as on Gentiles who lived among them (see Lev. 17:8–13 and 18:6–30).

The decision placed minimum restriction on Gentile converts and asked only that they avoid being a stumbling block to Jews. It granted freedom to Gentile converts from the observance of the Mosaic laws as a requirement for church membership, but it also cautioned converts not to misuse their freedom so as to scandalize Jewish Christians by participating in customs that might be offensive. By refusing to impose on Gentile converts the ritual act of circumcision and the observance of Mosaic ceremonial rules as a means of salvation, the council opened the way for the establishment of a truly universal Christianity, not tied to any ethnic or national group. That was good news for Paul, who felt free to undertake his independent mission, but bad news for his opponents, who felt he was misusing his freedom and encouraging his followers to do so as well.

In his letters Paul seems to walk midway between legalism (the views of the Judaizers) and libertinism, two extremes of an ethical nature prevalent in the early church. In writing to the Galatians Paul used the language of opposition, of flesh over against Spirit (see Gal. 5:16-26), because he had to detach his converts from legalism. But in writing to Corinth, plagued by divisiveness, he used the language of unity, of the single body that he was writing to unite (1 Cor. 12:12-13).

Because factions were dividing the churches in Corinth, Paul's own version of the gospel had been used to stir up trouble wherever he went. Whereas he left no doubt over his position in Galatia, lashing out against his opponents (see Gal. 3:1; 5:12), in Corinth he adopted a quite different approach. The slogan at Corinth: "All things are lawful for me" (1 Cor. 6:12), almost certainly derived from Paul's own teaching, led to sectarianism and licentious behavior. The problem at Corinth was not that one group was right and the other wrong, but rather lay in the fact of the dispute. The church, the body of Christ, was in danger of breaking up. This was the crisis, and all the groups in Corinth were culpable. What mattered there, above all, was to reconstitute the believers as a unity. Paul fears factions will divide believers in Rome as well.

Those who give priority to apologetics in Romans note that here, as in Galatians, Corinthians, and other of his letters, Paul is responding to claims about his gospel that he fiercely denies. Claims have been made by detractors, including by those who thought they might have found in Paul an ally, that Paul had forsaken the Jewish Torah (law), and this would have scandalized Jews and many God-fearers. Therefore Paul makes their attack, their misunderstanding of his gospel, the starting point for his letter, taking his readers in Rome across terrain that they rather than he had chosen.

"I am not ashamed," he says at the beginning of Romans, "of the gospel" (1:16). His approach makes it sound like he is responding to criticism. Could this gospel, then, be shameful? His opponents claim he belittles the Jewish law and encourages wrongdoing. Such a gospel, as Paul maintains, would be shameful. So he must make clear at the outset that he does not favor ungodliness or wrongdoing, or, as we might say today, that he is not "soft on crime." To distance himself from such error, he links God's justice with its counterpart, God's anger, right from the start. Paul moves into an elaborate condemnation of wrongdoing; there is no siding with evil here. From the outset, then, Paul's letter is shaped by his need to correct the rumors of his libertine stance.

Where his opening attack emphasized unconverted pagans, the next section addresses Jews. So who escapes Paul's direct attack? Only those converted pagans who have renounced idolatry and pagan immorality without taking up observance of the Jewish law, for this is just the group that shows the faith and lifestyle Paul seeks to nurture. Because they have in Christ the image of the one true God, they need no other images, no statues, and no Levitical regulations.

Paul's argument in chapter 3 makes room for a sly counterargument. If our wrongdoing serves to confirm the faithfulness of God, what is wrong with the wrongdoing? Paul sets up a dialogue with an imagined objector who pursues this line of thought (3:5-9). Paul eventually mounts a full response. The power of wrongdoing, he says later in Romans, is vastly strengthened by the arrival of the law (5:20). All the more, therefore, is achieved by the countering grace of God. In chapter 6 he raises another question: "Should we continue in sin in order that grace may abound"? Paul settles that question, but must confront its corollary: "Should we sin because we are not under law but under grace" (6:15)? His rebuttal of these two questions leads to the very heart of the letter.

But these questions and their answers—the whole central section of Romans—do not settle the issues raised in that early exchange about God's righteousness. Paul turns to it yet again in chapters 9–11. The matter of Israel in God's plan, the question of God's faithfulness to the promises to the Jews, is not for Paul, abstract. The rhetorical questions in this section, raised over and over, followed by indignant answers, serve the same purpose as before: every time they appear, Paul is rebutting the same rumor—that his gospel implies injustice in the justice of God.

The issue of Paul's reputation and gospel continue in the closing section, where Paul addresses the unity of Jewish and Gentile Christians, fearful that factions might divide the churches in Rome, as they had done at Corinth. Once more his gospel is at the heart of the matter. The solution, he states, is the equality of believers in the body of Christ: "Let us therefore no longer pass judgment on one another, but resolve instead never to put a stumbling block or hindrance in the way of another" (14:13).

Personal Transformation: The Fourth Way to Read Romans

A fourth way to read Romans focuses on metaphors used to describe the journey of Christian discipleship: sin to salvation, tragedy to triumph, despair to hope, alienation to reconciliation, defeat to victory, death to life, darkness to light, weakness to strength, effort to grace. Each requires transformation by God's Spirit and all are appropriate to Paul's perspective in Romans. In this letter, to our knowledge his final correspondence, Paul sets out not just to describe, ground, or defend his gospel, but to demonstrate its effectiveness as God's power at work in his listeners and readers. The good news is "the power of God for salvation [deliverance] for everyone who has faith" (Rom. 1:16), and Paul's letter is that power in action. To hear/read Paul's letter, to internalize its message, is to be transformed by it. While some read Romans theologically, historically, or apologetically, this way focuses on personal growth and spiritual transformation.[4]

This way to read Romans examines the same literary terrain as before, only it moves Christians step by step to a new understanding of their destiny. Why does Paul begin the letter with a tirade against idolatry? Because humans have taken the glory of God, in whose image they are made, and exchanged it for a power or ambition of this world. Elaborating on idolatry and its corollary, immorality, Paul eventually grasps an important metaphor in 1:28, to which he will return repeatedly throughout the letter: a vast delinquency of mind ("debased mind") in need of transformation. In 2:1 Paul catches his audience off balance, critiquing faultfinders and guilty alike: "you have no excuse, whoever you are, when you judge others; for in passing judgment on another you condemn yourself, because you, the judge, are doing the very same things." He broadens his view to cover all humans, leading to the first great summit in the letter's topography: "all have sinned and have fallen short of the glory of God" (3:23).

Knowledge—that is the theme of the opening chapters. If the Romans have lost sight of the knowledge they really have, then they must first be reminded of what they can and do know. They have the knowledge to be what we would call responsible moral agents, but their mind is unhealthy. So Paul sets out to heal it. This is the aim of the letter. By speaking of "mind" (the Greek word *nous*), Paul is thinking not merely about intellect, but about the entire array of thoughts and information upon which we draw in the course of our daily lives. Can an unsound mind heal itself? In chapter 2, Paul reassures the Romans that they have the capacity they need. Jewish Christians might think they have the advantage, because they have God's law, an observation Paul quickly counters. The Jews, he states, who have

---

4. The discussion in this segment is adapted from Griffith-Jones, *Gospel According to Paul*, 404–33.

the law, have the requisite knowledge, but they fail to apply it (2:17–24). On the other hand, there are Gentiles without the Jewish law who nonetheless "do instinctively what the law requires" (2:14). They have an active and discriminating conscience or knowledge of themselves. Paul's emphasis in chapter 2 is not yet about faith or grace. He insists in 2:5 that all will be judged by their deeds. Paul appears to deviate from his gospel here, but he arrives at his point in chapter 3 when he argues that Jews and Gentiles alike are infected by the power of sin (3:9–12).

Later, at the letter's midway point, Paul examines the progress made possible thus far. The mind, no longer in rebellion against God, seems sufficiently healed to recognize the limits of its own power, but is still unable to counter the power of wrongdoing. The inner person is ready now to endorse God's law, but sees a rival law at work in the body: "So then, with my mind I am a slave to the law of God, but with my flesh I am a slave to the law of sin" (7:25).

But restoration is under way. The children of God are declared "heirs of God and joint heirs with Christ" (8:17), and those whom God has chosen "he also predestined to be conformed to the image of his Son" (8:29). Here is the good news in action, the power of God for deliverance. As the Romans grow into a self-conscious determination to obedience and to faith, they discover the limits of their own ability—and the transformation offered at the crucial moment by God's power.

Paul's final chapters (12–15) are dedicated to the practicalities of communal life. How easily people stop reading once the "important" business of the letter is over and Paul turns to problems that have nothing to do with them. And how completely, by such neglect, they miss the result of Paul's work. As Paul reaches the last section of the letter the effects of the transformation, in the individuals and in the church, are readily apparent. Now that the Romans have a sound mind and can begin to think and live aright, Paul bases his appeal for effective living on what God has already accomplished: transformation by the renewing of their minds (12:2). If they have been paying attention, the Romans discover that their transformation has begun even as they hear the letter. In his letter, Paul has not been just persuading, teaching, or informing. He has set out to heal the Romans: "Keep up your transformation in the renewal of your mind"; that is how we should read Romans 12:2. Once more the mind, as at the letter's start; but this time, a mind healed. Once more discernment of right and wrong; but this time, uncontaminated. The community that was collapsing into factionalism and divisiveness can now recover the life to which it was called—a body with many members, diverse yet equal and united. The instructions in Paul's last chapters make it clear that believers are not united by mutual honor, pride, or obligation, but rather by love (13:10).

The good news of Paul's gospel is this: The power that moves believers from the downward spiral of disobedience to an upward spiral of obedience—from weakness to strength, from effort to grace—is available through God's indwelling Spirit: "There is therefore now no condemnation for those who are in Christ Jesus. For the law of the Spirit of life in Christ Jesus has set you free from the law of sin and of death" (8:1–2). The good news, activated in the letter's reception, is God's present power for deliverance (see 1:16). The way of grace, the journey of transformation from a debased mind (1:28) to a renewed mind (12:2), has begun—for the Romans, and for us.

In his letter to the Romans Paul redefines his audience, as individuals, as a community, and as part of creation as a whole. In so doing, Paul engages not just the Romans' intellect, to grasp his ideas and argument, and not just their will, to apply his insights, but also their imagination, to engage the mystery and magnificence of the divine in all of life, whether above us, below us, or within us (see 8:39; 11:33). The Romans are on their way to glory, transformed into the likeness of the image they gaze upon. The glory is growing even as they hear and accept Paul's letter. And by the end of the letter the Romans will have learned, in practical terms, what Paul's talk of transformation means.

Essay 2: A River Runs Through It: The New Testament Gospel of Grace

When Jesus Christ relied on the power of the Holy Spirit to accomplish what he did on earth (Rom. 1:4), and when the apostle Paul gave all credit for his success to the grace and power of God operating through him (Rom. 1:5), we know we are dealing with a profound divine truth. As Paul discovered, when Christians access the strength to rise above their infirmities or difficult circumstances, they experience God's grace, which is sufficient to endure or overcome whatever may be hindering or harming them (2 Cor. 12:9).

If grace can be said to underlie the Christian gospel and to embody the biblical portrayal of God's identity and activity, what does the word "grace" mean, and what is its transformative power? In a nutshell, grace is the power and ability of God operating through believers:

- for regeneration: the power of God's grace that saves through faith;
- for sanctification: the power of God's grace to overcome harmful addictions and temptations;
- for ministry: the power of God's grace to accomplish the work we are called to do in life;
- for joy: the power of God's grace to relinquish negative patterns and attitudes;
- for confidence: the power of God's grace to help us bless others through our goals and aspirations.

The following biblical principles set the stage for our thinking about grace:

1. God's grace is *abundant*. As God gave "great power" and "great grace" to the early apostles (Acts 4:33), God can do the same for us, since God shows no partiality (Acts 10:34; Rom. 2:11). God desires to make our grace abound (that is, increase greatly) and is able to provide us with grace in abundance and sufficiency in all things (2 Cor. 9:8; 12:9).

2. God's grace is *free*. In the New Testament, the words for "gift" and "grace" are closely related. This connection is made clear in passages such as Ephesians 4:7: "each of us was given *grace* according to the measure of Christ's *gift*" and 1 Corinthians 1:4–8, where the *grace* of God is said to enrich believers in all speech and knowledge, so that they are not lacking in any spiritual *gift*. The Greek term *charis* is most frequently translated "grace," and *charisma* is most often rendered "gift." The New Testament describes those who have been transformed by God's grace to be recipients of spiritual gifts (see 1 Corinthians 12–14 and Romans 12:3–21), and exhorts believers to employ their "gifts" for one another, "as stewards of the manifold grace of God" (1 Pet. 4:10). [On this topic see essay 11 below.]

3. God's grace is *powerful*. God exhorts us to "grow in grace" (2 Pet. 3:18), that is, to become mighty and strong in grace (2 Tim. 2:1), and this occurs when we allow God to train and nurture us. In 1 Corinthians 15:10 Paul describes grace as the enabling power of his work. Grace provides forgiveness, cleanses from all unrighteousness, and then fills us with power to press on in the "obedience of faith" (Rom. 1:5; 16:26). And the wondrous truth is that this power is present not only in the

work of regeneration, but at every stage of the Christian life (1 Pet. 4:10–11; 2 Thess. 1:11–12).

4. God's grace is *transformative*. The Bible teaches that we cannot reach our divine destiny by relying on our own wisdom, knowledge, intelligence, or strength, for those who try to build the house of their lives solely through their own efforts will end up laboring in vain (Ps. 127:1). We can, however, reach our destiny if God guides our steps and nourishes our vision with transformative power and grace: "Not by might, nor by power, but by my spirit, says the Lord of hosts" (Zech. 4:6).

As Paul makes clear in Romans, the concept of grace, lavish and free, can be easily misunderstood, and consequently abused (see Rom. 2:3–4; 3:8; 6:1–2, 15). In his Christian classic *The Cost of Discipleship*, German theologian Dietrich Bonhoeffer (1906–1945) wrote an exposition on the Sermon on the Mount in which he addressed Paul's concern, spelling out what it means to follow Christ. First published in 1937 under the simple title "Discipleship," Bonhoeffer wrote when the rise of Nazism was underway in Germany, and against this backdrop developed his theology of costly discipleship, which led to his untimely death in 1945. In this book Bonhoeffer presented his audience with a profound understanding of grace by distinguishing between "cheap grace" and "costly grace."

Cheap grace, Bonhoeffer argued, is grace without discipleship or the cross, grace apart from the living and incarnate Jesus Christ. Cheap grace is a byproduct of the spread of Christianity, which resulted in secularization and in the church's accommodation to the requirements of society. Cheap grace is represented as grace without price; grace without cost!

Costly grace is the call of Jesus Christ at which disciples leave their nets and follow him. Such grace is costly because it calls us to follow, and it is grace because it calls us to follow Jesus Christ. It is costly because it costs our lives, and it is grace because it gives us the only true life. It is costly because it condemns sin, and grace because it justifies the sinner. It is costly because it compels a person to submit to the yoke of Christ and follow him, and grace because Jesus says: "My yoke is easy and my burden is light" (Matt. 11:30). Above all, it is costly because it cost God the life of the Son: "You were bought with a price" (1 Cor. 6:20), and what has cost God much cannot be cheap for us. Costly grace represents the incarnation of God.

The term "cheap grace" had been coined by Adam Clayton Powell, pastor of the Abyssinian Baptist Church in Harlem, New York. Bonhoeffer attended that church while away from Germany at Union Theological Seminary. Bonhoeffer benefited from the protest culture of the African American church and gleaned from it social gospel elements that he took with him back to Germany. In Germany he opposed Hitler's social and political agenda and was arrested in 1943 after being associated with a plot to assassinate Adolf Hitler. After imprisonment he was sent to a concentration camp where he was executed by hanging days before the collapse of the Nazi regime. Like Paul, Bonhoeffer chose costly grace over cheap grace; in death both embraced the cost of discipleship, faithful to the end.

The 1992 film *A River Runs Through It*, directed by Robert Redford and starring Brad Pitt, tells the story of two sons of a Presbyterian minister raised in Montana. Based on a short story published in 1976 by Norman Maclean, the film is alluring, its scenery stunning. But it is the words, narrated by Redford, one remembers most, lines such as "I am haunted by waters" and "eventually, all things merge into one, and a river runs through it." As waters flowing through Montana bring unity to the film, so "grace" flows through Romans, indeed through the entire New Testament, enhancing its message. Paul is aware in Romans that he and his fellow-believers are living in an age in which a full tide is flowing into their individual lives from a great spiritual ocean. Again and again he speaks of grace abounding (see Rom. 5:17, 20), far surpassing any contrary force of evil, flooding life with lavish hope and strength. Not only Paul but the New Testament as a whole speaks of grace as an amazingly liberal gift (Eph. 2:8), characterized by phrases such as "the riches of his grace" (Eph. 1:7; 2:7), "surpassing grace" (2 Cor. 9:14), and the "indescribable gift" of which one cannot say enough (2 Cor. 9:15). Of all the attributes of Jesus Christ, perhaps the most significant is "full of grace" (John 1:12), a grace he shares lavishly with his followers, as John's Gospel makes clear: "From his fullness we have all received, grace upon grace" (John 1:16). As we learn in Ephesians 4:7, Christ delights in sharing grace with his followers. That grace Paul experienced at his conversion, explored throughout his career, and exposited in his letter to the Romans.

Grace is pervasive in Romans, present in every theme. As expected, it is evident in Christ's life and death, in God's righteousness (God's faithfulness and righteous justice), in justification, predestination, election, and saving faith. But grace is also present in Torah (Mosaic law) and perhaps most surprisingly, in God's judgment and wrath. The method I use to outline Romans captures its theme perfectly: "all (is) for grace" (1:16—8:39) addresses the universal need of grace; "grace (is) for all" (9:1—11:36) addresses the presence of grace in human history; and "all (is) from grace" (12:1—15:13) addresses the results of grace in society. Surely here is grace revealed.

Questions to Ponder

1. Having read Romans, what seems to be its primary message?
2. In your estimation, what passage represents the core of the letter? Explain your answer.
3. Do you find a message in Romans that has practical value in your present circumstances?
4. Explain the difference between reading the Bible literally and historical-metaphorically? If you consider yourself a theological conservative, how does this perspective influence the way you read and interpret scripture? If you consider yourself a theological moderate or liberal, how does this outlook influence the way you read and interpret scripture?
5. Having read the essay on grace, what role does grace play in your life?
6. What are your takeaways from this session?

Session Three

Grace and Paul's Apostolic Work

Summary: Session 3 provides a historical background to the church at Rome, including its origin and makeup. The textual discussion examines Romans 1:1–17 and 15:14—16:27, a segment that provides Paul's reason for writing his letter. These sections bracket the rest of the letter, framing Paul's main argument. Besides the formalities of greeting and valediction, this segment provides significant insight into Paul's work and plans while also explaining his relationship with the Romans. Because Paul is unknown to the majority of his readers, he provides his spiritual credentials, emphasizing his apostolic calling (1:1–6). He continues with a thanksgiving, a section he completes at the end of the letter (15:14–33), where he notes his desire to visit the Roman church to elicit support for an anticipated westward expansion of his mission. As he writes, he is preparing to visit Jerusalem, a task he views as necessary but with apprehension. Chapter 16, the closing chapter, consists primarily of greetings and a closing doxology. The letter's theme, in 1:16–17, emphasizes the righteousness of God, whose plan is to unite Jews and Gentiles in covenant faithfulness. The concluding essay addresses the topic of "justification by faith," noting the classic debate between Protestants and Catholics on this topic and examining four meanings of "faith" in Christian history: as belief, trust, faithfulness, and vision.

Assignment: Read Session 3 of *Grace Revealed* and Romans 1:1–17 and 15:14—16:27. Answer the following questions, writing the answers in your journal. [Be prepared to share your views with others in the class.] Imagine receiving a letter from the founder(s) of your church, indicating their original expectation ("then") and their current hope ("now"). In light of their *original* expectation, how would they assess your church's current status? Would they focus on its potential, progress, or failures? Which shortcomings would they mention, and which strengths? In light of their *current* expectations, what goals and strategies might they suggest? [If you don't identify with a particular congregation, imagine receiving a personal letter from a revered ancestor assessing your individual spiritual status.]

Key Verse(s): Romans 1:16-17; 16:25-26

Central Theme: Trusting God's faithfulness

Technical Words and Concepts: gospel, Septuagint, righteousness, righteous, adoptionism, "exaltation" Christology, Lord, holy, Satan, infusion, imputation

Learning Objectives

In this session participants will examine:

1. The Roman church in Paul's time, including its origin and makeup
2. The nature of Paul's gospel
3. Paul's reason for writing Romans
4. The meaning of Romans 1:16-17
5. The Lordship of Jesus Christ
6. The meaning of "justification"
7. Four meaning of "faith": faith as belief, trust, faithfulness, and vision

Outline to 1:1-17; 15:14—16:27

I. Grace and Paul's Apostolic Work 1:1-17; 15:14—16:27
   A. In Paul 1:1-7; 15:14-33; 16:25-27
      1. Paul's Apostolic Gospel 1:1-7
      2. Paul's Reason for Writing 15:14-33
      3. Paul's Doxology 16:25-27
   B. In Christians at Rome 1:8-15; 16:1-24
      1. Paul's Thanksgiving 1:8-15
      2. Commendation of Phoebe 16:1-2
      3. Personal Greetings 16:3-16
      4. Final Instructions and Greetings 16:17-23
   C. Thesis Statement: The Power of Grace 1:16-17

Historical Context: Jewish and Gentile Christians in Rome

Although the origins of Christianity at Rome are unknown, it seems likely that the first believers arriving in Rome would naturally have sought out the Jewish communities in the synagogues, where they would have encountered not only Jews but a number of Gentiles who were attracted to Jewish life and teaching. While there is considerable debate about the makeup of Paul's audience, it seems likely that Paul is primarily addressing Gentile Christians, though it is clear from texts such as 15:7–12 and 16:7–11, in addition to the discussion in chapters 1–4 and 9–11, that there are Jewish Christians in the audience. It is Gentile Christians in Rome that he admonishes, since he is the apostle to the Gentiles.

Chapter 16 suggests that Paul knew of at least five house churches in Rome: one sponsored by Priscilla and Aquila (16:5); one that includes Asyncritus, Phlegon, Hermes, Patrobas, and Hermas (16:14); one that includes Philologus, Julia, Olympas, and Nereus and his sister (16:15); Christians in the house of Aristobolus (16:10); and Christians in the household of Narcissus (16:11). Their combined membership was probably quite small, possibly several dozen but likely less than one hundred. The exhortation against division and dissension in 16:17–20 implies that the church in Rome lacked central organization and authority. It seems likely that the first Christians in Rome were ordinary Jews and God-fearing Gentiles who had heard the gospel in Jerusalem and brought the message back with them (see Acts 2:10–11). If that were the case, one reason the church in Rome lacked central organization is that it had no apostolic foundation. It is also possible that someone like Andronicus or Junia, "apostles in Christ" before Paul (16:7), had brought Christianity from Jerusalem to Rome shortly after the death of Jesus.

In AD 49, eight or nine years prior to Paul's writing, a significant number of Jews and Jewish Christians had been forced to leave Rome (see Acts 18:2). The Roman church, originally composed predominantly of Jewish Christians, was left primarily Gentile Christian in nature. When the ban was lifted in AD 54, perhaps a majority of the Jewish Christian exiles had returned to Rome, complicating the relation of Jewish and Gentile Christians within the church. Enormous problems of reconciliation would have resulted, and the mixed congregations comprising the Roman church needed instruction on the role of Jews and Gentiles in God's plan. Such a situation explains the thrust of the letter, including emphasis upon the faithfulness and impartiality of God; the equal accountability of Jew and Gentile before God (chapters

1-2); the equal right of Gentile and Jew as offspring of Abraham ("the father of all of us"; see chapters 3-4, especially 4:16); the terms on which true obedience to God is possible (chapters 5-8); the meaning of Israel for the life of the church (chapters 9-11); the debt of Gentile Christians to their Jewish heritage (11:18); the equal freedom and responsibility of Jewish and Gentile Christians in the everyday life of the community (chapters 12-15); and the urging of Gentile Christians to be more tolerant of Jewish religious practices (14:3, 5-6, 14). Paul no longer uses himself as a model (see Gal. 6:14; 1 Cor. 9:15-23; 10:32-33; 11:1), since these are not his converts, but points more directly to Christ (Rom. 15:3,7).

Romans 1:1-17; 15:14—16:27: Flow of the Argument

We begin where Romans begins—with the gospel: "Paul, a servant of Jesus Christ, called to be an apostle, set apart for the gospel of God . . . the gospel concerning his Son . . . through whom we have received grace. . . ." This announcement draws together two things: the nature of God as gracious and the nature of the gospel as God's gracious plan for humanity. Paul insists that his message reveals God's righteousness (1:17), that is, God's covenant faithfulness to the promise that through Abraham all the families (nations) of the world would be blessed (see Gen. 12:3; Rom. 4:16, 17; Gal. 3:6-9, 14).

At the start of the Christian era, before any gospel had been written, there was the gospel of Paul. The instrument of his conversion from persecutor of Christians to apostle to the Gentiles, this gospel animated his theology, shaped his ecclesiology, fueled his missionary endeavors, and informed his letters. Paul's gospel, which he received from the apostles and by revelation from the risen Christ, was not created by himself or by the first Christians, for it was perceived as underlying the Hebrew scriptures (Rom. 1:2). This gospel, early Christian exegetes discovered, permeated the scriptures and was said to guide theocratic leaders such as prophets, priests, and kings. It was present in the Babylonian exile, at Sinai, in the exodus, and at creation, and is depicted in such imagery as Isaiah's Suffering Servant, Abraham's sacrifice of Isaac, and the expulsion from the Garden of Eden, for the gospel of grace, those Christians discovered, defines God's creative, disciplinary, and regenerative activity. Grace, powerful in nature and transformative in effect, was to characterize God's covenant people during the church age.

Having indicated that the gospel is the good news proclaimed by Jewish prophets in the Hebrew scriptures, Paul then specifies what this gospel is about, likely using a preexistent statement of faith.[1] In this early church creed we find a double affirmation: Jesus is both the Davidic Messiah and the exalted Son of God. These are not necessarily Paul's views (nowhere else does he mention that Jesus was a descendant of David or that Jesus had become the Son of God at the resurrection), but part of an earlier tradition. Paul's use of this creedal statement at the start of his letter was deliberate, a way to dispel any suspicion about the acceptability of his views and a means of establishing common ground with his Roman audience.

Occasion and Purpose of Romans (1:8-15; 15:14—16:27)

While Paul was in a more reflective mood when he wrote Romans than when he penned Galatians or the Corinthian letters, Romans is not an essay on Christian doctrine but a genuine letter, reflecting the particular situation of both Paul and the Roman church.

Some details about Paul's situation seem clear. In 1:10-15 it is clear that he is carrying out a long-cherished plan to visit the church at Rome. In 15:14-33 he is more specific, indicating he felt that his work to the Gentiles in the eastern Mediterranean was complete (15:23). Wishing to extend his mission to the west and to Spain, Paul needed to solicit support from the Roman church, perhaps even financial support. Phoebe, a friend of Paul's, was about to leave Cenchreae for Rome (Paul was writing from Corinth, located on an isthmus, and Cenchreae was one of its port cities) and could be a trusted bearer of the letter, perhaps adding to the letter's content and responding to questions raised by the Roman church.

In writing Romans, Paul was conscious of two audiences. First and foremost were Roman Christians, predominantly Gentile Christians, to whom he would sent this letter in preparation for his expected arrival in the city. Since Paul hopes for help from a church he did not establish, he wants to present this church with an authentic representation of his message to gain trust and backing. As he writes, Paul has in mind a second audience, Jewish Christians in Jerusalem. Before visiting Rome, Paul faced a worrisome journey to Jerusalem. The predominantly Gentile churches Paul had founded throughout Macedonia and Greece had collected an offering for the famine-stricken churches at Jerusalem (15:25-26), and it was Paul's

---

1. Ehrman, *How Jesus became God*, 218-25.

job to deliver this gift. The collection, if received by the Jerusalem church, would concretely symbolize the unity of the one church of Jewish and Gentile Christians (see Gal. 2:1–10; 2 Cor. 8–9). But as he freely acknowledges (Rom. 15:22–32), he fears going to Jerusalem on two accounts. First, he was afraid for his life (15:30–32; see Acts 20:22–24; 21:10–14). Many Jews were suspicious of Paul, who once persecuted the church but now has become the "apostle to the Gentiles."

Paul was also uncertain whether the Jerusalem church would accept the offering collected from the Gentiles, Some Jewish Christians may have encountered pressure to avoid association with Gentile Christians. If they rejected the offering from Gentile Christians, Paul would have been devastated, for he had fought valiantly for a church where there was "neither Jew nor Greek." The gospel of which Paul is not ashamed and which he is eager to proclaim to those in Rome depends on a single message: The lordship of Jesus Christ, in whom the righteousness of God is made known to all people, to the Jew first and also to the Greek (Rom. 1:16).

When we examine the historical issues underlying Romans, it becomes clear that the letter is much more than a neutral exposition of theological ideas and ethical ideals. One may easily imagine that agitators and opponents from Paul's earlier conflicts over his mission to Gentiles may have had some influence in Rome that he would have been anxious to neutralize before his visit.

Paul's Thesis Statement: The Meaning of Romans 1:16–17

Romans 1:16–17 sets forth the basic theme or proposition that Paul will then advance by a series of arguments: "For I am not ashamed of the gospel; it is the power of God for salvation to everyone who has faith, to the Jew first and also to the Greek. For in it the righteousness of God is revealed through faith for faith; as it is written, 'The one who is righteous will live by faith.'" Paul seems to draw his justification for writing to the Romans and his right to be heard by them from his being an apostle to the Gentiles (1:13–14) and on their being a Gentile Christian community. Nevertheless, the argument itself is cast in profoundly Jewish terms, including its controlling vocabulary, its appeals to authority and tradition, the values invoked, the techniques employed in interpreting scripture, and the things taken for granted in the minds of its readers.

Paul begins this passage by indicating to his largely Gentile audience that they should not be ashamed of a gospel that is for the Jew first. In the biblical vocabulary on which Paul depends, "being ashamed" is not a matter of personal embarrassment, but rather means that he has "complete confidence in the gospel" as God's way of dealing with the human predicament.

The difficult phrase translated "through faith for faith" but also "by faith from first to last" or "from faith for faith" in 1:17 is important and has elicited much debate. It can mean that (a) faith is the sole condition for salvation; (b) human faith comes from God's faithfulness as demonstrated in the faith of Jesus; (c) God's faithfulness leads to our faithfulness; or (d) saving faith (the act of trusting in Christ) produces additional faith. Given Paul's understanding of faith, which turns out to have more than one level of meaning, it appears wise not to be definitive here, though the third option is most likely. God has been faithful to his purposes and promises made long ago, and if one wants to benefit from God's faithfulness, one must have an answering faithfulness (the "obedience of faith" he spoke of in verse 5).

To back this up, Paul quotes a passage from Habakkuk (the Hebrew reading "The just person shall live by his faith" 2:4, means that individuals are saved by their own faith or faithfulness, whereas the Septuagint reads: "The just shall live by my faithfulness," that is, by God's faithfulness. Readers will note that Paul's quotation differs in detail from the Hebrew and the Septuagint texts, the latter referring to the Greek translation of the Hebrew scriptures that Paul often uses). Habakkuk faced a great catastrophe coming upon Israel and had to learn to trust God, to have faith in God's faithfulness. Paul, setting Habakkuk's quote in a Christian context, seems to be telling his audience something about God's promise and something about their response: (a) that righteousness (right standing) comes through divine faithfulness, not human achievement, and (b) that while the saving promise is God's, the response is ours.

Paul's discussion in Romans begins with the inability of Gentiles and Jews to earn their salvation (their covenant status as children of God) and culminates in the discussion of God's plan for Jews in chapters 9–11, a plan not merely to save Gentiles but to unite Jew and Gentile in Christ. The discussion about the relationship of Jew and Gentile (Jewish and Gentile Christians) continues in chapters 12–15, when the subject of factions and divisions in the church comes to the fore.

While the quotation from Habakkuk ("the one who is righteous will live by faith") foreshadows chapters 3:21—8:39, Paul's earlier statement (that the gospel is "the power of God for salvation to everyone who has faith, to the Jew first and also to the Greek") foreshadows the discussion in chapters 9–11. Furthermore, the reference to living by faith ("the righteousness of God is revealed through faith for faith") is precisely the focus of chapters 12–15. The whole of Romans represents Paul's instruction about faith and faithfulness: God's impartial faithfulness in Christ to Jews and Gentiles as well as human faith and faithfulness (see the discussion on "justification by faith" in essay 3 and on God's righteous faithfulness in essay 9).

Textual Analysis: Topics to Ponder or Discuss

Romans 1:1–7

1. As we commence our study of Romans, we need to keep in mind Paul's relationship to his audience. Paul call himself an apostle of Jesus Christ in 1:1 (see 1 Cor. 15:8–10). In this context, the term refers not to one of the twelve disciples but has broader meaning. To whom, then, is Paul an apostle (see Rom 1:5)?

2. What does Paul mean by "the gospel of God" (see also 15:15)? In your estimation, why does he change the emphasis to "my gospel" in his summation (16:25)? As you answer these questions, keep in mind what was said about Paul's gospel in the "Flow of the Argument" above.

3. Scholars detect in 1:3–4 Paul's use of a primitive creedal statement used by the church, one associated with "exaltation" or "adoptionist" Christology, meaning that Jesus was "appointed" or "designated" Son of God at his resurrection. By quoting this creed, does Paul agrees with its Christology? (see Romans 9:5 and the discussion of Paul's Christology in the narrative segment of Session 9). Does such a view contravene that found in later Christian writings (see John 1:1–18; Col. 1:15–20; Hebrews 1:1:1–4; and even Paul's earlier statement about Jesus in Phil. 2:5–11) declaring Jesus the eternal Son of God? [Note: Surely the church's understanding of Jesus evolved in the first century, and not necessarily along a straight line or at the same rate in every part of early Christianity.] The use of the term "Lord" for Jesus goes back to the disciples. While originally the term expressed respect for Jesus, much like a student might use it of a teacher or a worker of a master, the reference came to take on new meaning once Jesus' followers believed he had been raised from the dead (see Rom.

14:9). Because of his exaltation by God, Jesus came to be called Lord, the same term used of God in the Hebrew Bible. In his writings Paul often used the phrase "the Lord Jesus Christ" in conjunction with the mention of God the Father (1 Thess. 1:1; 2 Cor. 8:5–6). The confession "Jesus is Lord" can be understood on two levels, politically and religiously. As a *political claim*, Christians were affirming that their primary allegiance belonged to Jesus and not to the Roman emperor, government officials, or the religious elite. As a *religious claim*, Christians were affirming that Jesus Christ was the personification of God, the one in whom heaven and earth met. In contrast to the many so-called gods and lords, for Paul there is but one God—the Father—and one Lord—Jesus Christ (1 Cor. 8:5–6).

4. In 1:5–6 Paul reminds his Gentile readers that they, like he, also have a divine call on their lives. In 1:7 Paul names the entire Christian audience in Rome as "beloved of God" and as "saints" (holy ones). Paul's vision of the people of God is clear from the first. He uses terms formerly used of Israel even of his largely Gentile audience, because he believes that Jew and Gentile united in Christ and in his gospel are the eschatological people of God and therefore stand in continuity with Abraham and Israel. If Paul uses the term "holy" in the Old Testament sense of "dedicated" or "consecrated," this anticipates his discussion in 12:1: a sacrifice is something dedicated or consecrated to God. Does Paul's discussion in 1:7 address your relationship to God and the world? Do you see yourself as "holy" in God's sight? Why or why not?

5. An expression we find in 1:5 (see also 16:26) and nowhere else in Romans is "obedience of faith" (better translated as "trusting/believing obedience"). Why doesn't Paul simply speak of faith alone here, as is his custom, rather than coupling it to "obedience"? If faith is primarily about trust, where does obedience fit? It is clear that while faith is central to Christianity, such faith is not alone but rather leads to obedience (see 2:6). [Note: When Paul speaks of "faith," he is not thinking of "belief," which leads to passive inaction, but of trust. Lack of faith, however, can lead to disbelief, and the consequences of disbelief in 1:18–32 are said to include immoral behavior.]

6. In his salutation Paul combines God our Father and the Lord Jesus Christ (see 1:7), whereas in chapter 15 he presents what appear to be Trinitarian allusions (see 15:16 and 30). From what you know about

GRACE AND PAUL'S APOSTOLIC WORK

Paul's theology, what is his understanding of the role of the Holy Spirit in our lives and in history? In your estimation, why does Paul refer to the Holy Spirit as both the "Spirit of God" and the "Spirit of Christ" in 8:9?

Romans 1:8–15 and 15:14–33

7. According to 1:8–15 and 15:14–33, did Paul envision his evangelistic ministry to be limited to Gentiles (see Gal. 2:7–9)?

8. While Paul usually divides humanity into Jew and Gentile (Greek), in 1:14 he divides the entire non-Jewish world into Greeks and barbarians. By "Greeks" he means Greek-speaking persons, which would include most Romans; "barbarians" were simply non-Greek-speaking persons. By designating the Gentile world in categories of culture and rationality (rather than race and geography), Paul is not being a snob or an elitist. Rather he is emphasizing that his message is for all persons, and not just for those who are well-educated or of higher status. Already Paul is anticipating the question he will later pose explicitly to those who would discriminate against others on the basis of status: Who are you to pass judgment on those who serve (Rom. 14:4)? As you examine your motives, are there individuals or groups whom you stereotype, or against whom you discriminate? Can you think of a concrete situation in your life where God's love can transform your attitude or where you can start treating a former enemy with dignity (see Matt. 5:43–47)?

9. In your estimation, why did Paul feel he had completed his mission in the eastern Mediterranean world (see 15:23)?

Romans 16:1–27

10. Some interpreters view Romans 16 as a once-separate letter. The manuscript tradition provides evidence that some copies of Romans ended at 15:13 or 15:33 (note the benedictions that still appear in these verses). This gave way to the theory that chapter 16 was an individual letter addressed to Ephesus on behalf of Phoebe, who was going there from Cenchreae (Rom. 16:1–3). It would be more likely that Paul knew this many people in Ephesus, the base of his mission in Asia Minor, than in Rome, which he had never visited. And first on this list come Aquila and Prisca, whom Paul knew at Corinth and Ephesus (see Acts 18:2–3, 18–19). I adopt the view now commonly

held that Paul is sending greetings to Rome rather than to Ephesus. By AD 57, Aquila and Prisca are safely back in Rome following Claudius's death (in 54) and the lapse of his edict. Other names Paul mentions in chapter 16, such as Aristobulus and Narcissus, fit the Roman scene. Almost a third of Rome's inhabitants were present or former slaves, so it is no surprise that at least ten of Paul's addressees have slaves' names. A plausible explanation for the differences in the manuscript tradition and the presence of multiple benedictions in chapter 15 is the likelihood that the 14- and 15-chapter abbreviated forms of Romans represent a later period, when Paul's letters were copied and circulated to other churches.

11. The name "Junia" in 16:7 is feminine, meaning that there were female leaders in the early church. Some later copyists (and indeed later Christian tradition) changed the name to "Junias," a masculine name, in part as a way to prevent women from taking leadership roles in the church. But other Pauline passages make it clear that Paul considered women co-workers and equals in church ministry (see the reference to Prisca [an abbreviation of Priscilla] and Aquila in 16:3, "who work with me"; also Euodia and Syntyche in Philippians 4:2-3, whom Paul calls loyal companions and co-workers in the work of the gospel). Given this tradition of gender equality in the early church (see also Galatians 3:28: in Christ "there is no longer male and female"), should limits be placed today on women's roles in church leadership?

12. The only direct mention to "Satan" in Romans is in 16:20. If the term originally meant "accuser" or "adversary," is Paul's use of the term theological or sociological? (In 1 Chronicles 21:1 David's plan to take a census is attributed to Satan; note that the earlier account of this action in 2 Samuel 24:1 contains no reference to Satan and places the blame solely on David). Rather than making a grand theological statement about the nature of evil, the context suggests that Paul is using the term metaphorically, personifying the cause of fragmentation and disunity in the Christian community by attributing it to Satan (see 16:17-19).

13. What does the presence of Tertius in 16:22 tell us about how Paul composed his letters? How was Tertius the author of Romans?

14. When Paul closes his letter, he refers to a "mystery" that was kept secret in the past but is now revealed. What, in this passage, does he

mean by "mystery," and how does his usage here compare with that in 11:25?

Romans 1:16–17

15. When Paul says in 1:16 that he is not "ashamed of the gospel," to what is he referring? Is he alluding to his preaching about the cross (see 1 Cor. 1:17–25; 2:2–5), taking what the world views as an act of torture, shame, and death and translating it into an instrument of revelation and divine disclosure? (see the discussion of this topic in essay 6).

16. Why does Paul give priority to "Jews" in God's plan of salvation (see 1:16)? Note that at least one third of Romans deals with the Jews. While Israel has priority in God's plan for humanity, Paul's point in 2:11 is that God is no respecter of persons.

17. When Paul speaks of the gospel as the "power of God" in 1:16, what does he have in mind? What power does the gospel currently exercise in your life? What power would you like it to have?

18. Explain what Paul means by "the righteousness of God" in 1:17 (see the discussion of this topic in essay 9).

19. Explain the meaning of the phrase "through faith for faith" in 1:17. What change does Paul make to the quotation from Habakkuk? Is that change significant?

Essay 3: Understanding Paul's View of Justification by Faith

No set of words is more important for understanding Paul's message to the Romans than those that share the root *dik*, especially the verb *dikaioo* ("to justify"), the noun *dikaiosyne* ("righteousness") and the adjective *dikaios* (one who is "righteous" or "just"). In the Old Testament, when the reference is to persons, this language has its context in the righteousness of God, an expression that speaks not only of God's ethical character as "just and true" but of God's relational nature, namely God's trustworthiness and faithfulness to his covenant with Israel and with all humanity. Underlying the concept of God's righteousness are essential questions: (1) what kind of God do we believe in? (2) what kind of God do we serve? (3) what is God's plan for humanity (how does God provide for human need)? The biblical answers are provided in *dikaiosyne* language, in the related concepts of "righteousness" and "justification."[2]

For Martin Luther and many Protestant interpreters who followed him, "justification by faith" is the center of Romans, of Paul's theology, and indeed of the Bible. Others disagree, noting the relative absence of justification language in Romans 5–8 while insisting that relational questions—how Jews relate to Gentiles, and Jewish Christians with Gentile Christians—dominate Romans, rather than questions of an individual's being right with God. Clearly Paul's doctrine of justification by faith has its context in his reflection on the relation between Jews and Gentiles and not within the questions of free will or of how individuals are saved (see Rom. 1:16-17; 3:28-29). But why choose between these alternatives? Biblically speaking, only when humans are in right relationship with God can they be rightly related to one another.

The concept of "justification" is clearly vital to Christianity, as it was to Paul. Luther's rediscovery of the doctrine revolutionized his thinking, and every revival within Christianity has evidenced the influence of this great article of the faith. Put quite simply, the religious perspective implicit in the concept is this: "Left to their own devices, humans are under the power of sin. Headed for destruction, they are powerless to save themselves, for salvation is of God. Salvation is a free gift of God, accomplished through the death of Christ on the cross. As a result, believers are 'justified' by God."

Confusion is generated by the fact that the Greek verb *dikaioo* ("to justify") can be variously translated as "to declare righteous" or "to make righteous." Since the Reformation, when the issue of justification rose to prominence, Protestants emphasized the former and Roman Catholics the latter. Essential to the Protestant interpretation has been the judicial, or forensic, understanding of justification and righteousness language generally. What God does for us in justification is similar to what a judge does in a court of law. When a judge pronounces someone innocent, this declaration does not change the person into a new kind of being, but simply declares the defendant innocent of any charges. In a Jewish lawcourt, the vindicated party possesses the status "righteous," not itself a moral statement but a statement of how things stand in the now completed lawsuit. But this status of "righteous" has nothing to do with the righteousness of the judge. When the defendant is declared "righteous" at the end of the case, there is no sense that the judge's righteousness has passed on to the defendant or plaintiff.

---

2. For a discussion or the righteousness of God, see essay 9.

What is granted when the court finds in one's favor is the status of being declared "righteous," not a moral quality.

In the past, this forensic understanding of justification was often denied by Roman Catholic interpreters, who insisted that righteousness includes inner transformation. This understanding, based on a medieval understanding of salvation, distinguished between two types of grace: operative grace (faith), whereby God is the sole actor, and cooperative grace (works), whereby humans participate actively in their salvation through meritorious deeds. For Thomas Aquinas and other medieval theologians, good works contribute to salvation.

In the sixteenth century Luther and Calvin denied any distinction between operative and cooperative grace and repudiated any suggestion that people could merit God's grace. Good works do not contribute to salvation, they argued, but result from God's gift of sovereign grace. How then is grace received? The answer depends on how "grace" is viewed, whether as an "act" or a "substance."

- *Infusion.* Catholic theologians, following Aquinas, regarded grace as a quality or *substance*. They viewed justification as a *subjective process* by which God actually *makes* individuals righteous by infusing grace into them through the sacraments. According to this view, grace plus works are required for salvation. The following formula captures this perspective: Faith + Works = Justification.
- *Imputation.* Protestant theologians, following Luther and Calvin, regarded grace as an *objective act* by which God *declares* humans to be righteous on the basis of Christ's death on the cross. According to this view, salvation is wholly the result of God's grace, which we appropriate not by our own efforts or works, but solely on the basis of faith in God's gift. Salvation produces good works. The following formula captures this perspective: Faith = Justification + Good Works.

The theological debate between Protestants and Catholics has changed. Most contemporary Catholic scholars now agree that Protestant theologians are right to insist that "justification" language in Paul is forensic. At the same time, many Protestant interpreters now minimize the significance of the doctrine of justification by faith. New debates have sprung up over the basis of God's verdict of justification. If believers are "declared righteous" (Protestant view), that is, freed from the charge and penalties of sin, then this understanding of justification makes God appear to regard us as something we are not, that is, sinless. If believers are said to be "made righteous" (Roman Catholic view), does it mean they have a new moral nature? The problem is that even those who are said to be "made righteous" by faith are often morally indistinguishable from those who are not so made righteous. Indeed, Paul complains to the Corinthians that some outside their fellowship (some non-Christians) are more moral than they are (1 Cor. 5:1). Again, to say God regards what we do as moral even when it is not is to introduce an element of sham into divine judgment that is quite foreign to Paul.

A better way to understand this terminology grows out of the way it is used in the Old Testament, where to be "just" or "righteous" is to uphold the covenant. In that context, righteousness is used to describe a relationship. What upholds that relationship is "righteous"; what destroys the relationship is "unrighteous." Similarly, to be "declared" or "made" righteous then means to be restored to a positive relationship with God and others, whereas an "unrighteous" act is one that destroys such a relationship. Likewise, when God acts righteously, it means that God acts to restore or uphold a covenant, to keep or restore his people to a positive relationship to himself. If sin as unrighteous activity means activity that estranges us from God and others, righteousness or being "made righteous" means to have the effects of sin nullified by entering into a restored relationship with God and others. It becomes increasingly clear when we examine Paul's argument in Romans that this is how he understand "righteousness" and its related terms. One can see that Paul equates God's righteousness with God's faithfulness (3:3, 5) and also in 3:21–30 how God's act in Christ is both the sign of God's righteousness and the means by which believers are justified (3:25–26).

In Romans, justification is neither a "moral quality" nor conformity to some legal norm but is a positive relationship to God growing out of God's power to restore rebellious humanity to God's gracious lordship (1:18—3:20). God's righteousness also represents God's power to restore harmony to creation (see 8:19–23).

What then about "faith"? Is it a gift or a work? If a gift, is it operative or cooperative grace? The answer is not simple. For Paul, before union with God can take place, two things must happen. First comes the divine initiative, this gift we call "grace." But in order for a gift to be viable, it must be received; this human response we call "faith." The two ideas are brought together strikingly in a famous passage: "by grace you have been saved through faith" (Eph. 2:8). Faith, like so many other biblical concepts, is paradoxical, for if salvation, which cannot be earned, is by faith, then faith must be a divine gift. But since faith (and its related term "belief") also functions as an imperative, as it does in so many biblical passages (see John 14:1; Acts 16:31; cf. Rom. 10:9; Heb. 11:6), there must be a human response. Grace, while lavish, is consensual; it requires assent.

In the history of Christianity, faith has four primary meanings. The first sees faith primarily as a "matter of the head," the remaining as a "matter of the heart."

1. *Faith as belief*. In this first sense faith means holding a certain set of "beliefs," that is, "believing" certain doctrines or dogmas to be true. This understanding of faith as belief is dominant today, both within the church and outside it. According to this understanding of faith, the opposite of faith is doubt or disbelief. In its fundamentalist permutation, those who doubt are said to lack faith, whereas those who disbelieve are said to have no faith. While this view is widespread, it is not biblical. Furthermore, it puts the emphasis in the wrong place, for it suggests that what God really cares about is the beliefs in our heads, as if having "correct beliefs" is what will save us. Faith starts with the willingness to recognize and question the core mysteries at the heart of existence: why we exist at all and how to make meaning out of our existence. We can't know the answers to the ultimate questions like we can know scientific answers, which build bodies of knowledge over time. Religious answers are more like wisdom. With the habit of faith, we are willing to ponder such questions in our hearts and minds. According to Aquinas, belief is "giving assent to something one is still thinking about." For this view, the opposite of faith is certainty.

2. *Faith as trust*. In the Bible, faith is relational; it means radical trust in God. Significantly, faith does not mean trusting in the truth of a set of statements about God, for that would simply be belief under a different name. According to this meaning, the opposite of faith is not doubt or disbelief, but mistrust, which results in worry and anxiety. Four times in the extended passage from Matthew's Sermon on the Mount, Jesus says to his hearers, "Do not worry," and then adds, "You of little faith" (Matt. 6:25–34). Lack of trust and anxiety go together; if you are anxious, you have little faith.

3. *Faith as faithfulness*. Faith is the trustful acceptance of God's promises, particularly of God's desire to bless all peoples and nations of the world. But faith is also trust in God's faithfulness to the promise, that is, in God's ability to deliver Good News to everyone, something that God

accomplishes through Jesus Christ and his followers. Because God is steadfast and faithful, we too are called to faithfulness. Faith as faithfulness means loyalty, allegiance, the commitment of the self at its deepest level. Its opposite is not doubt or disbelief. Rather, as in human relationships, its opposite is infidelity, being unfaithful to our relationship with God. To use a striking biblical metaphor, a vivid biblical term for infidelity to God is idolatry, meaning not so much the worship of idols as false gods, but centering in something finite rather than the sacred, which is infinite and beyond all images. As the opposite of idolatry, faith means being loyal to God rather than to seductive would-be lords of our lives, whether one's nation, affluence, achievement, family, or desire. Faith means being faithful to these two great relationships: God and neighbor. To be faithful to God also means to love that which God loves, which includes the whole of creation.

4. *Faith as vision.* As the word "vision" suggests, faith is a way of seeing reality, and how we view the whole affects how we respond to life. If we see reality as hostile and threatening, we respond to life defensively. Many forms of popular religion view reality this way: God (or Life, or Nature) is going to get us, unless we behave the right way, practice the correct rituals, offer the right sacrifices, or believe the right things. If we see reality as indifferent to human purposes and ends, we respond by building up whatever security we can, even enjoying and seeking to care for the world, but ultimately we are likely to be concerned primarily for ourselves and those who are most important to us. If we see reality as life-giving, nourishing, and full of promise, we are freed from anxiety and self-preoccupation. This can lead to radical trust and can generate a commitment to spend oneself for the sake of a vision greater than oneself. To understand faith as "vision" is to see reality as gracious. Its opposite, un-faith, views reality as hostile and indifferent.

This meaning of faith is closely related to trust. Trust and vision go together; trust in God—the God of promise and faithfulness—and how we view God go together. In this way of life, radical centering in God leads to a deepening trust that transforms the way we view reality. Seeing, living, trusting, and centering are all related in complex and salutary ways.

As we have noted, faith is relational, but this does not mean that beliefs don't matter. There are affirmations that are central to the Christian faith, affirmations such as the reality of God, the centrality of Jesus, and the significance of the Bible. But faith as a way of seeing at the deepest level requires avoiding the human tendency toward excessive precision and certitude. Christian theology has often been plagued by both—the desire to know too much and to know it too precisely. As we have seen, biblical and theological faith need not be viewed as assent to narrow propositions or as fulfilling specific requirements, but as a persuasive and compelling way of seeing reality.

Although we are saved by grace alone, such grace is not alone. While Paul would never think of faith as a basis for grace, he cannot conceive of faith apart from the aim of grace, that is, a right relationship to God in which faith is the motive and instinct of ethical obedience. "Work out your own salvation with fear and trembling," he argues in Philippians 2:12-13, "for it is God who is at work in you, enabling you both to will and to work for his good pleasure." This is a paradox only on paper. It is a reality in the sphere of grace, which caused Paul no more difficulty than it did the prophet Isaiah: "O Lord, you will ordain peace for us, for indeed, all that we have done, you have done for us" (Isa. 26:12). Believing grace, trusting grace, faithful grace, justifying grace, all are gifts of divine favor aimed at the creation of transformed personalities empowered to live out of God's resources.

While faith involves the mind, faith is primarily the way of the heart. In the words of the hymn writer: "Love so amazing, so divine, demands my soul, my life, my all."[3] Understood this way, to have faith in God is to love God and to love that which God loves. The Christian life is as simple and challenging as that.

Optional Group Activity

Divide the participants into four groups to discuss one aspect of faith found in essay 3 above, examining the merits of this perspective and its applicability in individual and group life. Ask Group 1 to focus on faith as belief; Group 2 on faith as trust; Group 3 on faith as faithfulness; and Group 4 on faith as vision. At the conclusion, reconvene the small groups into one and ask each group to share its insights with the others.

If time allows, give participants time to write down one takeaway (insight) from their reading or group discussion and then to share it with the class.

---

3. These lyrics are taken from Isaac Watts, "When I Survey the Wondrous Cross," published in 1711.

Part I

All for Grace
The Unity of Gentiles and Jews
(Romans 1:18—8:39)

THE SWEEP OF PAUL'S thought in Romans concerns not so much the spelling out of the implications of a doctrine like justification by faith, though that doctrine is clearly central to Paul's thinking, as it concerns the course of the history of God's gracious dealing with his creation, from its rebellion to its final redemption. The first eleven chapters of Romans can be seen from the course of that history between God and his creation. It is the story of God's gracious lordship rejected and restored. The result is alienation of humans from God, from nature, and from one another. The first three chapters discuss human rebellion and sin, tempered by the anticipation of Christ's redemptive act (3:21–26) in the trusting response to God by Abraham (3:27—4:25). Chapters 5–8 focus on the contrast between what was brought about by Adam (unrighteousness) and what was brought about by Christ (righteousness). Chapter 6 discusses how we have been delivered from the former by baptism and what our response to that reconciliation should be. Paul then addresses what our new situation means about our relationship to the past, which was dominated by sin and the law (chapter 7) and to the future, which is dominated by the Spirit (chapter 8).

When Paul refers to the gospel, he seems not to be referring to a system of salvation, though of course the gospel implies and contains this. Rather he is referring to the good news that there now is a way of salvation open to all. God's passion, says Paul, is to forge a unity of Jews and Gentiles from "the Jew first and also the Greek" (1:16; 2:9–10). However, at present there exists an unfortunate unifying feature on the human level, a unity under sin. Paul accuses humanity of universal failure, since "all, both Jews and Greeks, are under the power of sin" (3:9). To achieve global peace and unity, he seems to be saying, we need to confront global sin.

The central subject matter of Paul's proclamation in Romans is God's act of grace in Jesus Christ. At the heart of Paul's understanding of the history between God the Lord and creation (between creator and creature) is his conviction that the only way a creature can survive is if that creature enjoys the continuing favor of its creator. Because God is creator, God can deal with us as he wills (see 9:20–24). God the Lord has every right to judge creation on the basis of the way it behaves (2:6–11), and God's wrath toward a rebellious creation is fully justified (1:18–32). It is the nature of the creator, however, to demonstrate lordship more by mercy than by wrath. Such a favorable disposition by the creator toward creation Paul calls "grace." Such favor by the creator is then to be accepted by the creature as the only source of its continuing existence. Acceptance of that favorable disposition Paul calls "faith" or "trust" (the same word in Greek).

If the subject of Romans is God's passionate desire to heal a broken world, to end injustice, and to bring about a unified and peaceful earth, then the message of Romans 1–8 addresses the widest of the great divisions in Paul's world, that between Gentiles and Jews.

Session Four

The Universal Need of Grace

Summary: Session 4 examines Romans 1:18—3:20 from two perspectives, (a) apologetically (as a defense of Paul's gospel), and anthropologically (as an examination of the human condition). In this passage Paul examines the essence of human unrighteousness and the essence of divine righteousness. As human sin precedes God's salvation made known in Christ, so in Romans a discussion of sin precedes a discussion of salvation through Christ. In 1:18–32, Paul identifies three patterns of human rebellion (1:23, 25, 28) and three patterns of divine response (1:24, 26, 28). God is faithful and just: faithful to the covenants with Israel and humanity and just in judging evil and sin. God judges ungodliness (idolatry and immorality) through divine wrath, in the present restoratively and in the future punitively. There will be a day of judgment, when all will receive their due reward. God, creator of the universe, is impartial both in goodness and in judgment. In Chapters 2 and 3 Paul conveys his message using the diatribe style, asking rhetorical questions to set up dialogues with imagined objectors. Whereas the opening focuses on unconverted pagans (1:18—2:16), the next section addresses Jews (2:17—3:8). Both stand guilty before God. Paul's principle throughout is clear: it is not what one knows but what one does with what one knows that is important. Humans judge one another on outward appearance, but God on the heart. The closing essay addresses Paul's understanding of divine wrath and judgment, and how they are part of God's providential order.

Assignment: Read Session 4 of *Grace Revealed* and Romans 1:18—3:20. Answer the following question, writing the answer in your journal [Be prepared to share your views with others in the class.] What force drives Paul's argument in this passage: apologetics (defense of his gospel), theology (establishing a base for his doctrine of justification by faith), or something else?

Key Verse(s): Romans 2:9–11

Central Theme: The universality of human sin and God's righteous response

Technical Words and Concepts: retributive (punitive) justice, restorative justice, wrath of God, libertine, rhetorical question, Levitical purity laws, Hellenistic Judaism, circumcision, agape

Learning Objectives
In this session participants will examine:

1. The human predicament (universal sinfulness)
2. God's response to human sin and evil (how God's wrath relates to God's righteousness)
3. The metaphorical meaning of Genesis 1–3
4. Paul's approach to homosexuality
5. The role of human effort, conscience, and the moral law in God's plan of salvation
6. The role of Torah (Mosaic law) in God's plan of salvation
7. The role of agape in God's plan of salvation

Outline to Romans 1:18—3:20
I. All for Grace 1:18—8:39
   A. The Need of Grace 1:18—3:20
      1. By Gentiles 1:18—2:16
         a. Ungodly Gentiles 1:18–32
         b. Godly Gentiles 2:1–16
      2. By Jews 2:17—3:8
         a. Jews and the Law 2:17–29
         b. Two Objections Countered 3:1–8
      3. By All 3:9–20

THE UNIVERSAL NEED OF GRACE

Romans 1:18—3:20: Flow of the Argument

Anthropological Approach

Viewed anthropologically, Romans 1:18—3:20 addresses the human predicament. Paul announces the doctrinal theme in 1:17: "the righteousness of God is revealed through faith." Following his theme, Paul addresses the human problem, analyzing the universality of sin from the perspective of the coming Day of the Lord, the day of God's judgment (1:18—3:20). All human beings, without exception, fall short of God's standards and face divine wrath (when Paul speaks of "Jew and Gentile" or "Jew and Greek," he is describing the whole of humanity). Paul makes this point in 1:18-32, three times identifying a pattern of human rebellion and three times identifying God's response. Paul continues his indictment in 2:1-16, inferring that no one is in a position to judge others, as though the one judging were morally superior. He also cautions against moral laxity, based on the mistaken impression that God's delay in punishing evil means there will be no judgment at all. There will be a day of reckoning when all will receive their due reward (2:5-10). That means that all people, those with the Mosaic law and those without it, will have to give account for what they have done (2:12-16). Since God is the creator of all, God is impartial both in goodness and in judgment.

In 2:17—3:8 Paul directly addresses the Jews, noting that what he said applied to Gentiles also applies to Jews, namely, that they too are subject to God's wrath and judgment. Despite their election as God's covenant people and despite the benefits of having been entrusted with God's law, they are guilty of doing precisely what they condemn (2:17-24). Paul's principle throughout this passage is clear: it is not what one knows but what one does that is the important thing. Knowing God's will and believing in God are important, but in God's eyes they are not enough. What counts is not external but internal circumcision (2:29). Humans judge on outward appearances, God on the heart. Paul concludes his discussion by invoking scripture in support of his claim of universal sin, followed by an announcement of the inadequacy of the law for a right relationship to God (3:10-20). This overview of the human predicament prepares us for the solution: the role of Christ and faith in God's plan of salvation.

PART I—ALL FOR GRACE

Apologetic Approach

"I am not ashamed," he says at the beginning of Romans, "of the gospel" (1:16). This approach makes it sound like Paul is responding to criticism. So he must make it clear at the outset that he does not favor ungodliness or wrongdoing. To distance himself from such error, he proceeds to an elaborate condemnation of wrongdoing; there is no siding with evil here. From the outset, then, Paul's letter is shaped by his need to correct the rumors of his libertine stance.

As he writes further, he sees and confronts the most radical charge that could be laid against him and his gospel—that his reverence for a man (Jesus) has distorted the reverence that he owes to God alone. In his understanding of Jesus Paul seems to have "exchanged the glory of the immortal God for images resembling a mortal human being" (1:23). If that charge is valid, one can certainly see why some in Rome might choose to behave immorally. If his gospel has become a charter for libertines, Paul must put himself above all suspicion of idolatry, and he does so forcefully in 1:18-32.

At the start of his letter Paul speaks equally to Jews and Gentiles; the gospel, he declares, is for "everyone who has faith, to the Jew first and also to the Greek" (Rom. 1:16). The reason the gospel is for Jews and Gentiles is that both stand guilty before God. In chapters 2 and 3 Paul addresses Jew and Gentile alike. He borrows elements of the diatribe style, widely used by philosophical teachers and preachers in the Greek world (see 2:1-6, 17-24; 3:1-9; 3:27—4:25; the diatribe style also appears in 6:1-4, 15-16; 7:7, 13; 9:14-19; 10:14-21; 11:17-24; 14:4, 10-11). The format was one of vigorous debate on some important topic "peppered with apostrophes, proverbs and maxims, rhetorical questions, paradoxes, short statements, parodies, fictitious speeches, antitheses, and parallel phrases."[1] It becomes easier to follow Paul's arguments if readers imagine the apostle bantering with hecklers, each interrupting the other with quick and incomplete exchanges. It is quite probable that many of the arguments in Romans first took shape in this way, in the course of debates in synagogues or marketplaces.

In his "fictitious" construction in chapter 2 Paul critiques the type of morally superior Gentile in 2:1-11 and then the Jew in 2:17-24. Who is he impersonating? Ben Witherington suggests something quite subtle here, namely, that Paul at some level is impersonating himself as if he were already in Rome, addressing a mixed audience of Gentiles and Jews.

---

1. Fitzmyer, *Romans*, 91.

Perhaps he also imagines the speaker as Phoebe (see 16:1), who will orally deliver this letter, facing the audience, turning first to the Gentile Christian majority and then to the Jewish Christian minority, attempting to persuade the audience, speaking for Paul. Like practicing a speech in advance, alone at home or elsewhere in private, it requires imagination and putting oneself into one's own public character and into the location and occasion when the discourse will actually be delivered. Paul may be doing that in chapter 2.[2]

Does anyone escape Paul's direct attack in this chapter? One group seemingly does, the converted pagans who have renounced idolatry and immorality without taking up observance of the Jewish law, for this is just the group that shows the faith and lifestyle Paul seeks to nurture. Because they have in Christ the image of the one true God, they need no other images, no statues, and no Levitical regulations. The Greeks, or Gentiles, he makes clear, have it in them "to show what the law requires [for it] is written on their hearts" (2:15), while the Jews who boast in the law are found willfully and obviously to break it. Any supposed superiority in the Jews has been undermined.

Paul's tone changes in chapter 3, as he moves into a swift series of rhetorical questions. "Then what advantage has the Jew" (3:1)? Great in every way! And even though some Jews may be unfaithful, God is not. Paul's argument in chapter 3 introduces a counterargument. If our wrongdoing serves to confirm the faithfulness of God, what is wrong with the wrongdoing? Paul then sets up a dialogue with an imagined objector who pursues this line of thought (3:5–9). The statement in 3:8 rings clear: "And why not say (as some people slander us by saying that we say), 'Let us do evil so that good may come'"? The apologetic approach helps us see why Paul pursues this line of thought: these questions address rumors about himself!

Textual Analysis: Topics to Ponder or Discuss

Romans 1:18–32

1. As evident in 1:17, central to Paul's message in Romans is the righteousness of God, a concept that refers both to God's justice and to God's faithfulness to the covenants with Israel and humanity. The notion of God's justice is often interpreted as retributive justice, meaning

---

2. Witherington, *Romans*, 77.

PART I—ALL FOR GRACE

God's judgement on sin and evil, whereas the notion of God's faithfulness is generally viewed as restorative justice, meaning God's desire to restore what is broken and lost. The latter view, God's will and power to save, inspires Paul's understanding in 1:17 and this commentary as well. Paul's point in 1:16-17 raises a major question: From what do people need to be saved? The answer is found in 1:18—3:20. Paul begins with an overview of the Jewish polemic against the pagan world (1:18—2:16), followed by a polemic against nominal Judaism (2:17—3:9).

2. Whereas 1:16-17 speaks of the power of grace, the ensuing section, beginning with 1:18, speaks of the paradox of grace. Paul begins his discussion of the gospel of God's grace, paradoxically, with a discussion of God's wrath. The language and tone of Paul's opening argument raise an immediate concern, because instead of emphasizing God's gracious power to save, the focus is on anger, on the "wrath" of God. As we ponder the meaning of this concept, we note that for Paul and the Bible generally the primary focus of God's wrath is in the future (1:32 and 6:23 remind us of future wrath, speaking of death and reminding us that those who sin "deserve to die"; 2:5 and 2:16 speak of the day of judgment, an event Paul probably envisioned as coming soon), whereas in this passage God's wrath is a present reality. What is Paul's emphasis? Should we view God's present "wrath" as restorative and God's future "wrath" as punitive, both as punitive, or both as restorative? Is God's wrath an extension of his love (is God "out to change us") or is love an extension of his anger (is God "out to get us")? The answer to this question goes to the heart of one's understanding of the Christian message. [These concerns are addressed in essay 4 at the end of this chapter.] Whatever our view, Paul is not thinking of wrath as a vengeful act in which a vindictive God sets out to get even. God is loving and righteous, and the opposite of love is not wrath but indifference (just as the opposite of wrath is indifference). It is precisely because God is righteous that he deals restoratively with sin and punitively with evil.

3. For Paul, two things are being revealed in the present, simultaneously: the wrath of God and the righteousness of God. Paul's use of wrath in 1:18 must be clearly linked with his use of righteousness in 1:17. This link allow us to see God's reconciling purpose. God's saving purpose is powerful and cannot be taken lightly. On the other hand, God's wrath

THE UNIVERSAL NEED OF GRACE

guarantees that evil will be punished, but is itself part of the providential order.

4. In 1:18 Paul introduces the term "truth" as something that is knowable but distorted by human sinfulness. What does Paul have in mind when he speaks of truth as an absolute? Could Paul be referring to the concept of monotheism here, as something that should be universally affirmed? Polytheism and idolatry, the opposite of monotheism, were certainly rampant in the ancient world, and Paul might here simply be resorting to traditional Jewish polemic against paganism (this view seems to be substantiated contextually by Paul's discussion in verses 19–23). Note that Paul speaks of "truth" in 1:25 and 2:2 with a more nuanced meaning.

5. Verses 19–21 introduce the concept of "natural revelation," namely, of God's availability and accessibility through nature (understood as the realm of God's created order), to emphasize that humanity's rejection of God is inexcusable. Not only is God's revelation available to all, but also this evidence can be clearly seen and understood, which leaves humans no defense when they suppress this knowledge. Paul's point is that knowledge or awareness of God's self-revelation in creation is powerless to save people, but rather reveals and magnifies their culpability (later in the letter he will use the same argument about the law; see 3:20, 28; 4:15; 5:13, 20; 7:8–11, 13; 8:2–3).

6. Is Paul's reference to distorted thinking in 1:21 an indictment solely of polytheism and idolatry? While there were few avowed atheists in Paul's world, if he were writing today, would his indictment extend more broadly to include atheism and secular humanism (see 1:28)?

7. Three times in this passage Paul identifies a pattern of human rebellion, which involves some aspect of human corruption, the exchange of something good for something bad (see verses 23, 25, and 28). Each case is followed by God's response, described in the phrase "God gave them up" in verses 24, 26, and 28. The first exchange involves idolatry (making images to replace the invisible God or prioritizing anything over God); the second involves narcissism (viewing oneself as creator rather than as creature), and the third involves atheism (becoming autonomous, replacing God with oneself). For these substitutions God "gave them up" to immoral behavior (1:24), to excessive or fractured sexuality (1:26), and to a host of vices (1:29–32). Why are these forms

PART I—ALL FOR GRACE

of temptation dangerous? [Hint: verse 32 says that these things lead to spiritual death.] This is what happens, Paul laments, when humans are spiritually blind, giving up the invisible in the visible, the sacred in the profane, the mysterious in the tangible, the sacramental in the physical. Take time to examine sin and temptation in your present circumstances. Which sins and temptations do you need to resist?

8. As we read in essay 4: "the wrath that God visits on sinful humanity consists in simply letting humanity have its own way." If this is punishment, how is it so? How might God's wrath be restorative?

9. In 1:26–27 Paul mentions homosexuality in one of only two places (also 1 Cor. 6:9) in his undisputed letters. Thoughtful people today wonder why Paul singled out this particular practice here, and what he meant by it. Is all homosexual practice sinful? Are celibate homosexuals or those in committed relationships any different from celibate heterosexuals or those in committed relationships? All sex can be natural (God honoring) or perverted (heterosexual, homosexual, or bisexual). Sex is natural and proper in loving, gracious, responsible, committed relationships. Of course, sexual laxity and unfaithfulness in all its forms is morally deficient, so that is not part of this conversation. Since God is concerned with our wellbeing, God does not condone promiscuity, fornication, or unfaithfulness, nor should we. These contradict God's nature, and hence our own. Given what we know about sexuality today, homosexuality is no longer considered aberrant socially or psychologically, but rather how some people are hardwired. Today's concept of homosexuality as sexual orientation not chosen by individuals but part of their God-given sexuality would have been unknown to Paul.

10. Sexuality is a complex subject involving social, psychological, and medical points of view as well as theological and biblical perspectives. Several points need to be made about the topic biblically. While homosexual behavior is condemned in the Old Testament, such condemnation is part of Israel's Levitical purity laws, (see Leviticus 18, especially verses 19–24). Such legislation, including food laws and impurity caused by diseases like leprosy, does not apply to Christians today. The New Testament contains few references to homosexuality (Jesus, for example, never spoke of it), and in those cases they appear to address exploitative relationships, particularly forms of pederasty

in which adults prey on children. The Romans passage occurs in a section illustrating standard first-century Jewish thinking, not in the section instructing Christians how to live (chapters 12–16). Finally, Paul's argument reflects a line of thought found in Hellenistic Judaism, according to which polytheism (Gentile idolatry) inevitably led to immorality and to the "exchange of natural sexual roles," an argument developed in a first-century Jewish text called Wisdom of Solomon (11:15–16; 12:24–27; 14:12, 26), with which Paul was familiar and may here be citing. [Wisdom of Solomon, written in the first-century BC, is in the Septuagint and can be found in Bibles containing the apocryphal/deuterocanonical books of the Old Testament.]

11. Several times in this passage Paul speaks of a distorted or reprobate mind (1:21, 28). The human mind is an important topic in Romans, something Paul believes must be renewed or transformed (see 12:2). For Paul, a reprobate mind is one no longer capable of discerning good and evil. What evidence do you find of distorted thinking in society at large? In your own way of thinking and living?

12. Throughout this passage Paul seems to have in mind one particular biblical passage, namely Genesis 1–3. Paul believed that God's created order was good, and that humans were originally in a state of perfect harmony: with God, nature, other humans, and with themselves. But humans rebelled against the very structure of the created order, becoming autonomous (substituting their perspective for God's) and turning incurably inward (becoming increasingly independent in their priorities and decision-making), distorting their original harmony and losing their original blessing. Their revolt against God was a revolt against their own nature, resulting in disharmony with God, nature, other humans, and with themselves. They left the Garden, but all was not lost. God—loving them unconditionally—came looking for them . . . again, and again, and again!

Romans 2:1–16

13. A shift in address takes place at 2:1, from the third person plural to the second person singular. Paul now begins addressing his audience with "you." To whom is he speaking? While some claim he is thinking specifically about those Jews who condemn Gentile immorality while failing to acknowledge their own, it is better to think of the audience as inclusive, consisting of Jews and Gentiles. His focus initially is on

Gentiles (2:1–16; verse 5 confirms that Paul in the main is addressing non-Christian Gentiles here, but with implicit warning to Christian Gentiles who act in the same way; verses 15–16 also make it clear that Paul is not referring to Christians).

14. In chapters 2 and 3 Paul makes use of the diatribe, a teaching device common among philosophers. Question after rhetorical question cascade forward, some indignantly answered, others not at all, as Paul sets up dialogues with imagined objectors to hook his audience (see 2:1–6, 17–24; 3:1–9, 27–31). Such questions and answers do not always settle the issues raised earlier, but they move Paul's argument forward and his readers deliberately up the mountain peak at the center of the letter and to the landscape of hope beyond.

15. Paul's discussion about human hypocrisy in 2:1–3 leads to several important observations: (a) that since everyone is involved in self-indulgence, no human is in the position of judging another on the basis of moral superiority (see also 14:10–13); (b) that it is not what one knows but what one does that is important (2:6, 9–10, 13–14); (c) that God is impartial in goodness as in judgment (2:4–11); and (d) that the delay in God's judgment on evil does not mean there will be no judgment at all. There will be a day of reckoning, Paul insists, when all will receive their due reward (2:5–10).

16. When Paul states that judgment will be according to our deeds (2:6) and that such deeds can also serve as the basis of our justification (2:13), how does this square with his emphasis that salvation comes solely by grace, through faith in Jesus (1:16; see also 3:21–26)? Is Paul suggesting that one is justified by faith but judged by works? [Hint: According to Paul, when God judges our deeds, everyone is found wanting. This means that all saintly deeds, valuable and necessary for life on our planet, are inadequate to gain our salvation. No human effort, says Paul, can restore us to proper covenant relationship, because such harmony can only be achieved by God's grace.]

17. In your estimation, what does Paul mean by consigning honorable people to "eternal life" and dishonorable people to "wrath and fury" (see 2:7–8)? What is your expectation of life after death? Does it square with Paul's? Why or why not? Is God's judgment punitive or restorative?

18. Paul's discussion about law in 2:12–16 is complicated, in part because he does not define what he means by "law," and seems to use the concept inconsistently in his letters (see the discussion of law in essay 7). Generally, when Paul speaks of "law," he is referring to Israel's ethnic law, as found in the Torah (the Mosaic law) or as revealed in the totality of scripture. But what about its use in verse 14? Does Paul have in mind different laws to which humans are subject, or are all human moral standards ultimately subject to biblical standards? Paul's discussion of moral righteousness (good deeds) leads to the supposition in 2:14–15 that Gentiles, who do not possess the Mosaic law, may find themselves absolved of guilt on the day of judgment, if they live in accordance with the moral law (as revealed in their moral conscience): "doing instinctively what the law requires." (Verse 15 foreshadows 7:14–25, where we find precisely the sort of inner moral struggle mentioned here in passing).

19. In your estimation, why does Paul introduce a controversial point in 2:15–16, one that seems to undermine his central claims that no one is righteous (3:10, 23) and that no one can be justified by keeping the law (3:20)? [Hint: the key to understanding Paul's argument in 1:18—3:20 may be the point he makes in 2:11, that God is impartial both in goodness and judgment. Another possibility is to take the reference to Gentiles here as Gentile Christians, as Augustine so understood. While that interpretation could apply to 11:13 and 15:9, where the context suggests it, the thrust of Paul's argument in 2:14 demands a broader use.]

Romans 2:17–29

20. In this passage Paul addresses the Jews directly, noting that despite their advantages (possessing election, the covenants, and the law), they too are under "the power of sin" (3:9) and therefore liable to God's judgment. What Paul has said previously about pagans and Gentiles applies to Jews as well: they too are guilty of doing precisely what they condemn (2:17–24; Paul's list of violations, exemplary and not exhaustive, includes violation even of the Ten Commandments). In our reading of this section, we must be careful not to see in this passage a characterization of all Jews or Judaism in general. Paul is addressing an imaginary figure here, "censoring a censorious Jewish teacher," dialoguing in diatribe format. Just as Paul's dialogue with a

PART I—ALL FOR GRACE

judgmental and hypocritical Gentile in 2:1–16 was not intended as a broadside against all Gentiles, so too it is a serious mistake to see 2:17—3:20 as a broadside against all Jews. Look at the clues! Paul tells us in 2:19–20 that he is dealing with someone who fancies himself a teacher, and not just any sort of teacher, but one who teaches the spiritually blind and foolish. Verse 24 provides a further clue that the audience of this Jewish teaching is Gentile.[3] In speaking of a self-righteous Jew, the most notorious example was the unconverted Paul.

21. Paul's discussion of the contrast between words and deeds leads also to the contrast between appearances and reality, a topic made explicit in 2:25–29. Belonging to the chosen people is of no benefit if what one does is in complete contrast to what one claims for oneself. Simply belonging to the chosen people, Paul says, is not enough. True "chosenness," true "Jewishness," is not a matter of physical circumcision but of the heart (see Jer. 4:4; 9:26; Ezek. 44:9; Gal. 5:6); election is not about outward rituals but about inner reality, a reality perceived and honored by God. This, of course, is good news to Gentiles. They need not be fully Jewish to be Christian. Circumcision and other external rituals are no longer required, for true spirituality is not external but internal (2:29). Humans judge on outward appearances, God on the heart (see 1 Sam. 16:7).

Romans 3:1–8

22. Paul's argument about true Jewishness continues with force. If true Jewishness is internal, not external, and if circumcision must be understood spiritually rather than literally, then of what is the value in being a circumcised Jew? The answer we expect—of no value whatsoever—is not what we get. To be Jewish, Paul asserts, is of great advantage. The greatest advantage is that Jews are the ones with whom God communicated initially; they are the ones to whom God gave the promise of the covenant, first to Abraham (Gen. 12:1–3) and then to David (2 Sam. 7:8–16; Ps. 89:1–4, 19–37). God's covenant, even in promise, required reciprocation. In the case of Israel, the people promised to obey God's will (Exod. 19:8), a promise they broke repeatedly.

23. Paul continues in this section his argument that God's grace confers responsibility. We saw earlier that God punishes sin by withholding

---

3. According to C. K. Barrett, Paul has in mind a hypocritical Jewish teacher or missionary here; *Romans*, 55.

discipline from sinners (1:24–32) and that the giving of a law precisely for such discipline is an act of grace. Here Paul makes clear that "the gracious act of conferring discipline carries with it the responsibility to enact that discipline in one's life. To be shown favor by God does not absolve one from responsibility; rather it confers responsibility upon one."[4] Election, whether of Jew or Christian, does not excuse believers from realizing God's will in their lives. Rather, such knowledge bestows the responsibility to create that reality.

24. The issue of God's faithfulness reappears in 3:3–8: if Israel has been unfaithful, does this nullify God's faithfulness? Is God no longer bound to the covenant promise, and if not, will all humanity also be affected? Paul's gospel (his good news to Jew and Gentile alike) affirms that despite human disobedience, God remains faithful (3:4). Answers provoke further questions, and Paul continues his diatribe. If God is faithful despite our faithlessness, if our disobedience elicits God's gracious response, why not "do evil that good may come"? Some people are apparently accusing Paul of saying just that (3:8a). Paul's answer is unambiguous: No! Such thinking is perverse and adds to one's condemnation. Evil remains evil and must be eliminated at the final judgment.

25. Readers should note that charges Paul raises in 3:7–8, while not answered here, reappear later (see Romans 6:1 and 15, where some answers are provided).

Romans 3:9–20

26. The inference Paul draws about the advantages of Judaism in 3:3–8 seem to be denied in 3:9. However, the point he is making is that this historic advantage does not absolve Israel from responsibility to God. His overall conclusion is clear. Every human is separated from a positive relationship with God; even those "under law" are "under sin."

27. Paul's quotes from the Jewish scriptures—mostly from the Psalms—underscore his conclusion: on the basis of merit and effort, "no one is righteous, not even one" (3:10). Do you agree with Paul's negative assessment? Is it extreme for a reason? If so, what might it be?

28. Thankfully, 3:20 sheds new light on the law. Up to this point one could argue that the cause of universal sinfulness lies in lack of effort or

---

4. Achtemeier, *Romans*, 52.

compliance. One might conclude that keeping the law would eliminate condemnation, but that is not Paul's argument (see 3:20). Even total fulfillment of the law cannot restore relationship with the creator. The law cannot be the way to covenant relationship, indeed, that was never its role. The reason for the inability of the law to accomplish this is its close relationship with sin. [Note: Paul develops the law's link with sin in Romans 7, but he announces here the fundamental flaw with the law: It is not strong enough to resist the power of sin. Readers may want to consult the discussion of Paul's view of the law in essay 7.] While the law provides knowledge of sin, it is powerless to save. The law sets high standards, then seemingly mocks our law-inspired efforts at escape to bring us more firmly under its control. We humans have gotten ourselves into a frightful situation, one we cannot escape. That is why sin is so frightening. It makes God the enemy, the one to fear, rather than the one who is powerful and eager to save. [Note: Paul almost always uses the term "sin" in the singular, as a quasi-cosmic power to which humans are subject, not in the plural, as the accumulation of individual wrong.]

29. Before we leave this discussion of law, we add one final point for consideration. In Romans 13:10 Paul reveals a key to his thinking, that "agape [God's love in us] is the fulfilling of the law." In light of this principle, examine anew passages such as 2:1-2, 6-7, 13-16, 26-29, and 3:20 and how being motivated by God's love is far better than motivation by law and retribution (see 1 John 4:18-19; 1 Peter 4:8; John 13:34-35; and Mark 12:28-34).

Essay 4: Understanding Paul's View of Divine Wrath and Judgment

The mere fact that the Gentiles are now covenant participants with God requires a new interpretation of history. Also Paul has to explain, as best he can, how his gospel was anticipated in the Old Testament, instead of being a novelty, unrelated or even opposed to God's eternal purpose. Three times in his letters Paul describes how the history of Israel led to the grace found in Jesus Christ. The first survey is in Galatians 3:6—5:1 (where the culprit is "legalism" or "slavery to the law") and the other two are in Romans, in 1:18—4:22 (the culprit is "the power of sin") and 5:12-21 (the culprit is our "Adamic human nature").

THE UNIVERSAL NEED OF GRACE

Twice in Romans Paul outlines the situation that led to God's grace being revealed in Jesus Christ. In both passages his intent is to show the plight of humans, so desperate that nothing else could save them. Paul is not here providing speculative philosophies of history but rather surveys of the human predicament based on his own experience of grace; from this experience he argues back to the past. As God's grace had met his human need, Paul seeks to explain why and how this divine favor came about. Why was it grace? And why did grace take the form it did in Jesus Christ? Paul's surveys appear in different contexts and approach the topic from different vantages, but they agree that God had to come to the rescue. Paul had already touched on this question in Galatians 4:4: "when the fullness of time had come, God sent his Son." In Romans this vague allusion is filled out.

Curiously, grace is never mentioned in Romans 1:18—3:20 (which forms the negative basis for the more positive statement of 3:21—4:25). In 1:17 Paul declares that "the righteousness of God is revealed through faith for faith," yet we have to wait until 3:21 for any word about faith, since righteousness at once suggests its antithesis. As the resultant survey of moral history reveals, all human beings, Jew and Gentile alike, are shown to have come short of God's righteousness: "all are under the power of sin" (3:9). Then and only then, as Paul proceeds to speak about faith and the true righteousness offered in Jesus Christ, does the word "grace" appear (3:24). It is also striking here how Paul is silent for so long about Christ. No other passage of equal length in all his letters is without some mention of the Lord. The explanation is that Paul is analyzing the moral and historical conditions for the coming of Christ. Only then can he turn from the negative to the positive side of the issue.

The same happens when Paul discusses the position of the Jews in 3:27–29. There is no further mention of Christ until the end of chapter 4 (4:24-25), where talk of Jesus brings up the thought of grace (see 5:2). This does not mean that Paul conceives of God as ungracious during the pre-Christian period (since Israel had been chosen by grace for grace, that is, for service to the nations), but "grace" is so distinctively the mark of God's revelation in Jesus Christ that Paul reserves it exclusively for the Christian experience.

The antithesis to "righteousness" is not love or grace; it is "wrath." Yet the divine wrath is also part of the providential order. Paul begins his discussion of the gospel of God's grace, paradoxically, with a discussion of God's wrath. Yet grace and wrath are, for Paul, but two sides of the faithfulness of God to his promises made to Israel, and through Israel to all of humanity. Here, just as in an earlier letter (1 Thess. 1:9–10; 5:9–10) and later in Romans (9:22), Paul regards God's wrath as the reaction of divine love against the defiance of sin; the saving purpose includes the punishment of evil. Because sin is temporal, the saving purpose in God's wrath is restorative, whereas God's wrath against evil, historical and cosmic, is eschatological and therefore punitive. Meantime, in this time before the end, God intervenes with offers of grace.

God's faithfulness to his promises (his "righteousness"), however, is not something to be trifled with. To abuse God's offer of salvation brings with it terrible consequences. If God is faithful to his covenant promises, God is also faithful to his nature as God; and to refuse to acknowledge God's lordship is to remove oneself from fellowship with the divine. As Paul makes clear, to reject the God whose lordship is one of mercy and love is to place oneself "under the tyrannical lordship of something completely unworthy of our submission. Such lordships are incapable of exercising their lordship in any but the most destructive way. When we exchange lords in that way, Paul claims, we have handed ourselves over to some creature instead of to the Creator."[5]

In addition to losing our connection with God and participating in idolatrous and immoral practices, as Paul delineates in Romans 1:18–32, there is an even more insidious result of rejecting God's lordship, and that is to take as Lord—ourselves. The results of such servitude are generally disastrous. It is not a question of whether or not we have a lord over us. As creatures, we have no choice in the matter. The only question is what sort of lordship will it be? Whatever lordship it is—wealth, power, drugs, violence, abuse, sex, gambling, influence, acclaim, fear—it will claim us and use us to our own destruction.

If the way of salvation lies in accepting the good news that we need no longer be under the lordship of any creature but rather under the lordship of a benevolent creator, rejecting that good news brings in its wake terrible consequences. The most frightening thing about this passage is the way Paul describes God's punishment for the sin of idolatry. It is frightening simply because, had Paul not told us they were signs of wrath, we could easily have mistaken them for signs of grace. When God displays wrath in the way described in this passage, there is no divine calamity, no fire from

---

5. Ibid., 37–38. The segment on God's wrath is adapted from Achtemeier's commentary on Romans, 34–43.

THE UNIVERSAL NEED OF GRACE

on high sent to consume sinful society. Rather, the wrath that God visits on sinful humanity consists in simply letting humanity have its own way. According to Paul, God delivers sinful humanity over to its own desires. "For this reason God gave them up" to impurity and degrading passions (1:24, 26). Is this punishment? Yes, certainly, but it is not God's anger retaliating. Rather it is sin punishing the sinner, or, if you will, sinners punishing themselves. If sin is the attempt to get out of life what God has not put into it, then God's wrath is not something outside the moral order, but the natural order at work.

God's wrath therefore does not mean some divine restraint or punishment on humanity. Rather God punishes sin by letting us have control over our own destinies, through permissiveness. God's wrath, in sum, consists in letting humanity carry out the results of its rejection of the creator as Lord. And the results of the kind of life Paul describes in this segment, are disastrous—for individuals, and for society.

According to our interpretation, Paul has no desire to minimize the seriousness of sin. God's will has expressed itself in the very constitution of the universe, and therefore it is inevitable that evil, wherever and in whatever shape it appears, should feel the full weight of the divine reaction. But this is not "wrath," as we commonly conceive it. Rather it is the negative aspect of an order that has a positive purpose of good in it. The will of God must be conceived as the embodiment of a single principle: the will to good. God's wrath is God's grace.

God's wrath is not Paul's last word, but his first. In that respect, God's wrath is not devoid of grace, but its extension. God's saving purpose includes the punishment of evil at the end, and that is good news. In the meantime, God intervenes with the offer of grace to faith, and believers in Christ are assured of acquittal:

> But God proves his love for us in that while we still were sinners Christ died for us. Much more surely then, now that we have been justified by his blood, will we be saved through him from the wrath of God [the final, eschatological destruction of evil]. For if while we were enemies, we were reconciled to God through the death of his Son, much more surely, having been reconciled, will we be saved by his life. (5:8–10)

Believers already have right relationship with God—or as Paul calls it, "newness of life" (6:4)—which frees them from condemnation (8:1). And that is great news!

Optional Group Activity

Divide the participants into four groups to discuss the question of God's wrath. Ask Group 1 to discuss the merits of examining God's wrath as restorative. Ask Group 2 to discuss the merits of examining God's wrath as punitive. Ask Group 3 to address how God is dealing with human sin and evil in the present. Ask Group 4 to address the question: How will God deal with human sin and evil in the future? At the conclusion, reconvene the small groups into one and ask each group to share its insights with the others.

If time allows, give participants time to write down one takeaway (insight) from their reading or group discussion and then to share it with the class.

Session Five

The Gift of Grace

Summary: In Romans 3:21—4:22 Paul turns from God's wrath to God's grace, from the universality of sin and judgment to justification by the faithfulness of Christ; in other words, from the problem to the solution. We learn that a new period in human history has begun with the coming of Jesus Christ, whose mission was to make known in a new way God's righteousness. The essence of the gospel is explained in 3:21–26, namely, that salvation is available for all human beings through God's grace as revealed in Christ. Four effects of Christ's work are formulated in these verses: justification, redemption, atonement, and pardon. Having introduced God's solution to the human condition, Paul expands upon his ideas, beginning with faith. Appealing to the example of Abraham in scripture, Paul indicates that Abraham was reckoned righteous not because of anything he had done but in virtue of a promise made to him by God. As a result, Abraham is declared to be the father of all believers, and his faith a "type" of Christian faith. The concluding essay addresses Paul's view of sin and salvation, examining biblical metaphors used to describe human rebellion and God's gracious response.

Assignment: Read Session 5 of *Grace Revealed* and Romans 3:21—4:22. Complete the following task, writing the answer in your journal. [Be prepared to share your views with others in the class.] Four effects of Christ's work are found in Romans 3:21–26: justification, redemption, atonement, and pardon. Define these terms and explain how they address the human condition.

PART I—ALL FOR GRACE

Key Verse(s): Romans 3:21–26

Central Theme: Jesus' faithfulness enacts God's righteousness

Technical Words and Concepts: redemption, atonement, Day of Atonement, law of faith, Shema, belief, circumcision, corporate personality

Learning Objectives

In this session participants will examine:

1. The essentials of Paul's gospel as found in Romans 3:21–26
2. The meaning of "justification by faith" and "faith in Christ"
3. Four effects of the faithfulness of Christ: justification, redemption, atonement, and pardon
4. The relevance of the Mosaic law for Christians as discussed in Romans 4 and Galatians 3
5. The role of Abraham as exemplar of justification by faith
6. Biblical metaphors for sin and salvation

Outline to Romans 3:21—4:22

I. The Gift of Grace 3:21—4:22
   A. The Faithfulness of Christ 3:21–31
   B. The Faithfulness of Abraham 4:1–22
      1. Abraham Justified by Faith 4:1–8
      2. Abraham a Model for Jews and Non-Jews 4:9–15
      3. Abraham's Trust in God's Promise 4:16–22

Romans 3:21—4:22: Flow of the Argument

Having shown what happens to humanity apart from the gospel and under the influence of sin, Paul addresses the solution. The word "but" in 3:21 is pivotal in Paul's argument, as he turns away from the human predicament to the divine prescription. Paul recognizes that a new period in human history has begun with the coming of Jesus Christ, whose mission was to make known in a new way God's faithfulness. The essence of the gospel is explained in 3:21–26, a dense passage that is just one sentence in the original Greek. Paul's discussion in 3:21–31 revisits, revises, and expands upon his thesis (stated in 1:16–17) in preparation for a second line of argumentation, this time not from experience but rather from the ancient Hebrew scriptures. Paul's argument from scripture continues through chapter 11.

In 3:21–31 Paul formulates the essence of his gospel: salvation for all human beings by grace through faith in Christ Jesus. Martin Luther claimed that this section represented the core of Romans, indeed "the very central place... of the whole Bible." In these verses the theme of God's faithfulness is developed variously, in (1) its relation to the Mosaic law and the Hebrew scriptures (3:21), (2) its universal destination (3:22); (3) its necessity (3:23), (4) its gracious nature (3:24a), (5) its mode of revelation (3:24b–25), (6) its tolerance (3:25b), and (7) its consequences for Jews and Gentiles alike (3:27–31). Four effects of Christ's work are formulated in these verses: justification, redemption, atonement, and pardon. For Paul such effects are appropriated exclusively through faith in Christ Jesus. Faith is how human beings experience what Christ has accomplished.

Having introduced God's solution to the human predicament in 3:21–31, Paul expands on his ideas, starting with faith, taking many of these ideas and explaining them further. In chapter 4, as in chapter 3 of Galatians, Paul appeals to the example of Abraham in scripture. Paul has not changed his earlier views about the role of the law and the Mosaic covenant, but because he is dealing with a different situation than in Galatia, where Judaizers were attempting to persuade the Galatians to become Jews, in Romans he presents the law differently. There is no need to polemicize against the law here, for Roman Gentile Christians show no interest in getting circumcised or in submitting to the Mosaic law. On the contrary, they are more likely to devalue the law and the Jewish heritage in general.

In order to demonstrate that justification by grace through faith does not undo the law but upholds it, Paul argues that this principle was operative in the Old Testament. Paul had appealed to scripture in 3:21, but in chapter 4 he demonstrates that what he had affirmed in 3:21–31, namely, that reconciliation is a matter of divine grace, is supported by scripture. Abraham was reckoned righteous (declared to be in right relationship with God), we are told, solely on the basis of his trust in God (4:1–8), and not because of anything he had done. Abraham's righteousness did not result from his circumcision (4:9–12) or obedience to any law, but resulted from a promise made to him by God (4:13–17). In this manner Abraham became the father of all believers, and his faith is a "type" of Christian faith (4:18–25). Because of grace, Abraham's example eliminates boasting (see 3:27; 4:2).

PART I—ALL FOR GRACE

Textual Analysis: Topics to Ponder or Discuss

Romans 3:21–31

1. In 3:21–26 Paul reaches the point of the argument he began in 1:18. Using traditional theological language, Paul offers a rich summary of his gospel, showing it not to be a novelty but rather forever God's way of accepting those who trust in him. This paragraph, one of the most tightly woven in all Paul's letters, is not easy reading but deeply rewarding to those who ponder each phrase. [Hint: it helps to read the passage in more than one English translation.]

2. The meaning and placement of the phrase "righteousness of God" in 3:21 is central to Paul's argument in this unit. [Note: As you ponder this pivotal section of Romans, keep in mind that the word "righteousness" is best translated as "faithfulness," and that the concept "the righteousness of God" is best understood when tied specifically to God's covenant with Abraham.] In the Old Testament God's righteousness is often connected with God's justice, whereas in Romans it most often refers to God's commitment to uphold the covenant arrangements with Israel, and, in this sense, it seems often to be virtually equivalent to his faithful grace. The second half of the larger expression "the righteousness of God [disclosed] through faith in Jesus Christ" in 3:22 is mistranslated. Generations of English translations reflect the presumption that what Paul meant here and elsewhere is human faith "in" Jesus Christ, but scholars, arguing from grammar and context, are coming to understand that Paul meant something quite different, namely, that it is Jesus' faithfulness, not human faith, that brings about God's righteousness. The phrase in this context carries a "subjective" sense, designating the faithfulness of Christ to God, not a human's faith in God or Christ. Since the ensuing phrase "for all who believe" already emphasizes the human response to God's gift, Paul's intention in this verse might well be that our faith is made possible by the faithfulness of Christ. If our faith is the acceptance of the fact that we are accepted, then our justification is not by our faithfulness but by the faithfulness of Christ. The danger is always that faith becomes a work we perform in order to earn salvation, something deemed impossible by Paul. Faith, for Paul, is not just believing in something as factual; faith is trust in God's faithfulness, acceptance of God's work in Christ.

3. It is important in Romans to trace Paul's theological argument as it develops from section to section. In this endeavor, we should not lose track of Paul's apologetic purpose, that is, the continuing defense of his Gentile mission. Hence his emphasis at the beginning that the righteousness of God has been disclosed "apart from the law" (3:21), an emphasis he maintains in chapter 4, brilliantly portraying Abraham as the classic example of justification through trust in God's promises.

4. The "Flow of the Argument" above mentions four effects of Christ's work in 3:21–26: justification, redemption, atonement, and pardon. Using a Bible dictionary or online resource, define each term and its meaning in this passage. If you were to reduce Paul's argument in this section to one sentence, what would it be? [In other words, what, for you, is the essence of Paul's gospel?]

5. The reference to redemption in 3:24 reminds us of the exodus, an event that released captive Israelites from slavery (see Exod. 3:8; Ps. 78:35). To redeem is "to ransom" or "buy back," so when God redeems the Israelites, whom he calls "my firstborn son" in Exodus 4:22, he is emancipating or delivering that which was previously his. That is the idea here as well. If "the earth is the Lord's and all that is in it" (Ps. 24:1), then all peoples and nations belong to God. The cross represents not only God's unconditional love for humanity but God's desire to rescue humanity from all that enslaves, whether things present or things to come; powers and principalities of all sorts, personal or political; material, social, and emotional factors; powers above us, below us, around us, and within us, none can "separate us from the [redeeming] love of God in Christ Jesus our Lord" (8:38–39).

6. The reference to "atonement (reconciliation with God) through Christ's blood" in 3:25 reminds us of the centrality of the cross for Paul [see the discussion on Paul's view of the cross in essay 6]. Older translations use words such as "propitiation" or "expiation" to describe what the newer versions call "atonement." The language and imagery is taken from the Old Testament sacrificial ritual on the Day of Atonement (Lev. 16:13–15), in which sacrificial blood was poured upon the lid of the ark of the covenant in the innermost sanctuary of the tabernacle. This mercy seat was envisioned as the place where God dwells (1 Sam. 4:4; 2 Sam. 6:2; Ps. 80:1), where God speaks (Exod. 25:22; Numb. 7:89), and where God atones (forgives and reconciles) by the

shedding of blood (Lev. 16:13–15). Propitiation language addresses two concerns: (a) how God can be propitiated, that is, what humans can do to turn God's wrath (justice) from the sinner, and (b) how sinners can be purified from sin. Some translators prefer "expiation" language because it refers only to wiping away or forgiving sins; no allusion to God's wrath is included. Whatever translation one choses for the Greek *hilasterion*, the general meaning is clear: Jesus becomes the place where and also the means by which God meets his people and forgives their sins. Forgiveness comes by the blood of Jesus, namely, by the giving of his life.

7. According to Paul, the sacrificial death of Jesus is at the heart of God's saving plan. God's covenant justice is on display here, both as a means of dealing with human sin and as a way of vindicating God's people. The verdict of the final judgment has been brought forward into the middle of history. We do not have to wait to discover who really belongs to God's people. This is the meaning of the gospel, of justification by faith, that whoever trusts in the faithfulness of God, as manifested through Jesus, is among those who will be vindicated in the future.[1] What is your understanding of the meaning of Christ's death on the cross? Can an instrument of torture and shame represent the means of salvation?

8. The consequences of Paul's assertion about the manifestation of God's faithfulness in Christ and about the role of faith in human life are discussed in 3:27–31. The style again is that of diatribe. The framework is the human tendency to rely on one's own power and ability and thereby to think one can achieve right standing in the sight of God. The central term is "faith," mentioned four times in the preceding paragraph and five times here. In 3:27 Paul introduces the odd phrase "law of faith," better translated as "principle of faith" (as in the RSV). Thus by an oxymoron Paul contrasts law and faith, which is in reality no law at all. Such use of "law" is unparalleled in Paul's other writings, though in 8:2 he refers to "the Spirit of life" as a law, and in 1 Corinthians 9:21 and Galatians 6:2 to the "law of Christ." The law (God's law) was always meant to be fulfilled by faith, the sort of faith that transforms one's heart. The law always was God's law; thus it is not abolished but fulfilled by faith, through love (13:8–10). As Paul

---

1. Wright, *Romans for Everyone*, 1:58.

makes clear in 12:3, human faith is not an effort we bring to God, but a gift we return to God. Despite the daunting terminology, Paul's point here is clear: the righteousness that comes to human beings by virtue of faith in Christ Jesus is alien to them; it is the faith(fullness) of Christ that is ascribed to them and that in no way depends on their own merit or striving. It comes to them from God as grace, so all boasting is excluded (see Gal. 3:25–29).

9. In 3:30 Paul traces to the monotheism of Israel ("God is one") the unique relationship of all human beings to him (see the Shema, the basic Jewish confession of faith, in Deuteronomy 6:4). He insists that God not only justifies human beings gratuitously, but also offers that grace to all humans alike. In 3:31 he tells us that justification by faith upholds the law, though he does not here explain how this is so. That explanation will emerge during the course of his argument in Romans. Chapter 4 offers a partial explanation, particularly in relation to the problem of boasting, but Paul will return to the matter in a theoretical way in chapters 8, 10, and 13. Paul's point, however, is that salvation by faith does not mean that God's revelation in scripture can simply be set aside. Though in the heat of argument Paul sometimes seems to have only a negative view of the role of law (see Rom. 7:4–6; 8:3; Gal. 3:23; 4:4; 4:21—5:1), he insists that the law is from God, plays its proper role in God's saving plan, and must be understood positively in the light of God's act in Christ (this role he elaborates in 7:1–25).

Romans 4:1–22

10. Since Abraham is the progenitor of the people of Israel and the recipient of God's covenant promise, Paul must deal with the figure of Abraham. He does so in chapter 4. As you read this chapter, compare it with Paul's discussion in Galatians 3, noting the similarities and differences in tone and emphasis between these two Pauline versions. If you could reduce Paul's message in each version to a few sentences, what would it be?

11. Paul's discussion in chapter 4 extends the comments made in 3:1–2 about the benefits that belong to Jews, and it also anticipates the longer discussion in Romans 9–11. Crucial to this discussion is Paul's interpretation of Genesis 15:6, quoted in 4:3. Read that verse and determine its meaning for the original author, for Paul, and for you. As noted above (see point 2), how we translate the Greek terms for

"faith" and "belief" makes a huge difference in our understanding, interpretation, and application of the Christian message, for these terms are central to being Christian. If we keep the covenant relationship in mind, how in the Bible terms such as "faith" and "belief" emphasize relational and corporate realities rather than abstract and individual ones (the notion of "trust" in the faithfulness of God/Christ rather than faith or belief as human qualities), the result brings us closer to understanding the concept of grace in God's plan for humanity. Reading Pauline and New Testament terminology in this fresh way is God's new exodus for our time, redeeming us from bondage to guilt, anxiety, uncertainty, and fear, and freeing us for grace and peace (see 1:7). Freedom from bondage and freedom for grace, that's Paul's message: "Now you are children of the promise, like Isaac . . . ; do not submit again to a yoke of slavery" (Gal. 4:28—5:1). In Romans 4, Paul draws on Genesis 15:6 in three slightly different ways to underscore the fact that Abraham did not earn God's favor; can you discover them? [Note: The answers appear in the commentary below.]

12. In 4:3 Paul quotes Genesis 15:6 as evidence that it was by faith and not by works that God puts the ungodly in a right relationship to himself. He elaborates with the analogy of work, indicating that faith is a gift, not something to be earned.

13. In 4:9 Paul notes that Genesis 15:6 mentions Abraham's faith prior to the time when circumcision became essential for inclusion into the covenant people of God (see Gen. 17:9–14). Paul draws a conclusion from the order of the two stories: Abraham's experience of faith occurred before the legal requirement for circumcision, and this makes Abraham the ancestor and model for non-Jews as well as for Jews (4:11–12). Circumcision as a legal requirement has no validity for Christians, but only as a sign or "seal" of faith in God's goodness (4:11). Modern Christians sometimes find talk of circumcision perplexing or possibly irrelevant (circumcision, as a religious rite, was a sign of the old covenant, signifying that a person belonged to Israel), in part because the New Testament, addressed to Christians, substitutes baptism as the sign of God's new covenant with humanity (see Col. 2:11–13). Paul may have baptism in mind when he uses the word "seal" in 4:11 (see also 2 Cor. 1:22), although that is not clear. We will defer discussion of baptism until 6:1–14, where Paul explores its meaning.

14. Paul's reference to Abraham and his descendants inheriting "the world" in 4:13 certainly extends beyond the original "Promised Land" (see Gen. 15:18–21). Is Paul saying that Jews should inherit the world? If not, could he have meant by "descendants" God's "global covenant community"? [Another possibility is to view the entire world as God's "Holy Land," which God's people are to claim and possess.]

15. A key to understanding Paul's argument in Romans 4 is found in 4:17, where Paul seems to be saying that "God's original promise envisioned a multi-ethnic family." If that is true, take a moment to ponder how such a vision can influence your actions, attitudes, and priorities in today's climate of increasing global fear, suspicion, and xenophobia.

16. In 4:22 Paul notes that Genesis 15:6 is based not only on God's promise of posterity (see Gen. 15:5), but also on Abraham's faith in that promise, despite the barrenness of his aged wife Sarah and the inadequacy of his own body, that was "already as good as dead" (4:19). Abraham remained strong in faith, fully convinced that God was able to do what God had promised. What Paul seems to be saying is that faith in the God who promises impossible things is the foundation on which God's family builds. Another version of God's promise to Abraham and Sarah appears in Genesis 18:10–19, a fascinating account highlighted by the divine promise: "Is anything too wonderful ("too hard," RSV) for the Lord?" (18:14). If these words "were written not for his sake alone, but for ours also" (4:23–24), what application might such assurance have in our lives and in our world today? [Notice that in 4:24–25 Paul shifts from descriptive third-person language to a first-person plural style that signals the confessional stance of the Christian community. With the exception of 5:12–21, this stance guides the discussion in chapters 5 and 6.]

Essay 5: Understanding Paul's View of Sin and Salvation

The centrality of sin in Christianity is unquestionable. Its place in the Bible as the central issue in our life is equally paramount, though its place as dogma goes back to the fourth century, when Christianity was engaged in the task of accommodating to dominant culture. One of the unfortunate results of that process was the reduction of the multiple and powerful biblical metaphors for describing the human condition to one dominant metaphor;

one explanation described the problem (sin), and one solution sufficed (salvation). While sin matters, biblically, theologically, and existentially, it needs to be demoted from its status as the dominant Christian metaphor for the human condition. Sin is not the sole biblical image for the human condition, nor is it the primary one. Demoting sin enables us to affirm the power and importance of other metaphors, thereby enriching our understanding of what ails us.

In the story of Israel's bondage in Egypt, sin was not the issue. The ancestors of the Jewish people were not in slavery because they had sinned. As slaves, what they needed was not forgiveness, but liberation. In Israel's experience of exile in Babylon, sin does play a part. Exile, however, was their problem. What they needed was not primarily forgiveness but a path out of exile, a way to return "home." We find the same image in the well-known parable of the prodigal son (Luke 15:11–32). The younger son goes to "a distant country," where he becomes an exile. His life as an exile becomes so miserable that he eventually resolves to return home, to journey back to his father. Though the son prepares a confession of sin, the father doesn't need to hear it—indeed, the father has been waiting for the son all along and, filled with compassion, rushes out to meet him. The parable is not about sin and forgiveness. The son could have received forgiveness in exile and yet remained far away. Nothing would have changed, except that he had been forgiven and felt better. Would anyone remember a story like that? Rather than being a story about sin and forgiveness, it is about exile and return, reconciliation and celebration.

Another biblical image for the human condition is infirmity in its many forms: illness, blindness, paralysis, deafness. What the infirm need is not forgiveness, but healing and wholeness. When sin becomes the "one size fits all" metaphor for the human condition, it obscures the rich and important meanings of other metaphors. According to the Bible, our predicament—what we need deliverance from—is not simply or primarily sin. There are other issues such as bondage, exile, blindness, infirmity, fear, detachment, anger, cruelty, addiction, and abuse.

People in bondage need liberation, people in exile need to return home, people who are blind need to see, people who are sick or wounded need healing, people who are fearful need to trust, people who are outcasts need community, people who are abused need deliverance. The heaven-and-hell emphasis on sin and forgiveness doesn't address these issues very well. To the extent that we are responsible for these conditions, the message of forgiveness does mean we are accepted by God, despite our baggage or bondage. This message is true and important. But forgiveness doesn't address the problems themselves. If our problem is bondage or exile, we need more than forgiveness. In such cases, the metaphor of sin misses the richness and depth of the biblical message.

When we turn to Paul's discussion of sin, we find he refuses to be tied down to rigid consistency. Thus to the difficult question of the origin of human sin he gives no fewer than three distinct answers. In one place he suggests human sin is the direct consequence of the sin of Adam (Rom. 5:12–21); in another, sin springs from the "flesh," the constituent part of human nature that rebels against God (Rom. 7:14—8:8); in another, it is the work of cosmic powers controlling the universe (Gal. 4:3, 9; cf. the "powers" of the universe in Rom. 8:38–39). In Romans 7, Paul's classic passage about sin and its effects, we discover an important element in the apostle's thinking—his view of sin as personal: "sin . . . deceived me" (7:11). Here sin is viewed as a personal force, a living power, which exists outside the human realm but which launches its attack upon humans. And the point of attack is the flesh, human frailty and weakness. Yielding to this force destroys fellowship with God, hardens the heart, and warps moral judgment. It destroys life as God intended it; its result is "death" (6:23).

Concerning the concept of salvation, Christian scholars are convinced that the evangelical emphasis on "being saved," that is, viewing salvation primarily as an assurance of entrance to heaven, is a rather recent emphasis in Christian tradition, going back to the nineteenth century. In the Bible the concept of salvation is seldom about life after death. Rather it is about life now, about transformation this side of death. This also affects our understanding of Jesus as Savior. Salvation assures believers of security from external threats and dangers and their place in the coming kingdom of God on earth, and Jesus embodies such, through his life, death, and resurrection.

The doctrine of salvation is complex, and different aspects of the Christian understanding have had particular attraction during different periods of church history or for specific situations. Recent studies of the biblical notion of salvation have placed considerable emphasis upon the importance of contextualization, meaning that, because the Christian gospel always addresses specific situations, the doctrine of salvation should be contextualized in those circumstances. For example, to the oppressed—whether spiritually, economically, or politically—the gospel response is liberation; to those burdened by personal guilt, the message is forgiveness; to the despondent, the message is hope.

Christianity holds that the created order, particularly humanity, has fallen into disorder. Things are not what they were meant to be, and something needs to be done about this. The same God who made the created order must act to reorder it, and this he has accomplished through the life, death, and resurrection of Jesus Christ. In his widely used *Christian Theology*, Alistair McGrath provides answers given by Christians throughout history to the question, "*from* what are we saved?" In each case, the doctrine of sin provides an answer. Each model, in turn, also points to the doctrine of salvation, with its hopeful answers.[2]

From what, then, are we saved? McGrath provides six answers: Christians are saved from (1) their human condition, (2) their guilt, (3) their lack of holiness, (4) their inauthentic human existence (characterized by faith in the transient material world), (5) oppression, and (6) from forces that enslave humanity—such as satanic forces, evil spirits, fear of death, or the power of sin. In summary, the Christian doctrine of salvation deals with the restoration of all things, including humanity, to their proper relationship to God.

Salvation, consequently, represents new possibilities, a new state of being. McGrath provides models of salvation that correspond to the six models of sin. Together, they answer the question, "*for* what are we saved?" Christians are saved for (1) relationship with God, (2) righteousness in the sight of God, (3) personal holiness, (4) authentic human existence, (5) social and political liberation, and (6) spiritual freedom. All six concepts can be reduced to one biblical truth: salvation is life; to be saved is to gain or regain life, abundant and free.

This understanding of salvation exhibits a radical this-worldly orientation. The reason is clear: traditional Christians followed their Jewish counterparts in placing their faith into a historical context. The basic conviction of the Greeks was that truth was changeless and hence not tied to events. The earliest Christian creeds, such as the Apostles Creed, were composed to counter such views, which tended to overspiritualize Jesus and detach Christianity from history.

---

2. McGrath, *Christian Theology*, 339–42.

Optional Group Activity

Today we tend to think of salvation individually and personally, which is important, but that is not the biblical emphasis. While individual sin does arise in the heart (at the center of our being), it can be fostered by peer pressure and the need to conform. The Bible was written when people lived communally, identifying with a tribe, clan, or nation (a notion termed "corporate personality"). Divide the participants into four or more groups to discuss the question, "From what are we saved?" from a communal perspective. Thinking biblically, ask each group to address one aspect of national or corporate sin, reflecting on the origin, nature, and consequences of this mindset and suggesting ways to counter its influence in society by asking "For what are we saved?"

Ask Group 1 to address corporate greed; Group 2 to address racism; Group 3 to address sexism (including sexual lifestyles); Group 4 to address materialism; Group 5 to address militarism, etc. Depending on the interest of the participants, other social sins may be studied instead. At the conclusion, reconvene the small groups into one and ask each group to share its insights with the others.

If time allows, give participants time to write down one takeaway (insight) from their reading or group discussion and then to share it with the class.

Session Six

The Work of Grace

Summary: Romans 4:23—5:21 serves a transitional purpose in Romans. This unit presents what it means to be Christian, not so much individually as communally. Romans 5:1-11, a tightly constructed passage, speaks of God's love. The purpose of this passage is twofold: to produce endurance for the present and hope for the future. These qualities are the result of God's love revealed through Christ's death on the cross, an act of sheer grace. In 5:12-21 Paul returns to the question of sin, explaining how weak, ungodly sinners can be justified. Paul uses Adam and his story as representative of the human race. Using Adam as a prototype of Christ, Paul explains how Adam and Christ personify the old and the new in strikingly antithetical ways. The "act" that each performs determines the identity and destiny of all people. Because the question of "original sin" is said to arise in 5:12, this session includes a discussion of the topic from biblical, theological, and biological perspectives. The closing essay addresses Paul's understanding of the cross, a central theme in his letters (see 3:25; 4:25; 5:6-10; 6:2-11; 1 Cor. 1:23; 2:1-2).

Assignment: Read Session 6 of *Grace Revealed* and Romans 4:23—5:25. Answer the following questions, writing the answers in your journal. [Be prepared to share your views with others in the class.] What is your understanding of the role of the cross in Christianity? Does the cross hold significance for your life? Why or why not? The closing essay of this session indicates that the cross can be viewed as a means of revelation about the character of empire, about the path of personal transformation, and about the character of God. Which of these seem most relevant and applicable to you at this time? Why?

Key Verse(s): Romans 5:18

Central Theme: God's grace is morally and spiritually transformative

Technical Words and Concepts: chiasm/chiastic structure, sanctification, original sin, typology, reconciliation, Vulgate, substitutionary atonement, temple theology

Learning Objectives

In this session participants will examine:

1. Paul's use of chiastic structures
2. The theme of eschatological hope in Romans 5
3. The relationship between justification and sanctification
4. The doctrine of original sin
5. The assurance of Christian salvation
6. Paul's use of typology in 5:12–21
7. The meaning of the cross and the crucifixion of Jesus

Outline to Romans 4:23—5:21

I. The Work of Grace 4:23—8:39
    A. In Human Nature 4:23—8:17
        1. New Life in Christ 4:23—5:21
            a. The Results of Life in Christ 4:23—5:11
            b. The Adam and Christ Typology 5:12–21

Romans 4:23—5:21: Flow of the Argument

Romans 5:1–11 serves as a transitional unit into the next major section of the letter, which extends through 8:39. As the previous sections addressed God's saving act in response to universal human sinfulness, this section presents what it means to be Christian, not so much individually, as a disciple following the teachings and example of Jesus (the gospels approach discipleship more from that perspective), but corporately, as one who participates in the community of faith. The basic theme of this section is that the Christian life is one of freedom from various threats to life: freedom from alienation and judgment (chapter 5), from sin (chapter 6), from the law (chapter 7), and from the flesh, suffering, death, and the cosmic powers that separate us from God (chapter 8).

Chapters 5-8 of Romans form a unit not only thematically, but structurally. Scholars detect in this section a "ring composition," or chiasm. A chiastic structure is an X- or V-shaped pattern frequently found in the literature of Paul's time, in which clauses, verses, or units are related to each other through a reversal of structure in order to make a larger point. If the pattern consists of seven segments, the topic of scene one (A) corresponds to that of scene seven (A'); scene two (B) to scene six (B'), and three (C) to five (C'). Such structure draws special attention to the fourth scene (D), the innermost scene and pivotal point in the chiasmus. If the pattern consists of six scenes, the focus may be on inner (the third and fourth, C and C') or the outer scenes (A or A'), and the latter is the case in Romans. The main development of chapters 5-8, viewed chiastically, appears thus:

A.	5:1-11	assurance of future glory
B.	5:12-21	basis of assurance in work of Christ
C.	6:1-23	the problem of sin
C'.	7:1-25	the problem of law
B'.	8:1-17	basis of assurance in work of Christ
A'.	8:18-39	assurance of future glory

As 8:18-39 shares a common theme with 5:1-11, so 8:1-17 has much in common with 5:12-21. In between is 6:1-7:25, parenthetical but hardly incidental to the surrounding themes. The concern for Jewish/Gentile relations and the related topic of the Mosaic law, essential to Paul's argument in chapters 1-4, are by no means dropped. In the midst of his depiction of life in Christ, Paul returns to the law in 5:13-14, 20; 6:14-15, climaxing in the chapter-long discussion in chapter 7 and lingering in 8:1-4, 7, and 15. In chapters 5-8 Paul invites Christians to join him in assurance of what the gospel provides, a new life given to God's service and a certain hope for future glory.[1]

Paul's discussion in 5:1-11 begins in 4:23, for the shift from past to present occurs there, not in 5:1. To find the transition at 5:1 makes the first eleven verses of chapter 5 seem a random collection of ideas, rather than

---

1. In addition to chapters 5-8, a chiastic structure is evident in 12:1—13:14 (see below). Paul also utilizes the chiastic structure in individual passages, such as in 5:1-11.

part of a larger argument with its own internal coherence. The structure of 4:23—5:11 consists in the statement of three themes, with their subsequent development. These themes appear in 4:23-25; they are righteousness (4:23-24), Christ's death for sins (4:25a), and Christ's resurrection for righteousness (4:25b). The structure of 5:1-10 is chiastic (A, B, A'):

First theme: A (Righteousness, 5:1-5)
Second theme: B (Christ death for sins, 5:6-8)
Third theme: A' (Christ's resurrection for righteousness, 5:9-11)

The unit speaks of God's love. The first and third themes speak of the results of God's love (peace that comes from God's reconciling grace), and the second (central) theme points to the cross (the death of Christ) as the source of God's love, administered through the Spirit (this theme is developed in chapter 8). As this structural examination makes clear, Paul is not speaking randomly here on Christian virtues. Rather he is using literary devices familiar to his readers in support of a carefully crafted argument. That argument runs as follows: Now that we have been justified (set right with God) through Christ's death and resurrection, we may, in addition to having peace, have confidence in our hope for the future; but more, our present status in God's grace is such that we can maintain that confidence even in the face of adversity, for grace produces hope, grounded in God's love and made abundant through the Spirit; since that is the case, we have nothing more to fear, whether things present or things to come; our reconciliation with God, which we have because of Christ, is the basis for our confidence.

Two dimensions of 5:1-11 are striking. First, attention is directed to the future, as Paul writes of "our hope of sharing the glory of God" (5:2). The "glory of God," the very reality that humanity has lacked because of sin (3:23), becomes the object of hope, which for Paul is not mere wish but confident expectation (see 8:18). This hope makes possible a positive attitude toward the sufferings of the present time. At the end of the unit, in 5:9-11, Paul returns to the theme of the future, noting that grace casts out fear of eschatological judgment (see 5:17). The Christian life does not spare believers from present troubles, but rather "produces hope" (5:4-5), placing suffering in the framework of God's ultimate purpose for the world. Paul's theology makes no sense apart from eschatological hope—the sure confidence in the consummation of God's glorious kingdom.

Second, Paul again takes up the death of Jesus (as in 3:21-26), but he does so in a way that is striking. Paul's point that Jesus died for the ungodly (all those mentioned in 1:18—3:20) is unexpected in that it is not accompanied by a call to repentance to activate its result. It happens unilaterally and unconditionally, an act of sheer grace. Christ's death for weak, ungodly sinners is unanticipated and incomparable.

"Therefore, since we are justified by faith" (5:1) recapitulates the language of righteousness and justification in the previous section. After the start of chapter 5, we notice a significant change in Paul's style and vocabulary. The change of style observed in 4:23-25 continues through chapter 8, except for a brief return to the more objective third person in 5:12-21. "Faith" and "believing" are scarcely used, whereas "death" and "life" (also "to die" and "to live") frequently appear. The "righteousness of God" is not mentioned again until 10:3; "Jew" and "Greek" disappear, along with mention of God's impartiality and faithfulness, until after chapter 8. Clearly there is a move away from the relationship of Christianity to Judaism and a greater focus upon the Christian community and its experience (except, of course, for 5:12-21). New terminology appears, such as "enmity" and "reconciliation," "slavery and freedom," "adoption and peace." The language of "hope" is emphasized, together with God's love and the role of the Spirit.

Yet this does not mean that the treatment of justification has been abandoned; rather, it has become more focused. The forensic language of indictment and acquittal becomes more specific than before (see 5:13-14, 18-19; 7:1-3; 8:1, 3, 31-34). In these passages Paul provides a reformulation of justification. If "righteousness" is no longer "the righteousness of God," its new referent is the quality and integrity of life that accompanies obedience to God. Paul's new term is "sanctification" (6:19, 22; see also 1 Cor. 1:30), a term anticipated in Paul's salutation, where Christians are called "saints" (holy ones, 1:7). As Paul's exposition in 6:1—7:6 demonstrates, justification includes both God's free and undeserved initiative and the restoration of integrity to human lives. The separation of justification and sanctification, of "forensic" and "sacramental" grace, of "imputed" and "infused" righteousness that Christian debates have produced, is shown to be artificial. In Paul's mind—and therefore in ours—justification and sanctification belong together, theologically and practically. The heart of Paul's theological position is his interpretation of the death and resurrection of Jesus. Each stage in Romans, from 3:25 on, has involved recourse to the death (and resurrection) of Jesus as the decisive clue to God's nature and action. The clue provided in 4:25 turns out to be the one to follow: the justification of the unrighteous means for Paul not only forgiveness and acquittal but God's gift in Jesus Christ of a reordered life and hope as well, as chapters 5-8 of Romans make clear.

In 5:12-21 Paul addresses the question of how weak, ungodly sinners can have confidence on the day of judgment. Paul begins that explanation by returning to the question of sin, this time using Adam and his story as the representative story of the human race. Paul speaks of sin as a transcendent power (see 3:9) that overcomes and enslaves human life. Using Adam as a prototype (model) of Christ, Paul treats Adam and Christ less as individuals than as corporate figures, each representing all of humanity. What distinguishes them is the result of their action: through Adam death spreads to all people; through Christ life comes to all (5:18). The two-age scheme introduced in 5:1-11 is even more evident here. Adam and Christ personify the old and the new in strikingly antithetical ways. The act that each performs (disobedience and obedience) determines the destiny of all people. In chapter 6 Paul turns to the obligations upon those who have received reconciliation through Christ.

Original Sin: Theology Meets Biology

Sin, traditionally understood, is the problem from which we need deliverance. It is commonly understood as the reason for Jesus' death: he died for our sins (Rom. 3:23-25; 5:6-8). Indeed, in many forms of Christianity, we could not be forgiven if it were not for Jesus' sacrifice on the cross. Sin is thus the reason for the incarnation. If we had not sinned, Jesus' life and death would not have been necessary. Thus for centuries, Christians have seen the central issue separating humans from God as "sin." This doctrine, traditionally understood, has come to be called "original sin."

Some attribute the doctrine to Paul, but that is not correct. While Paul maintains that sin entered the world through Adam (Rom. 5:12), he never uses the wording "original sin," and he does not speak of a fall from previous grace. But it was in reflection on 5:12 that in the fourth century Augustine developed the doctrine of original sin. Augustine's discussion belongs to the realm of systematic theology, while Paul's discussion resorts to typology, comparing Adam as a type to Jesus the antitype (see Rom. 5:14-21, especially v. 14). What dominates Paul's picture of Adam is his theology of Jesus. In other words, Paul did not read Genesis and come to understand Jesus; rather he understood Jesus and then read Genesis in that light. This retrospective approach means that Paul really has nothing novel to teach us about the historical origins of the human race. Paul's primary interest is not in the sin of Adam but in the grace of Christ. He contends that Christ's act of righteousness led to justification and life for all. Rather than teach universal sinfulness, some use this passage to argue for universal salvation.

The classic doctrine of original sin has two separable parts. One is the historical claim that the first human beings, Adam and Eve, sinned by eating fruit forbidden them by God. The second is the psychological claim that human nature was once virtuous, but was corrupted by the first sin. Both claims, however, can be shown to be false. As Patricia Williams demonstrates in her groundbreaking book *Doing without Adam and Eve*, the alleged corruption of human nature is found neither in Genesis 3 nor anywhere else in the Hebrew scriptures. Genesis 3 explicitly states that Adam and Eve became more like gods after they ate the fruit of the tree of knowledge (Gen. 3:22). The idea of a fall—a corruption in human nature—is also not prominent in the New Testament; the event of Genesis 3 is only mentioned in two passages, both Pauline (Rom. 5:12–21, 1 Cor. 15:21–22). Only later, in the writings of Augustine, does the doctrine of original sin become formulated in any significant way.

In a chapter titled "The Demise of Adam and Eve," Williams asserts that it took the birth of modern science to challenge the predominant model of the universe and of human nature that had survived for over a thousand years. The scientific theory of biological evolution made clear that successful species like humans do not pass through single-pair bottlenecks; there is certainly no evidence that this was true of *Homo sapiens*, a species that seems to have been well spread around the earth. Genetic evidence indicates that human populations never consisted of fewer than several thousand individuals.

Scientifically speaking, Adam and Eve can no longer be viewed as the progenitors of humanity, for they were not historical figures. If not historical figures, they could not have disobeyed God. If they did not disobey God, then we have no basis for original sin and therefore no fall and no corruption of human nature.[2] Thus, the narrative about them cannot be used to explain the human inclination to sin or the origin of evil. That said, there is no need for despair. If one is prepared to accept a metaphorical interpretation of the Adam and Eve story, while insisting on the relevance of evolution, a ready understanding of original sin emerges.

---

2. Williams, *Doing without Adam and Eve*, xiv, 79–80.

As Darwinians have demonstrated, the struggle for existence and the consequent selection of variations leading to adaptations designed for success in this struggle often involve self-interest, if not outright selfishness, with the host of features, attitudes, and characteristics that most humans find offensive and that Christians judge as sinful. Of course, to be self-interested is not necessarily to be immoral. No one judges ill the person who eats a meal because he or she is hungry, or who falls in love with a pretty girl or a handsome young man and wants to have that person as a mate. But, all too quickly, self-interest degenerates into qualities like greed, lust, and boastfulness. There are good biological reasons for this. Those who feed themselves or their families are better off than those who have no food or just leftover scraps. The man who impregnates a hundred women is ahead (in the Darwinian game of survival) of a man who impregnates just one. The person who lies and cheats his way to the top of the corporate ladder is more successful than he who loses.

Original sin as part of the biological package comes with being human. We inherit it from our parents and they from their parents. Moreover, overlapping our selfishness is a genuine altruism, a very necessary adaptation given the human path of sociality. We are loving, kind, and generous because that is just as much a part of our nature as is our selfishness. Acknowledging that sin remains central to the human condition, Williams supplies insights from the field of sociobiology, such as the influence of genes, the environment, and the misuse of human freedom, to account for the origin of sin and to deal with the problem of evil. With respect to original sin, sociobiological *Homo sapiens* are practically identical to Christian *Homo sapiens*. Both camps see humans as deeply self-centered, selfish even, but with a genuine moral overlay, guiding (at least, instructing) our actions in social situations and interactions. The surface stories are very different, but the underlying concerns are the same: humans are truly sinful, with goodness fighting for control.

As understood by Augustine, who coined the term, original sin is a biologically transmitted tendency to evil desires (*libido*) that arose with Adam and has contaminated all of humanity. However, most theologians today would consider such an interpretation extremely shallow. According to contemporary theological interpretation, original sin refers not to a specific act committed by a parental couple in the remote past, but to the general state of our present human estrangement from God, from each other, and from the natural world. We are all born into a world that is already deeply flawed, in great measure by human greed and violence. The notion of original sin, in this sense, also reminds us of our human incapacity to save ourselves from this state of affairs.

The assumption of an original perfection of creation, as envisioned by creationism, has in fact led religious speculation to imagine that the source of the enormous evil and suffering in the world must be either an original principle of evil—an idea unacceptable to biblical theism, which views the creation as inherently good—or else some intraworldly being or event. The latter supposition has led to the demonizing of various events, persons, animals, genders, and races. Understanding evil as the result of an initial transgression has made reparation and expiation a priority for all who follow biblical religion. The vital problem, both for Christ and for us, is to find a culprit and remove its influence. The assumption of original sin opened up the possibility of interpreting suffering essentially as punishment, necessitating an ethic of retribution.

By contrast, it is enough for us simply to wonder what a salutary thing it would be if religious thought were now to take the reality of evolution with complete seriousness. Evolution means that the world is unfinished. And if unfinished, then we cannot justifiably expect perfection. There is inevitably a dark side. The notion that present evil can be attributed to a culprit that somehow spoiled the primordial creation has led to a misunderstanding of the "history of salvation" as a drama of "restoring" the original state of affairs. This emphasis has caused theologians to subordinate the expectation of the far more accurate and fulfilling understanding of the history of salvation as *transformation*—the novelty and surprise at the fulfillment of God's promises—to that of *restoration*—the recovery of a primal perfection of being. This is why evolution is potentially such good news for theology. Evolutionary cosmology invites us to complete the biblical vision of a life based on openness to the future and hope for surprise rather than allowing us to wax nostalgic for what we mistakenly imagine once was.

In an unfinished universe, we humans remain accomplices of evil, of course. But our complicity in evil may now be interpreted less in terms of a hypothesized break from primordial innocence than as our systematic refusal to participate in the ongoing creation of the world. According to this new way of thinking, sin and evil now include our resistance to the call of "being more," our deliberate turning away from participation in what is still coming into being. In an evolutionary context, "original" sin is also the aggregation in human history and culture of all effects of our habitual refusal to take our appropriate place in the ongoing creation of the universe. It is this kind of corruption—and not the defilement of an allegedly original cosmic perfection—by which each of us is "stained."

Textual Analysis: Topics to Ponder or Discuss

Romans 5:1–11

1. In light of the theological riches contained in this passage, it is not surprising that it is regularly included among the appointed readings for Christian worship. One finds here themes of great assurance, themes that address perennial concerns. Like the pearl of great price, this passage is superlative in its message and inspiration, truly one of Paul's most magnificent creations. As noted earlier, chapter 5 of Romans serves a transitional purpose. Some scholars associate it with Paul's preceding argument, others with ensuing concerns. It is important that we view it as a bridge joining both sections, serving both causes. Paul's "therefore" in 5:1 must be taken seriously.

2. The passage, taken independently, might seem a random collection of pious thoughts, so it is imperative that it be seen as part of a larger argument, with its own internal coherence. Paul has put a good bit of thinking into this unit, considering its carefully crafted composition. Familiarize yourself with its chiastic structure and try to determine Paul's key verse or concept in this unit. Notice how the three "supernatural virtues" (faith, hope, and love) appear together, as in 1 Corinthians 13:13. Does Paul prioritize one in this passage? Can you determine how these virtues are related to the concept of "grace"?

3. When Paul speaks of "peace" in 5:1, he is not speaking of the subjective "peace of mind" but of the objective state of peace with God, which results in reconciliation, transforming enemies of God into friends (5:10). We learned earlier that one dimension of God's righteousness is God's faithfulness to his covenant promises. Here we are given another dimension of that righteousness, that God is our friend. Considering the consequences of such a relationship, what benefits and responsibilities is Paul implying in this passage?

4. Paul repeatedly emphasizes the three dimensions of God's faithfulness, past, present, and future. This pattern appears in 5:2 and in

5:8–9. This three-dimensional, "already-but-not-yet" understanding of salvation is characteristic of biblical theology. What assurances is Paul proclaiming in these verses? How do they produce confidence?

5. Verses 3–4 speak of suffering, endurance, character, and hope, in that order. Paul notes that suffering produce character. Has this been true in your experience? If so, how? The point is not that suffering produces character in the cultural sense of improving one's personality or making one tougher, but that one's life is incorporated into God's larger purpose for the world and history. Hope, based upon assurance, will be a major topic in chapter 8:18–39. The Christian life cannot be maintained apart from hope. Like a muscle that needs exercise to be strong and effective, Paul tells us that life's trials and tribulations are like doing workouts in the gym; they strengthen rather than diminish hope. Suffering should not be viewed in isolation, but as part of the process of our transformation. Take a few moments to ponder how the circumstances in your life at this time are affecting your spiritual transformation.

6. Verse 5 speaks of love as the result of God's work in us, not the product of our own efforts. Take a few moments to ponder the role of God's Spirit in your life at this time. Is your love for God and others growing or diminishing? If the latter, how can you get back in the game?

7. In 5:6–9 we find a principle that speaks profoundly of God's covenant faithfulness and love, that "while we were still sinners Christ died for us." As we read in John 15:13, there is "no greater love than this, to lay down one's life for one's friends." But Paul's point takes us beyond this great love to a concept so stunning as to be practically unthinkable, that the cross of Christ represents God's love for his enemies. At the heart of Christianity lies this principle, that the power of God's love routinely turns enemies into friends (see Matt. 5:44–45). Who wouldn't commit to this cause?

Romans 5:12–21

8. In this passage Paul is giving humanity a choice about identity and destiny; where one begins determines where one will end. The choices are two: Belong to those whose destiny is determined by Adam or to those whose destiny is determined by Christ. Adam and Christ, in Paul's mind each an individual, nevertheless impact decisively the identity and fate of humanity.

9. Verse 12 represents the thesis for what follows. Paul has in mind here the story of the Garden of Eden, where Adam and Eve's sin result in human mortality. In the Genesis text mortality and death are understood not as natural but as spiritual conditions (see Rom. 3:9) that overcome and enslave human life. Some older translations, based on the Latin Vulgate and not on the original Greek text, translate "*and so* death spread to all" as "*in whom* death spread to all," thereby supporting the view of "original sin" as the genetically transmitted sin and guilt of Adam's transgression. The better translation is "because of" or "with the result that death spread to all," meaning not that God punishes all later human beings for the sin of Adam, but that Adam's story is the representative story of everyone (in Hebrew the word Adam means "human"). Paul seems to be making this point in 5:12d: "because all have sinned." Paul's intention in these verses is not to produce a simplistic analysis of the human condition but rather to describe how enemies can become friends of God. Paul uses an ancient Jewish rhetorical device known as typology to address the dilemma: Christ got us out of the mess that Adam got us into; what Adam did, Christ undid; where Adam failed, Christ succeeded. That had been Paul's reasoning all along: the universality of human mortality is Paul's empirical proof of the universality of human sin. It is useless here to speculate on the biological origins of sin (for example, in the act of procreation) or on whether apart from sin humans would be immortal. For the present time, to be human means to experience pain and loss of death. As long as death remains, sin exercises power in God's creation.

10. Adam's sin was to disobey God, and thus to suffer the consequences of that decision. It is the universal consequences of Adam's disobedience that anticipate the universal consequences of Christ's obedience. It is because of those universal consequences that Paul calls Adam a prototype of Christ. The parallelism is not precise, however, because trespass and grace are not equivalent (5:15). Paul explains why in the following verses. It takes more power to overcome the effects of sin than it took originally to allow sin to enter; an act that brings life is greater than one that brings death. If trespass and grace are not equivalent, neither are sin and grace. Grace is greater because it can undo the power and effects of sin.

PART I—ALL FOR GRACE

11. Having clarified the imbalance in favor of grace over sin, Paul draws his conclusions about Adam and Christ, this time in grammatical parallelism (see 5:18–19). The Greek word "all" (*pâs*)," a keynote of Romans, is significant here, as elsewhere in Paul's letter (the Greek word for "all" occurs over seventy times in Romans; see 3:22, 23; 5:12; 10:12; 11:32; 14:12). One should not be misled by Paul's use of "many" in verse 19 instead of "all." The use of "all" in verse 18, to which verse 19 is parallel, makes clear that Paul also means to include all humanity in what he says in verse 19. The same is true of "many" meaning "all" in verse 15 (on Paul's use of "all" in Romans 11:26 and 32, see the discussion in Session 10 and essay 10).

12. The concept of "law," introduced into the discussion in verse 13, is central in chapters 6 and 7. [The discussion there focuses on the interrelationship of law, sin, and grace.] Having examined the parts played by sin (Adam) and by grace (Christ), what role does law play in Paul's argument? As the provisional answer in 5:20 points out, even the addition of the law, with its effect of increasing the trespass by making it recognizable (see 5:13), cannot tip the balance in favor of disobedience and sin. Grace simply outperforms sin, demonstrating its superiority not only in quantity but in result. As grace overcomes sin, it also overcomes death, sin's result. Thus Christ's obedience makes it possible for humanity to have a new goal: life instead of death (6:4). It is this act of setting humanity off in a new direction that makes Christ the "second Adam," the second originator of humanity. While eternal life will be consummated in the future, until then we walk by faith and not by sight (2 Cor. 5:7). [Note: The same Greek term used in 5:20 (grace "superabounding") is used in 2 Corinthians 7:4 of joy "overflowing"; this term, not found elsewhere in Greek literature, may have been coined by Paul.]

Essay 6: Understanding Paul's View of the Cross

For Christians, the doctrine of salvation is closely related to the crucifixion of Jesus. This connection is evident in the gospels, where the accounts of Jesus' passion are paramount. The crucifixion is also central to Paul: "We proclaim Christ crucified" (1 Cor. 1:23). A few verses later, Paul repeats the statement, using even stronger language: "When I came to you . . . I decided to know nothing among you except Jesus Christ, and him crucified" (1 Cor.

2:1–2). "Christ crucified" wasn't simply information about how Jesus died. For Paul, the cross is our salvation. Rich in meaning, the death of Jesus became the subject of theological reflection throughout Christian history.

For centuries, Christians have viewed the death of Jesus as salvific, making salvation possible. According to many Christians, the death of Jesus was the purpose of his life on earth and central as well to God's purpose for history. The Nicene Creed speaks of the saving significance of Jesus' death as the very reason he came: "For us and for our salvation he came down from heaven, (and) for our sake he was crucified under Pontius Pilate."

Looking back on the crucifixion of Jesus, the early Christian movement sought a providential purpose in this horrific event. At least five interpretations of the cross are found in the New Testament itself:[3]

1. A *political meaning*: Jesus was a threat to the Roman authorities, who executed him. The authorities said "no" to Jesus, but God has said "yes" (Acts 2:36).

2. A *cosmic meaning*: temporal rulers, whether Roman rulers or Jewish aristocrats in Judea, are viewed as subject to cosmic "principalities and powers," evil systems of domination built into human institutions. According to language found primarily in letters attributed to Paul (Col. 2:15), Jesus' death defeats such cosmic powers.

3. A *psychological meaning*: the death and resurrection of Jesus are seen as the embodiment of the path of spiritual transformation that lies at the center of the Christian life, the path of dying to an old way of being and being raised into a new way of being (Gal. 2:19–20).

4. A *spiritual meaning*: the death of Jesus reveals the depth of God's love for us (John 3:16; Rom. 5:8).

5. A *sacrificial meaning*: this view emphasizes that "Christ died for our sins" (1 Cor. 15:3). This sacrificial understanding of the cross—God became man in order to expiate the sin of Adam—was formulated in the Middle Ages by Anselm of Canterbury (1033–1109), who defined the doctrine of substitutionary atonement that became normative in the West.[4]

---

3. Borg, *Heart of Christianity*, 91–95.

4. This view, with its notions of punishment, substitution, and payment, appeared rather late in Christian history. While vigorously defended by some Christians as central to the gospel message, the concept is troublesome to others, who question the idea that God requires a blood sacrifice. The doctrine of substitutionary atonement first appeared

PART I—ALL FOR GRACE

Biblical scholar Marcus Borg argues that in its first-century setting, the statement that "Jesus is the sacrifice for sin" would not have meant that Jesus' death was part of God's plan for salvation. Rather, it would have been understood as a challenge to the sacrificial system centered in the temple in Jerusalem. According to temple theology, "certain kinds of sins and impurities could be dealt with only through sacrifice in the temple. Temple theology thus claimed an institutional monopoly on the forgiveness of sins; and because the forgiveness of sins was a prerequisite for entry into the presence of God, temple theology also claimed an institutional monopoly on access to God."[5] Jewish Christians, using the metaphor of sacrifice, affirmed that forgiveness is not rooted in institutional monopoly but in gracious freedom. It is ironic that the Christian religion later claimed for itself a monopoly on grace and access to God that is undermined by this contextual understanding of the meaning of the cross.

The cross (the death) and resurrection of Jesus go together for Paul. The cross would have had no meaning for Paul without his conviction that God had raised Jesus. Without this conviction, the cross of Jesus would have been just another execution by imperial authority. Resurrection gave meaning to the cross. Paul's conversion transformed not only Paul, but also his way of seeing Jesus' death. The cross was no longer simply an execution, but a means of revelation. Paul's understanding of the cross can be divided into three categories:[6]

1. The cross *reveals the character of empire*. To proclaim "Christ crucified" signaled that Jesus was an anti-imperial figure, and therefore that Paul's gospel was an anti-imperial gospel. In his overture to 1 Corinthians (1:17—2:16), Paul distinguishes the "wisdom of God" and the "wisdom of the world" through a series of contrasts: "wise" and "wisdom" are contrasted with "foolish" and "foolishness"; likewise, "powerful' and "power" (or "strong" and "strength") are set in opposition to "weak" and "weakness." Note that Christ as the "power of God" and the "wisdom of God" is synonymous with "Christ crucified"—and it is foolishness to the wisdom of this world. But the foolishness and weakness of God are wiser than the wisdom

---

in 1097 in a theological treatise by Anselm under the Latin title *Cur Deus Homo?* ("Why God Became Human?"). Anselm answers his question with the following argument: All humans have disobeyed God; forgiveness requires that compensation be made. Our debt to God is infinite, which only an infinite being can pay; Jesus, God's incarnation, is that infinite being whose death as a substitutionary sacrifice pays the price of our forgiveness.

5. Borg, *Heart of Christianity*, 94.

6. The following discussion is adapted from Borg and Crossan, *First Paul*, 131–47.

and power of this world. Rome embodied the wisdom of this world, the way things commonly are. The normalcy of this world is to achieve domination through threats, violence, and war. Paul's indictment of the wisdom of this world is clear: the rulers of this age "crucified the Lord of glory" (1 Cor. 2:8). Paul exhorts believers to live life differently, imitating their Lord: "For we have the mind of Christ" (1 Cor. 2:16).

The common view of the cross as a Roman instrument of torture and execution might explain the unusual phrase Paul uses to introduces his thematic statement in Romans 1:16: "For I am not ashamed of the gospel." Whereas Paul's gospel exalts the cross (Gal. 6:14), the general populace of his day found his message perverse, "a stumbling block to Jews and foolishness to Gentiles" (1 Cor. 1:23). At his conversion Paul came to consider the cross a messenger of grace and truth rather than a scandal and stumbling block.

2. The cross, for Paul *reveals the path of personal transformation*. To have "the mind of Christ" is to undergo spiritual death and resurrection, dying to an old identity and way of life and rising to a new identity and way of life. This view of atonement, participatory rather than substitutionary, is metaphorical language for a process of radical inward change. This was Paul's own experience, expressed concisely in the following statement: "I have been crucified with Christ" (Gal. 2:19). While Jesus was crucified literally, for Paul its meaning is metaphorical. In his conversion and as a Christian, Paul felt he had experienced internal crucifixion, internal death. The old Paul had died, and a new Paul had been born: "It is no longer I who live, but it is Christ who lives in me" (Gal. 2:20). Crucifixion and resurrection, dying and rising, are radical images of internal transformation.

In Romans 6 Paul writes about dying and rising with Christ as the meaning of baptism, the ritual of initiation into the new life "in Christ." Dying and rising with Christ is the means to life "in Christ," a phrase Paul uses over a hundred times in his letters; he uses the synonymous phrase "in the Spirit" more than fifteen times. The phrases refer to an identity and way of life centered in Christ, in the Spirit. As baptism symbolized joining Jesus in his death, it was to be followed by resurrection: "as Christ was raised from death . . . so we too might walk in newness of life" (Rom. 6:4).

In Romans 12:1 Paul writes about internal transformation using the language of sacrifice: "I appeal to you . . . to present your bodies as a living sacrifice, holy and acceptable to God, which is your spiritual worship." To present one's body (one's self) as a sacrifice is an image of dying. The result is transformation and renewal: "Do not be conformed to this world, but be transformed by the renewing of your minds, so that you may discern what is the will of God" (Rom. 12:2).

3. The cross, for Paul, *reveals the character of God*. Paul often speaks of Jesus dying "for others" and as a "sacrifice." This understanding views the cross as a revelation of God's love (and Christ's) love for us. The two—God's love and Christ's love—demonstrate Paul's Christology; he saw Jesus as the decisive revelation of God: "For to me, living is Christ" (Phil. 1:21). Paul's claim is that God's character and passion are revealed in Jesus. That claim has been central to Christianity ever since; indeed, it defines Christianity. For Paul the cross (the death of Jesus) reveals God's character as love and God's passion for the world. Hence Paul can speak of Christ's love and God's love interchangeably. The three—God's love, Christ's love, and the cross—are combined in Romans 5:6–8, one of Paul's most important texts about Jesus' death for others: "But God proves his love for us in that while we still were sinners Christ died for us" (5:8). That Christ died for us reveals the depth of God's love for us. The world matters to God, deeply so, and that love can be seen in Christ's life and death.

In a climactic passage, familiar to millions of Christians, Paul asks the question, "If God is for us, who can be against us?" (Rom. 8:31). The answer is "no one." The evidence that "God is for us" is the cross (8:32). Paul's meaning is clear: the cross, seen as the death of God's Son, reveals the depth of God's love for us.

Optional Group Activity

Divide the participants into five groups (fewer if necessary) to examine the implications of the cross for Christianity. Ask group 1 to discuss the political significance, Group 2 the cosmic significance, Group 3 the psychological significance, Group 4 the spiritual significance, and Group 5 the sacrificial significance. At the conclusion, reconvene the small groups into one and ask each group to share its insights with the others.

If time allows, give participants time to write down one takeaway (insight) from their reading or group discussion and then to share it with the class.

Session Seven

Law, Sin, and Grace

Summary: Paul's discussion in Romans 6–7 answers the classic objection to salvation by grace, namely, that grace is cheap and encourages immorality. In this passage Paul gives a three-part response, using analogies from baptism, slavery, and marriage to dispute his opponents' claims that he is "soft on sin." If the law is powerless to save, what role does it play in God's plan of salvation? Paul's response examines three realities in various combinations: sin and grace (6:1–14); law and grace (6:15—7:6); and law and sin (7:7–25). Paul shows how the law, holy and good, is unable to keep its observers free from sin. It is the Spirit of God, rather than human efforts to keep the law, which is the power that in Christ breaks sin's hold on God's creation. Apart from Christ, humanity lives under the power of the "old age," dominated by sin and death, whereas with Christ a new age has begun. Christians live in both eras simultaneously, for though the new era has begun, they are not yet free from the old. Paul's purpose in chapter 7 is to describe the human predicament (the old age) from the Christian perspective of grace. In the process, the law is defended and the Christian life is portrayed as a new way of righteousness. The closing essay examines Paul's understanding of the law, demonstrating his careful walk between legalism and antinomianism.

Assignment: Read Session 7 of *Grace Revealed* and Romans 6:1—7:25. Answer the following questions, writing your answers in your journal. [Be prepared to share your views with others in the class.] Read Romans 7:7–25 and explore the meaning of this challenging passage in light of Paul's larger argument in Romans 5–8. Evaluate the merits of the various positions regarding the identification of the rhetorical "I" in this passage (see the discussion in the textual analysis below). In your estimation, which view best represents Paul's position? Which interpretation do you find most promising for your own spiritual condition at this time?

Key Verse(s): Romans 7:6

Central Theme: Slavery to righteousness sets Christians free from slavery to sin

Technical Words and Concepts: apocalyptic, baptism, flesh, law of Christ, law of the Spirit, law of love, antinomianism

Learning Objectives
In this session participants will examine:

1. How grace increases rather than decreases righteousness
2. The role of God's moral law in salvation
3. The effects of sin (Adamic disobedience) on the law
4. The effects of grace (Christ's obedience) on the law
5. Paul's two-age apocalyptic framework
6. The meaning of the "divided self" passage in 7:7–25

Outline to Romans 6:1—7:25
I. The Work of Grace 4:23—8:39
   A. In Human Nature 4:23—8:17
      1. Law, Sin, and Grace 6:1—7:25
         a. Analogy from Baptism: Dying and Rising with Christ 6:1–14
         b. Analogy from Slavery: Slaves of Righteousness 6:16–23
         c. Analogy from Marriage 7:1–6
         d. The Divided Self 7:7–25

Romans 6:1—7:25: Flow of the Argument

Paul begins the argument of chapter 6–7 with the classic objection to salvation by grace, sincerely made by those who fear that without the requirement of the law and the threat of punishment, morality is undermined and so also efforts to live ethically responsible lives: "Should we continue in sin that grace may abound?" (6:1). "Law restricts sin," say the legalists; "grace encourages immorality." Paul's earlier discussion in 3:5–8 shows the objection was not merely theoretical, but an actual personal charge made against Paul. In Romans 6–7 Paul provides a three-part response, using three analogies to make his case: baptism (6:1–14), slavery (6:16–23), and marriage (7:1–6).

To understand Paul's reasoning in chapters 6 and 7, we need to review his argument thus far. The past has been a time of rebellion and sin on the part of humanity (1:18—3:20). Yet the past also included the coming of Jesus (3:21–30), which brought to completion God's reconciling plan for humanity in Abraham (4:1–25). Between those events—the call of Abraham and the coming of Jesus—another religious event of profound significance occurred, namely, the giving of the law. And it is to the problems posed by that event that Paul turns in chapters 5–8 of his letter.

The reason for the problems associated with the law, as Paul understands it, lies not in the law itself but in the law's inability to prevent humans who follow it from falling into the power of sin. Paul begins this part of his letter with a review of that problem, cast in terms of Adam, who disobeyed, and Christ, who obeyed (5:12–21). Until Christ delivers us, we are under the power of sin and the consequences of that primal disobedience. In chapters 6 and 7 Paul examines three realities in various combinations: sin and grace (6:1–14); law and grace (6:15—7:6); and law and sin from the perspective of grace (7:7–25). If we get sidetracked from these concerns, it is easy to lose our way.

An analogy from World War II may prove beneficial. The story is told of a remote harbor on the coast of France where Allied ships could go for safety in times of danger. The harbor itself was treacherous, however, on account of hazardous shoals and sandbars. There was a secret to navigating these waters, a secret known only to Allied commanders. As ships approached the harbor, three lights were visible; when these lights aligned as one, the passage was secure. As we navigate through the shoals in chapter 7, the same holds true; only by keeping sin, grace, and law in proper alignment can we hope to reach the harbor of chapter 8 securely.

In chapters 6 and 7 Paul's focus is on the effect of Adam's disobedience (the source of sin) and the obedience of Christ (the source of grace) on the law. Looking at these three realities, Paul shows how the law, in itself good (7:12), is unable to keep its observers free from the power of sin. He argues that baptism into the death and resurrection of Jesus Christ is the only way that God's reconciling act, which breaks the power of sin, can become real in the individual's life (6:1–14). Apart from baptism, sin controls human life (6:15—7:6), an enslavement the law is powerless to remove (7:7–25). It is the Spirit of God, rather than the law, which is the power that in Christ has broken sin's hold on God's creation. Only by that Spirit can humans enjoy in the present a foretaste of the freedom that will one day characterize all of creation.

Paul's discussion in chapters 5–8 must be understood within the two-age apocalyptic framework which Paul describes. Apart from Christ, human existence is lived in the "old age," under the tyranny of sin and death (5:12–14), an era determined by Adam's rebellion. With Christ, however, a new age has begun, in which humans can be made righteous and be granted newness of life (5:17; 6:4). Christians live in both eras simultaneously, for although the new era has begun, they are not yet free from the old. For the present the newness of life to which believers are called is a cruciform life (united with Christ in a death like his, 6:5). The Christian life is lived between two poles, the "already" and the "not yet." Having been united with Christ's death in baptism, we will yet be united with him in resurrection. In the meantime, our present life is determined by these two real events, one past and one future (6:5–11). If it is Paul's purpose in chapter 7 to describe the past (dominated by law) from the Christian perspective, in chapter 8 it is his purpose to describe the present and future (dominated by God's Spirit) from the Christian perspective.

Some later biblical writings relaxed this tension and saw the Christian life as already participating in the power of the resurrection (see Col. 2:12; 3:1; John 6:47; 11:25–26). Paul questions this view (although see 2 Cor. 5:17), and members of the later Pauline tradition rejected it as heretical (see 2 Tim. 2:18).

In the course of speaking about the law we find the famous "divided self" passage in Romans 7, often used as a proof text for Paul's deep insight into the human predicament: "I can will what is right, but I cannot do it. For I do not do the good I want, but the evil I do not want is what I do" (7:18–19). While much attention has been given to the question whether Paul here speaks about some pre-Christian or Christian experience of his, or about the human predicament in general, we must remember that Paul is here arguing about the law. The diatribe style of the chapter helps us to see what Paul is doing. In verses 7–12 he answers the rhetorical question raised in 7:7: "Is the law sin?" His answer is "no," for the law is "holy, just, and good" (7:12). This leads to the next question: "Was this good law the instrument of my spiritual death?" (7:13), and the answer is summarized in 7:25: "with my mind I am a slave to the law of God, but with my flesh I am a slave to the law of sin." What the law of sin and death, weakened by human frailty (the flesh), was unable to accomplish (freedom from guilt, condemnation, and spiritual death), the law of the Spirit (the law of Christ) does accomplish (8:1–14).

Such an analysis of Romans 7 shows that Paul is defending the holiness and goodness of the law. In 7:13–25 he carries out this defense by making a distinction between the law and the power of sin and flesh that come to assume the entire responsibility for the fatal outcome. It is striking that the "I," the ego, is not identified with sin and flesh. On the contrary, "it is no longer I [the ego] that do it [the evil the ego does not want to do], but sin that dwells within me" (7:25). The argument is one of acquittal of the ego, not of Paul's "divided self." Nowhere in Paul's writings do we find a struggle of conscience. Quite the opposite. In Philippians 3 he speaks most fully about his life before his Christian calling, and there is no indication that he had had any difficulty in fulfilling the law. The same holds true for his experience as a Christian. Though he is aware of personal sin, it is not for him a source of personal struggle. This is probably one of the reasons why "forgiveness" as a term for salvation is not found in Paul's undisputed letters.[1]

About Paul's sense of actual sin, one point is clear: his persecution of Christians. This shameful activity, the climax of his dedicated obedience to the Jewish law (Gal. 1:13; Phil. 3:6), was what made him the least worthy of apostleship (1 Cor. 15:9). Nevertheless, Paul knew that God's grace made up for this terrible deed, as he says in 1 Corinthians 15:10: "But by the grace of God I am what I am, and his grace toward me has not been in vain." These are not the words of a tormented soul. Paul did not arrive at his view of the law by testing and pondering its effect upon his conscience. Rather it was grappling with the question of the place of Jews and Gentiles in the plan of God (Romans 9–11), combined with the relation between Jewish and Gentile Christians (Romans 12–15), which drove him to his own unique interpretation of the law.

---

1. The reference to "forgiveness" in Romans 4:7 is from an Old Testament quotation; as the context makes clear, Paul's preference is "justification" language.

PART I—ALL FOR GRACE

Textual Analysis: Topics to Ponder or Discuss

Romans 6:1–14: Sin and Grace

1. In 5:20 Paul made the astonishing claim that one of God's purposes with the Mosaic law was to use the "increase" of sin's power over us to augment grace. If that is so, someone might ask, shouldn't we "continue in sin that grace may abound?" (6:1). Paul raised this point previously (3:5–8), in the context of God's righteousness. Romans 3:8 showed Paul's personal concern with this charge, leveled against him by opponents who presumably thought his teaching denied the reality and seriousness of sin. In 6:1, however, Paul is not simply turning aside from his main argument to put down a local objection. Rather, his answer forms a carefully constructed stage in his presentation of the justification of the unrighteous. Chapters 3–5 showed that righteousness is a matter of grace (3:24; 4:16; 5:15–16). In the present section Paul turns the argument in the opposite direction, noting that God's grace involves for its recipients a reordering of their lives based upon the restoration of integrity. Paul always resists the artificial separation of justification and sanctification. At each stage in Romans, from 3:25 on, Paul points to the death and resurrection of Jesus as clues to the Christian life. Chapters 6 and 7 contain additional reflections on the meaning of that event.

2. There are three stages in Paul's response to the charge of antinomianism (that Christianity is "soft on sin"). Each stage provides an illustration or analogy that expands on the polarities—of sin and grace, death and life, disobedience and obedience—that were set up in 5:12–21, contrasting Adam and Christ. Paul's first analogy, from Christian baptism, appears in 6:1–14. Here Paul reminds his readers that they have been baptized into Christ's death. [Note: As you read these verses, keep in mind three things: (a) for Paul the death of Jesus was not the isolated event of a single individual but that of a representative figure, the founder of a new humanity. Earlier Paul explained the meaning of Jesus' death as effecting not only forgiveness and reconciliation with God but also liberation from the power of sin (3:21–26; see also 3:9); (b) for Paul baptism is both a personal and a communal experience, because it places individuals "in Christ," that is, in the body of Christ, the church (see 1 Cor. 12:13; Gal. 3:27). Baptism is not individualistic but a matter of incorporation within the Christian community; (c) for

Paul, baptism is not a mere initiatory ritual, entrance requirement, or subjective experience, but an event in which something really happens, an event in which God is active. The Christian is "united with" Christ in baptism, so that the story of Christ becomes the Christian's story. As in a marriage ceremony, something objective happens that changes the person's status. It may take a lifetime of experience and reflection to probe the meaning of the event, but its reality is not determined by the candidate's feelings or doctrine at the time.] If you have been baptized, take time to ponder the meaning of your baptism. If you have not yet been baptized, consider joining a church that nurtures and challenges its members to the fullness of faith and mission.

3. The first answer to the rhetorical question raised in 6:1 is that *justification is a new life of righteousness because it means death to sin* (6:6). Its penalty has been paid. Whoever has died is freed from sin (6:7), and that is the key to his argument. Obviously if one is dead, one is free of sin. Solidarity with Christ means "burial with Christ" (6:4), solidarity with Christ's death. Paul takes it for granted that all his readers have been baptized and that they understand this baptism to have been a baptism "into [Christ's] death" (6:3). Interestingly, Paul never argues *for* baptism, but *from* baptism, as the common history of all Christians. Christians are often prone to jump quickly to identification with Christ's resurrection, but as Paul indicates in verses 5 and 8, the resurrection represents the future polarity ("will be united," "will also live") more than the present one. Nevertheless, as Paul indicates in 2 Corinthians 5:16-17, the Christian life anticipates the new order. If we do not yet share the glory of Christ's resurrection, the share in his death is enough for now. It has broken the enslaving power of sin over us. For the first time, Christians have a real choice: they can choose not to sin! Verses 12-14 show us the fruit of our freedom: Freed from enslavement to sin, we can now turn to serve another master. As baptism alters our past, it also alters our future. Baptism changes our status—from the realm of sin to the realm of grace—our race, and our citizenship. What Paul discussed as past event in 5:12-19 has become present reality.

Romans 6:15—7:6: Law and Grace

4. The second answer to the rhetorical question in 6:1 is *that justification is a new life of righteousness because it means freedom from the lordship*

of sin (6:17). Whereas the first answer was cast in terms of life and death, the categories now shift to freedom and bondage. But the most striking feature of this second answer is that it appears at all. Once one accepts Paul's premise of death to sin, why does he need to repeat the rhetorical question yet again in 6:15? The clue is found in the issue of allegiance Paul raised in 6:12–14. Paul does not think of human beings as autonomous creatures, or of freedom as devoid of obligation. Paul presupposes that everyone has some "master," some controlling allegiance. We are born into a human race already enslaved to sin and death (see 5:12–21), and live in a world alienated from God and subject to forces that prevent us from living the good life for which we were created (see 8:19–22). By Christ's death and resurrection, believers are delivered from one form of slavery—to the power of sin—and set free for another—to serve God. Paul envisions two alternatives, either life in service of sin, whose end is death, or life in service of righteousness, whose end is life (6:16). There is for the human no neutral ground. It was precisely the search for "neutral ground," the search to be gods for themselves, that got humans into enslavement to sin in the first place. So the choice is not slavery or freedom in some absolute sense, but rather slavery to which lord, to which ruling power?

5. If, as Paul argues in Romans 13:8, "love" is the fulfillment of the law, he does not have in mind a bland set of subjective principles. For Paul, love is the core value of a new moral order, responsibility to a new law, service to a new master. What Paul has in mind may be likened to the situation of a person recently released from prison. This new freedom does not mean one is freed from all constraints. One actually passes from one responsibility to another, one regime to another. One is always under responsibility, whether forced to obey prison rules or free to obey society's rules. The same holds true with Christian freedom. Freedom from sin means freedom for life in Christ.

6. Once one comes under the lordship of a new master, Christ, can one revert to the lordship of the former master, sin? That is the point Paul is arguing in 6:16–19. The new situation, like the old, requires obedience. Justifying faith denotes sanctifying obedience. That is the key. The phrase "obedience of faith" that brackets Romans (see 1:5 and 16:26) reminds us that justification (faith) and sanctification (obedience) are joined at the hip.

7. Galatians 4–5 contains an important exposition of Christian freedom. Particularly important is the phrase "faith working through love" (5:6). That expression aptly captures the meaning of Christian freedom. [Note also Paul's discussion of the "law of Christ" in 6:2, which includes "bearing one another's burdens."] Paul's discussion in Romans 6 points ahead to the prolonged discussion of practical concerns in chapters 12–15. As you note Paul's imperatives in 6:12–23, remember that every imperative (what we should do) is based on a preceding indicative (what God has already done on our behalf).

8. As chapter 6 indicates, being under grace and not under law is not a license to sin (see 6:15–23). Paul has also told his readers that the Christian is freed from the domination of sin by baptism into Christ's death (6:1–14). How does Christ's death free the Christian from the law? That is the question Paul seeks to answer in 7:1–6.

9. The third answer to the rhetorical question in 6:1 is *that justification is a new life of righteousness because it means freedom from the old legal code* (7:6). The chosen example is one of the clearest definitions of justification in Paul's letters. It concerns the legal responsibilities in marriage. A woman is bound by law to her husband and cannot simply take up an intimate relationship with another man while her husband is alive. The death of the husband creates a new situation for the widow. She is released from the binding marital code and is free to marry another husband. Likewise, the death of Christ brings freedom from the law and enables union with another—in this case with the risen Christ. The key is found in 7:6, where believers are declared to be "slaves not under the old written code, but in the new life of the Spirit" (see 2 Cor. 3:6; the "letter" that kills is not the law itself, but the law as controlled by sin). These words recall 6:4 and anticipate the discussion of the Spirit in chapter 8.

Romans 7:7–25: Law and Sin

10. The general theme of Romans 7 is freedom from the law. Paul's views about the law are complex. He never writes a systematic treatise that pulls together his multifaceted statements about the role of the law in God's plan, but as he makes clear in 7:7, his many negative statements about the law should not lead the reader to think that he considers the law to be sinful. The discussion in 7:7–12 forms the first part of his argument: The Mosaic law is not the origin of sin; the law should

not to be confused with sin, for it remains God's good and holy law. Nevertheless, law does play a role in relation to sin: it identifies sin and makes it known (Paul may well have Genesis 3 in mind: law produces the very thing it is supposed to prevent).

11. The most striking feature of chapter 7 is that, even though the matter of the law is addressed at the outset, the underlying preoccupation is its relation to sin. In the course of his presentation of justification, Paul has said many things about sin. Almost personified, it has turned out to reign and have dominion (6:14), with death the symptom of its rule (5:21). Yet its power is curiously dependent on the Mosaic law, apart from which it lies dormant (7:8). The law magnifies sin (5:20) and accords sin its power. Indeed, so closely have the functions of sin and the law blended in Paul's reflections that death to the law is required if one is to escape the power of sin (7:4). It is hardly a surprise that the same logical necessity that produced the question of 6:1 now gives rise to 7:7.

12. Despite the close relationship between sin and the law, Paul makes it clear that it is sin that is evil, not the law (the law is "spiritual," 7:14, and "holy and just and good," 7:12). The law's fault is that it is weak. It cannot resist the power of sin, and hence, like humans, it is enslaved by sin. To help us understand Paul's point, the following analogy may be helpful. As a puppet is controlled by a puppet master, so sin controls the law for its own purposes. If a puppet makes obscene gestures, one cannot condemn the puppet. It is the puppet master that caused such gestures. Likewise, Paul understands that if the law results in evil acts, it is not the law but rather the controlling power that causes such behavior. That is the point Paul is making in 7:7–11, and it explains the conclusion of verse 12. It is sin that is the cause of the evil the law brings about; it is sin that takes the initiative, that reverses the intent of the law. One can no more condemn the law for evil than one would condemn the puppet for its actions. The law still reflects God's will, despite its use by sin to bring about the opposite effects. Sin uses not something evil but something good to work its evil intent (7:13). Indeed, what it does to the law it also does to human beings: It takes good creatures of God and enslaves them; it takes the good law it has corrupted and uses it to corrupt God's good creation, so that good creatures can no longer do the good they want to do and know they

should. That is the essence of Paul's discussion in the remainder of chapter 7.[2]

13. Over the centuries the chief problem of interpretation for Romans 7:7-25 has been the identification of the rhetorical "I." There are four main positions:

- The "I" describes *Paul's pre-Christian experience*. Here Paul recounts his attempts to keep the law as a Jew, which ended in despair.

- The "I" describes *Paul's experiences as a Christian*. Here Paul describes his internal struggle to live by the Spirit rather than the old life of the "flesh."

- The "I" describes *the situation within the Roman church*. Here Paul creates an imagined self to give voice to the factions at Rome. He associates himself with the self he has created because he comes as a member of that body to heal the divisions. Paul spins an imaginary web around the Roman Christians, within which the types in his dialogues and monologues emerge to play their part and then disappear. There is a unity—deeper than any division—between those factions that their members cannot see, and a unity between them and Paul.

- The "I" describes *human experience apart from Christ*. Here Paul recounts the story of Adam (or the story of Israel apart from Christ), but seen from the Christian perspective.

As you ponder Paul's meaning, recall that in his day people were viewed less as individuals and more as members of larger units. One's nature and destiny were seen more as products of participation in these societal structures than of one's own personal decisions. Jews in particular emphasized the importance of solidarity with the nation. Numerous Old Testament passages suggest that "I" denotes the nation of Israel (see Mic. 7:7-10; Jer. 10:19-22; Lam. 1:9-22; 2:20-22). Whatever our conclusion, we must remember that the rhetorical "I" in Romans 7 is a stylistic device rather than a reflection of Paul's own experience. Paul's frequent use of the diatribe style in Romans also points us in this direction, a view supported by Paul's ability to write in the first person elsewhere without alluding simply to himself (see 1 Cor. 13).

---

2. Achtemeier, *Romans*, 118-19.

14. Consider role-playing this passage. Read Romans 7:7–25 from each perspective suggested above, placing yourself in the position of the "self" Paul describes. Which view best characterizes Paul's intention? [Note: While the first position seems convincing in isolation, remember that in his writings Paul never indicates that keeping the law was a burden or problem in his pre-Christian life (Phil. 3:1–6 indicates precisely the opposite). The second position also seems convincing to Christians besieged by temptation. Such a view seems to be confirmed by the struggles all Christians experience as well as by Paul's statement in Galatians 5:16–18. However, the literary context in Romans precludes this interpretation. Paul has just written in 6:6–7, 17–18 that the Christian is delivered from the power of sin, and in chapter 8 he celebrates the Christian's victory over sin and death. The third view is not widely held. Its view of the Roman Christians as deeply divided and dysfunctional seems extreme, though it does speak to the importance of the sociological nature of Paul's message.]

15. The fourth position is intriguing and seems to make the most sense, though it too has problems. According to this view, in 7:7–25 Paul is recounting in universally personal terms the experience of the human race he described in 5:12–14, the dilemma of all human beings who seek to follow God's will apart from Christ (see 7:25). To illustrate the view that Paul is here describing the general human condition apart from Christ, we turn to 7:7–11. These verses could well apply to Adam. His disobedience of God's command did result in spiritual death. The serpent did tempt him in terms of the very command God had given him about the Tree of Life. Adam, as we saw in 5:12–20, represents humanity at large. The view that Paul has (Adamic) Israel in mind is also possible, for it makes sense of verses 22 and 25b and points ahead to Paul's discussion in chapters 9–11. Despite Paul's dramatic presentation, we must not lose sight of the fact that the real subject of chapter 7 is God's good law, and how sin misuses it and turns it into an instrument of condemnation.

16. In 7:14–25 Paul shifts from past to present tense to introduce the conflict between what one desires to do and what one actually does. The conflict described is not an internal one, between the "lower" (fleshly) part of our nature and the "higher" spiritual part. In Paul's terminology "flesh" refers to the whole of our human existence, including our highest ideals and aspirations (see 8:5–13; 1 Cor. 3:1; 2

Cor. 5:16; 10:2; Gal. 3:18; 4:23, 29). The conflict here is between the will of God revealed in the law and our earthly, human existence apart from God. The solution to the human dilemma is not to follow one's "higher nature" but (a) to rely on God's grace revealed in Jesus Christ and (b) to live in the power of God's Spirit given to all Christians (see 8:1–17). Thus what is described here is not the internal struggle of the Christian but universal human experience prior to and apart from Christ, as seen from the Christian perspective. The statement in 7:17: "it is no longer I that do it" has at its Christian counterpart the statement found in Galatians 2:20: "no longer I, but Christ."

17. Verses 21–25 represent a summation of the preceding argument. But what about 7:25b? Its contrast between the "mind" and the "flesh" conflicts with Paul's conclusion in 7:25a and with his description of Christian existence as described in chapter 8. Verse 25b is quite likely a marginal gloss mistakenly copied by a scribe into the text.

Essay 7: Understanding Paul's View of the Law

While Paul's conversion experience may be said to have contained within itself the totality of his apostolic message, that totality was not grasped by him immediately. The revelation he received on that occasion coincided with his call to preach Christ among the Gentiles, but not until he was fully launched in his evangelistic career could he understand what this call entailed. Justification by faith was certainly implicit in his conversion, but it would take a decade or more of ministry to fully flesh it out, as he does in his letters to the Galatians and to the Romans. Speaking of his Christian standing by contrast with his earlier situation, he describes himself as "not having a righteousness of my own that comes from the law, but one that comes through faith in Christ, the righteousness from God based on faith" (Phil. 3:9).

Let us recall that Paul did not come to Christ through a process of failure, frustration, or disillusionment. Describing his former quest as a young Jewish male, he declares himself "as to righteousness under the law, blameless" (Phil. 3:6). The law he speaks of here is not natural or social in nature but God's law, the revelation of God's will. Such reference is not always the case in Paul's writings, however. In Romans there are passages where "law" seems to include all law, for in Paul's mind Jewish, Roman, human, or natural law ultimately derives from God and reflects God's will.

Paul's discussion in 1:18–32 clearly points to natural law; 2:15 to the unwritten law of conscience; 3:27a, 7:21, 7:23a to law as a principle; 7:15 to humanity's highest values and ideals; and 13:1 to civic rules and regulations. For Paul as a Pharisaic Jew, keeping God's law, though it was not an easy task, seemed possible. However, after his conversion, Paul became convinced that keeping the law led to a false confidence that one could thereby achieve a valid relationship with God, for only by trusting in Christ can one's relationship to God be rectified, even if one does fulfill the law, as Paul felt he had done previously (Phil 3:9–11). As we read later, Paul also became convinced that keeping the whole law was impossible. This point is decisive in his argumentation in Romans 2:17—3:20 (see 2:1) and in Galatians 3:10–12.

The "advantage" of the Jew (Rom. 3:1), however is clear. To be born under the law was an immense privilege. Unlike Gentiles, who lacked this privilege, a Jew who was instructed in the law could know God's will. He could qualify to be a "guide to the blind, a light to those who are in darkness, a corrector of the foolish, a teacher of children" (Rom. 2:17–20). In a context where Paul expresses sadness that his own people, the Jews, do not accept Jesus as God's Messiah, he lists seven historic privileges that belonged to Israel—eight if one counts the last statement that the Messiah sprang out of Israel: sonship; God's presence; the covenants; the giving of the law; the worship of God in the temple; the promises to Israel through Abraham, Moses, David, and the prophets; and the patriarchs.

While Israel's advantage could not be revoked by disobedience (Rom. 3:1–4), that gave the Jews no edge on salvation. Because the law was unable to save, the Jews stand before God as guilty as the Gentiles, and even more so (Rom. 2:9). All this is said in the light of the new avenue of salvation, which had been opened in Christ, an avenue equally available to Jews and Gentiles, since it is no longer based on the law. In such a situation, Paul says, the old covenant, even with its provision for forgiveness and grace, is not a valid alternative any more. The only grace that counts is the one now available in Messiah Jesus.

At the time when Paul wrote these words he embraced another way. No longer did he rely upon the law and boast of his relation to God as one who had been born a Jew; no longer did he make his aim the attainment of that righteousness before God that was based on keeping the law. He had found a new way of righteousness, based on faith in Christ. Allegiance to a person had displaced devotion to a code and a way of life.

There were many early disciples of Jesus in the early church who though it quite possible—indeed desirable—to combine faith in Christ with the pursuit of righteousness through keeping the law, but Paul regarded this attitude as an impossible compromise. No one had kept the law with greater devotion than Paul, and the law, far from securing his righteousness before God, actually led him into sin. It was his devotion to the law that made him such a zealous persecutor of the church. But with his Damascus revelation came the recognition that Jesus was the Messiah; the crucified Jesus was the risen Lord. The followers of Jesus had been right after all, and Paul had been terribly wrong. Instead of pursuing the path of righteousness, as he thought, he had been committing the sin of sins—attacking the witnesses of the Messiah and, through them, attacking the Messiah himself. His disillusionment with the law, when he understood where his devotion to it had led him, is reflected in his words: "For through the law I died to the law, so that I might live to God. I have been crucified with Christ, and it is no longer I who live, but it is Christ who lives in me. And the life I now live in the flesh I live by faith in the Son of God, who loved me and gave himself for me. I do not nullify the grace of God; for if justification comes through the law, then Christ died for nothing" (Gal. 2:19–21).

It is plain that Paul believed and taught that the law had been in a major sense revoked by Christ: "For Christ is the end of the law" (Rom. 10:4). The age of law, which was never designed to be other than a parenthesis in God's dealings with humanity (Gal. 3:19), had been superseded by the new age, which Christians call "the age of Christ" or "the age of the Spirit." In this age, it is not the Mosaic law that liberates us from "the law of sin and death," but rather "the law of the Spirit of life in Christ Jesus" (Rom. 8:2). For, Paul continues, God has done what the law could not do, because of the "flesh," that is, the powerlessness of the human nature. The law belongs to the old age, the age of spiritual weakness (what we might call the first-half-of-life task: acquiring a solid foundation for one's moral identity), whereas the Spirit belongs to the new age, the age of spiritual power (what we might call the second-half-of-life task: acquiring freedom for one's spiritual identity in Christ). Law, Paul declares, informs conscience externally, but faith empowers it internally. Law establishes information, but not transformation.

The transition from the old age to the new—from inability to ability—is brought about by the coming of Christ. Not only did Christ accomplish the will of God, but on behalf of others he endured the curse pronounced by the law on law-breakers, thereby redeeming from that curse those who were under law, so that they might through faith receive the promised Spirit and adoption as children in the family of God (Gal. 3:10–14; 4:4–6). Thus, by his life and death, Christ has "condemned sin in the flesh" (Rom. 8:3), thereby inaugurating the new age of spiritual freedom, the age, we may say, of the new covenant. The reference to the Spirit should remind us that Paul's teaching here points to the fulfillment not only of Jeremiah's "new covenant" oracle (Jer. 31:31–34) but also of the companion oracles in Ezekiel 11:19–20 and 36:25–28, where God promises to implant within the new community a new heart and a new spirit.

It is to this new heart that Paul refers when he says that the message of the new age is written "with the spirit of the living God, not on tablets of stone but on tablets of human hearts" (2 Cor. 3:3). A written law-code is an inadequate vehicle for communicating the will of God. The will of God was codified only for a temporary purpose—to reveal human sinfulness. Doing the will of God is not a matter of conformity to outward rules but a way to express inward love, such as the Spirit begets (Rom. 5:5). Hence, says Paul, "the letter kills, but the Spirit gives life" (2 Cor. 3:6). In 2 Corinthians 3:7–18 Paul demonstrates how the new covenant is the opposite of the old. In his writings, the two covenants are contrasted so sharply that there is little apparent continuity left between the Sinai covenant and the new covenant in Christ. For that reason he reaches back to the covenant with Abraham, using the narrative of Abraham's faith to demonstrate the priority of faith over law. Such faith, he argues, is reckoned as righteousness (Rom. 4:1–25). In Galatians 3 Paul extends his argument further, arguing that the law in its spiritual sense, as the embodiment of God's will, is upheld and fulfilled more adequately in the age of faith than was possible "before faith came," when law kept the people of God "imprisoned and guarded . . . until faith would be revealed" (Gal. 3:23). In these passages it becomes clear that for Paul the Sinai covenant is an interruption in the history of faith.

The affirmation that "Christ is the end of the law" (Rom. 10:4) has been variously understood. The word "end" (*telos*) can mean "goal" or "terminus," and in Romans Paul probably means both, for Christ was the goal of the law in the sense that the law had a tutorial role until Christ came (Gal. 3:19, 24). But Christ was, for that reason, the terminus of the law because his coming meant that the period of its validity was now at an end.

This possibility, easily misunderstandable, has left Paul open to the charge of antinomianism, a charge that Paul met and rebutted in his own day (Rom. 3:8; 6:1–23). As he makes clear, Paul does not condone lawless behavior: "Should we continue in sin in order that grace may abound? By no means!" (Rom. 6:1–2). Romans 1–3 sets out to show that all—both Jews and Gentiles—have sinned and fallen short of the glory of God (Rom. 3:23; cf. 3:19). Romans 3:21—8:39 demonstrates how and in what sense this tragic fact is changed by the arrival of the Messiah. If Jewish Christians continued to observe various customs prescribed by the law as part of their way of life, Paul raised no objection; he himself conformed to those customs when he judged it appropriate. But what he is concerned with is the place of law in our approach to God: the righteousness attested by the law and the prophets comes solely through faith in Jesus Christ, for we are now justified by God's grace as a gift (Rom. 3:21–26).

Because the law is the promulgation of God's will, it is "holy and just and good" (Rom. 7:12). But the Spirit is holy both as being the Spirit of God and as creating holiness in human beings. It is the Spirit who renews the minds of the people of God so that they not only approve but do the will of God (Rom. 12:2). The holiness that the Spirit creates is nothing less than transformation into the likeness of Christ, who is the image of God. The purpose of the law, that humans should be holy as God is holy (Lev. 11:44–45), is thus realized in the gospel.

Because the concept of law is central to understanding the thrust of Paul's message in Romans, an analysis of the traditional Lutheran doctrine might be useful, which envisions the threefold function of the law as:

- *spiegel* (mirror): as a summons to repentance, God's law provides moral guidance;
- *oregal* (curb or bridle): as a means of restraint, God's law provides civil guidance;
- *regal* (rule): as a means of instruction, God's law provides practical guidance.

The first use is recognized by Paul as a fact of experience: "through the law comes the knowledge of sin" (Rom. 3:20). Insofar as the second use involves the administration of law by magistrates for the restraint of evil and the maintenance of order, this is not an aspect of the gospel, though Paul speaks of this subject in Romans 13:17. As for the third use of the law, Paul's thoughts on the guidance of the church may sometimes be expressed by means of the term "law," but when he speaks of the "law of the Spirit" (Rom. 8:2) or the "law of Christ" (Gal. 6:2), he is referring to the "law of love," the law which Christ exemplified and which he laid down when he said that the whole law and prophets depended on the twin commandments of love to God and love to one's neighbor (Matt. 22:40). This reinterpretation of the law is echoed by Paul when he says that the whole law is summed up in a single commandment: "You shall love your neighbor as yourself" (Gal. 5:14) or that "Love does no wrong to a neighbor; therefore, love is the fulfilling of the law" (Rom. 13:10).

But the law of love is a different kind of law from that which Paul describes as a yoke of slavery (Gal. 5:1). Love is generated by inward qualities and cannot be enforced by legal sanctions. The law of love builds on the third use of the law in the Lutheran tradition—its use to provide guidance for the church. So far as Paul is concerned, guidance for the church is provided by the law of love, not the law of constraint. In his letters he lays down guidelines for his converts and others, often couched in the imperative mood, but these guidelines mostly concern personal relations. Food sacrificed to idols, for instance, is ethically and religious indifferent; what matters is the effect of our conduct and example on others. If we ignore their true interests, or cause weaker brethren to sin, then we are "no longer walking in love" (Rom. 14:15).

In his guidance, Paul walks a careful line between legalism and antinomianism, recognizing the importance of Christian freedom while remaining subject to the needs of others. The reformer Martin Luther best entered the mind of Paul when he declared that a Christian is "subject to none" in respect to personal liberty, yet "subject to all" in respect to charity. This, for Paul, is the law of Christ because this was the way of Christ. And in this way, for Paul, the divine purpose underlying Moses's law is vindicated and accomplished.

Optional Group Activity

Divide the participants into three groups to discuss the merits of the threefold function of the law as found in traditional Lutheranism. Ask Group 1 to examine the merits of God's law as *spiegel* (mirror), providing moral guidance. Ask Group 2 to examine the merits of God's law as *oregal* (curb or bridle), providing civil guidance. Ask Group 3 to examine the merits of God's law as *regal* (rule), providing practical guidance. At the conclusion, reconvene the small groups into one and ask each group to share its insights with the others.

If time allows, give participants time to write down one takeaway (insight) from their reading or group discussion and then to share it with the class.

Session Eight

The Spirit and Grace

Summary: Romans 8 is a passage of hope, promise, and enduring beauty. Here Paul addresses two concerns, the Christian's life in the Spirit and the believer's security in Christ. As Paul makes clear, to be led by God's Spirit means to have changed our future from death to life, our relationship to God from rebellion to obedience, and our status from rebellious enemy to beloved child. While the present holds suffering, that suffering hardly compares to its recompense—glory. That glory involves the transformation of physical and human nature, indeed, the transformation of reality to its original goodness. For Paul, such transformation is not simply futuristic hope but proleptic hope, meaning it is being realized here and now. The passage ends with Paul's insistence that nothing can intercede between God and those whom God has chosen. God's love for his people is incomparable and irrevocable. The concluding essay explores Paul's view of "inaugurated" eschatology, emphasizing the nature and implications of the Spirit's operation in the lives of believers.

Assignment: Read Session 8 of *Grace Revealed* and Romans 8:1–39. Answer the following questions, writing the answers in your journal. [Be prepared to share your views with others in the class.] After reading Romans 8, summarize Paul's understanding of the work of the Holy Spirit. What evidence is there in your life of the Spirit's transformative power? How can you give appropriate attention to this presence through your life?

Key Verse(s): Romans 8:1–2, 28, 38–39

Central Theme: Life in the Spirit and its consequences

Technical Words and Concepts: life in the Spirit, Day of Pentecost, the old age, the new age, libertine, glory, proleptic hope, justifying grace, justifying faith, foreknowledge, predestination, cosmic eschatology, *eschaton*

Learning Objectives
In this session participants will examine:

1. Paul's understanding of the work of the Holy Spirit
2. Communication with God through prayer
3. Paul's eschatological hope for humanity and creation
4. The believer's security in Christ
5. The meaning of "inaugurated" eschatology
6. The distinction between eschatological and apocalyptic literature

Outline to Romans 8:1–39
I. The Work of Grace 4:23—8:39
   A. In Human Nature 4:23—8:17
      1. Spirit and Grace 8:1–17
   B. In Cosmic Nature 8:18–39

Romans 8:1–39: Flow of the Argument

Romans 8 is a passage of great beauty, offering images and affirmations unparalleled in scripture. Its inspirational themes include freedom from condemnation, divine indwelling, godly adoption, resurrection power, cosmic hope, effective living, unconditional love, and other blessings attributed to life guided by God's Spirit. This chapter has two purposes: (1) it elaborates the reference to the "new life of the Spirit" in 7:6 (see also 5:5), and (2) it returns to the main line of Paul's argument, established in chapter 5, by continuing his exposition of the believer's security in Christ.

In Romans 5–8 Paul invites Christians to join him in assurance of what the gospel provides, a new life given to God's service and a certain hope for future glory. If chapter 7 describes the human condition (the problem), chapter 8 describes the remedy. As noted earlier, chapters 5–8 form a unit not only thematically but also structurally. Viewed chiastically, two themes of chapter 8 are prefigured in chapter 5: (a) the hope Christians have of future glory (see 5:1–11 and 8:18–39) and (b) the power God provides in the present (see 5:12–21 and 8:1–17). As 8:18–39 shares a common theme with 5:1–11, so 8:1–17 has much in common with 5:12–21. Chapters 6–7 deals with two continuing threats (sin and law), and 8:1–17 shows how the work of God's Spirit overcomes these threats.

It is clear that we have turned a corner when we reach Romans 8. There is no more diatribe and no more impersonation. Instead Paul sets out to describe the Christian life at some length. As we noted earlier, Paul often begins with arguments grounded in human experience, then turns to scripture, and then argues on the basis of analogies with customs or other common practices. Here he returns again to the argument from experience, specifically Christian experience.

Paul's eloquence rises to a climax here precisely because his theme—life in Christ and its consequences—is the grandest yet in the letter, the theme that most completely fulfills the promise of the announced theme in 1:16–17. Now finally Paul can speak fully of the gospel for all Christians, about the power of God for salvation, about life in the Spirit, about how the righteous shall live by faith because the faithfulness of God has been revealed through Christ.

As Paul describes the life of the Christian, it is clear that the stress is on the believer's relationship to the Holy Spirit and the effect the Spirit has on the believer. The Greek word for "Spirit" (*pneuma*) occurs only five times in chapters 1–7 and eight times in chapters 9–11, but some twenty times in chapter 8. In speaking of God's Spirit, a few clarifications are in order. First, when Paul in this chapter speaks of "the Spirit," "the Spirit of God," or "the Spirit of Christ" (see 8:9), these phrases are identical and are simply ways of referring to the presence and power of God at work in the life of the Christian community and the believer. Also, we need to be clear about the spiritual nature of the early church: in Paul's day, all believers were charismatic. That is, they claimed to be instilled with the Spirit that was poured out on all flesh on the Day of Pentecost (see Acts 2:1–4, the biblical reference to the event that marked the birthday of the church), an event they interpreted as marking the end of the old age and the birth of the new (Acts 2:16–22).

Since Paul is writing this letter from Corinth, we might recall that the Corinthian church was deeply divided by issues having to do with the Spirit, primarily the possession of spiritual gifts. The problem in Corinth was not with Spirit possession, but with spiritual factions and excessive spiritual behavior that elevated some and debased others (see 1 Cor. 12–14). Paul seems to be especially careful in Romans 8 to avoid encouraging the Spirit enthusiasm that was so destructive in Corinth. He insists on the partial nature of the present experience of the Spirit, and contrasts the present sufferings with the future glory (8:18). He notes that the community's experience of the Spirit is only the "first fruits" of the harvest (8:23). He also notes the ongoing struggle in the Christian life between "flesh" and "Spirit." In 8:1–4 he forges a strong link between the Spirit and fulfilling the requirement of the law (8:4), a detail the Corinthians were prone to forget, and he answers as well the charge that his gospel encourages libertine behavior.

When Paul in these verses emphasizes the transforming power of the Spirit and the assurance of God's favor that presence reveals, he is drawing on a prophetic insight that identified the presence of the Spirit as the mark of God's presence with his people after the new covenant had been made. That insight came from the prophet Ezekiel. When Ezekiel described the reality of God's new covenant, he described it in terms of a "new spirit" that God would give them (11:19; 36:26–27). It is Paul's insight that Ezekiel's "new spirit" is in fact the Spirit of God now given through Christ. If Ezekiel is clear that the new spirit would ensure that God's people could finally keep the law faithfully, Paul is equally clear that God's Spirit will enable them to keep his law as well. Since the Spirit has freed people from the law with its servitude to sin (8:2), Paul is clear that sin is no longer able to bring about condemnation for those who live by God's Spirit (8:1). Only when the power of sin (that is, only when life in the orientation of "flesh" has been overcome by the greater power of God's Spirit), can people trapped in that life be free to pursue another kind of life. It is the presence of the Spirit that marks those who belong to Christ (8:9), and where the Spirit is present, the promise of new life is also present (8:11).

As Paul makes clear, to be led by God's Spirit means to have changed one's future from death to life, to have changed one's relationship to God from rebellion to obedience, and to have changed one's status from rebellious enemy to beloved child (8:12–17). While the present holds suffering, that suffering is hardly comparable to the recompense—glory (8:18). What that glory involves becomes clear in 8:19–23.

For Paul, and for us, such transformation is not simply futuristic but proleptic hope, meaning that it is being realized here and now. Justifying grace and its benefits are more than a preliminary to full fellowship with God. Such grace is not permission to wait in an antechamber; it is admission to the transforming presence of God. Grace looks ahead in hope, but already the reconciliation is an actual experience. No estimate of Paul's theology is adequate unless it takes full account of faith, and no account of faith is adequate that regards it as separated from the gift of the Spirit, God's sign that we are indeed eating the manna and drinking the living water of the new age. Justifying faith is a gift of divine favor aimed at the creation of transformed personalities empowered to live out of God's resources. Adoption and freedom are the objects of God's gracious and saving purpose. It was for this end that Christ was crucified and raised from death, to inaugurate the new order of life—not simply at the end of time, but here and now. Reconciliation, for Paul, is the beginning of eternal life. He is expressing the same truth as is implied in Jesus' preaching of the kingdom of God. In both conceptions, those whom God declares righteous become kingdom people, disciples, followers, believers, yet more—children of God, for whom "the whole creation has been groaning in labor pains until now" (8:22).

The passage ends with Paul's soaring insistence that nothing can intercede between God and those whom God has chosen. In 8:35–39 Paul returns to the love of God, which he has already identified in 5:5–8 as the ultimate basis for hope. The gift of the Spirit stands in the gap between the present and the future and yet provides the ultimate basis for confident hope. God's love is assured: nothing can stand between us and the love of God in Christ Jesus our Lord.

Foreknowledge, Predestination, and Election

In Romans 8:28–30 we encounter some of Paul's weightiest terminology, language that has fomented debates, fragmented believers, and troubled modern readers: "Those whom (God) foreknew he also predestined ... And those whom he predestined he also called; and those whom he called he also justified; and those whom he justified he also glorified." It is not our intention to take sides in these debates, but to offer perspective, as the following points indicate.

1. Paul uses the language of foreknowledge and predestination not as an explanation for why some are not believers but rather as assurance to believers that they participate in God's saving plan that extends from eternity to eternity. Paul is not here writing an essay on God's foreknowledge, predestination, and election, but a pastoral letter to a particular situation. He is not speculating on such deep questions as whether God knows all the details of the future, or whether God knows what will happen without

causing it to happen, or whether humans have free will. Paul's argument is that God is the author of our salvation, from beginning to end. The theological language emphasizes God's sovereign righteousness. This passage provides Paul's climactic summation of the truth that justification is by grace alone.

2. As the context makes clear, Paul's assurance to believers in verse 28 continues his discussion of the suffering of the church, groaning in longing and prayer for the redemption of the world, which is the means by which Christians are "conformed to the image of God's Son" (8:29). Paul is building on the point at which he began, that those who suffer with Christ are joint heirs with him, so that they may also be glorified with him. This is the theme that dominates 8:28–30. As noted earlier, Biblical language of predestination, like election, generally applies to groups and not to individuals alone. The language about "Jacob" and "Esau" in 9:10–13 has to do not just with the individuals, but with the nations designated by those names (that is, Israel and Edom). In the Bible God is pictured as the one who controls the destinies of nations and groups, not the one who predetermines who will belong to those nations and groups. Thus in 8:28–30 God predestines that those "in Christ" will be conformed to the image of his Son. Nothing is being said about God deciding in advance which individuals will be "in Christ." As we discover in chapters 9–11, what is at stake is God as Lord of history, not God who makes lists in advance of those accepted and those rejected.

3. The concept of election is central to Paul's discussion in Romans 9–11 (see essay 10), a discussion he anticipates at this point. Two ideas are central to understanding the biblical doctrine of election: (a) that the initiative for being "called" or "chosen" is not ours but God's (Israel did not first choose God, but rather was chosen by God), and (b) that election is not for privilege but for service. If we apply these to the biblical doctrine of salvation, understanding it as primarily a call to a way of life rather than a determination of one's eternal destiny, this lessens the anxiety produced by debates about foreknowledge and predestination.

4. Surprisingly, in 8:29–30 the past, present, and future dimensions of salvation are all collapsed into past tense statements, so that even the believers' future glory is viewed as though it were in the past. Using the past tense for the "not yet" offers believers assurance—it is "as good as done"! So certain is it that it can be spoken of as already accomplished.

5. In order to complete his argument from justification to glorification (the argument that began at 5:1–2), Paul goes back behind justification to God's purpose and call, and behind that to God's foreknowledge. God's plan for humanity and creation is Paul's overriding concern in these verses, summing up the argument of the whole chapter, particularly from 8:17. Paul is thinking of the family of God being shaped according to the likeness of Christ. God's people are to reflect the Son's image, just as the Son is the true image of God (2 Cor. 4:4). This is the point anticipated by the long argument beginning with 1:18, that the image of God, distorted and fractured through idolatry and immorality, is restored in Jesus Christ, the Son of God; and the signs of that restoration are visible in those who place their trust in the faithfulness of Christ. Christians, as true image-bearers, are to reflect that same image into the world, bringing to our world the healing, freedom, and life for which it longs. That is the thrust of 8:28–30, which, as the history of interpretation shows, can easily degenerate into an abstract theory of personal predestination and salvation.

6. In the Bible the language of predestination and election is not an alternative to "free will." Alongside predestination statements affirming God's sovereignty are "free will" statements affirming human responsibility. It is not either/or, not 50/50 or 60/40, but both/and, 100/100. God is absolutely sovereign, and we are absolutely responsible. Those who wish to think biblically must embrace paradox, just as those who relate to God must embrace mystery.

7. The language of predestination and election is confessional language, not analytical language. Paul's terminology in 8:28–30, as in other climactic passages such as 11:36–38, is the language of confession and praise, not discursive language that fits into a logical system from which further inferences can be made. The language of grace addresses the heart, not the head; worship, not intellect.

Textual Analysis: Topics to Ponder or Discuss

Romans 8:1–17

1. Verse 1 begins with the glorious affirmation: "There is therefore now no condemnation." The law has lost its power to condemn, and Christians no longer live under the threat of God's judgment.

THE SPIRIT AND GRACE

2. The phrase "in Christ" (8:1), like the similar phrase "in the Lord," possibly means no more than later generation meant by the term "Christian," a term Paul nowhere uses. In 8:9 the phrase "in the Spirit" seems to be used synonymously, particularly because of the close connection the Spirit has with Christ and God. Elsewhere, however, Paul differentiates the Spirit from Christ in various ways, although they are often said to have the same effect on believers. Paul is not a Trinitarian theologian, though his overlapping terminology was certainly a contributing factor when theologians and church councils hammered out the doctrine several centuries later.

3. In 8:2 Paul continues to use the language of law, but this time in a radically different way, connecting it with the Spirit and with Christ. The law, the revelation of God's will, was originally and inherently "spiritual" (7:14) before being hijacked by sin. The Christian has been set free from the law as dominated by the powers of sin and death to live by the law as it was intended to be, namely, "life in Christ."

4. Throughout Romans Paul magnifies God's grace, bestowed equally on all believers: "For God shows no partiality" (2:11). The liberality of God's gift is emphasized again in 8:9, where we hear that God's Spirit is not the possession of some elite group within the church, but dwells within every member. Paul's emphasis on the Spirit indwelling every believer is designed to eliminate the boasting and factionalism actually present at Corinth and potentially present at Rome, but in the modern church as well.

5. Paul reintroduces the language of "flesh" (see the discussion on 7:14) in 8:4–13, contrasting it with life "according with the Spirit." This contrast has led people to conclude that Paul has a negative attitude to the human body, but that is not the case (see Rom. 12:1 and 1 Cor. 6:15). The contrast suggests that Paul has in mind two ways of thinking, two realms of existence. To think "the things of the flesh" is to be governed by a set of values that is pint-sized (no larger than oneself), while the "things of the Spirit" is a mindset that is God-sized (larger than oneself). The contrast between the two mindsets becomes plain in 8:9–13. Nothing less than life and death are at stake here. (Paul's contrast between "death" and "life" is analogous between "perishing" and "eternal life" in John 3:16; see Deuteronomy 30:15–20 for the Old Testament biblical context.)

6. As the Spirit brings about transformation in mindset, the Spirit enacts a second transformation, from "slave to sin" to "child of God" (8:14–15). [Note: Literally speaking, Paul's language here is exclusive rather than inclusive ("sons of God" rather than "children of God"; see RSV or NIV), likely because he is thinking Hebraically, since it was sons and not daughters who inherited traditionally in antiquity; see also Galatians 4:4–7.] As children are the heirs of their parents, so Christians are joint heirs with Christ. While such teaching sounds attractive, Paul uses it to introduce an unexpected topic: suffering and rejection. Despite the sufferings early Christians experienced on account of their faith, Paul indicates that suffering can and will lead to a further transformation, the whole of God's creation (see 8:18–25). Like other biblical apocalyptic thinkers, Paul believes that God is not concerned with saving individual souls out of the world, but is determined to save the creation itself.

Romans 8:18–39

7. What an amazing idea, that one's transformation is part of God's plan for all humanity, and not just humanity, but the cosmos. As the earth had been corrupted by Adam's disobedience (see Gen. 3:17–18), that result of Adam's rebellion will also be set right by God. Creation yearns to be free of the restraint of corruption placed on it by Adam's disobedience, yearning it shares with all humanity (8:22–23). As one man's disobedience leads to futility and death, one man's righteousness leads to justification and life for all (Rom. 5:18). Through Christ's obedience creation will finally, with the transformation of reality, regain its original goodness (that is the meaning of the rather enigmatic verse 20). That final, freeing transformation of nature will also include the transformation of human nature (8:23). This passage contains the promise that God will restore his violated creation to its original goodness. And though it does not absolve us of responsibility, that is good news to those now living with air and water pollution and global warming.

8. The hope we have is more than a form of wishful thinking, since that hope is sure because we already have a foretaste of its fulfillment in the Holy Spirit. The restoration means above all the restoration of intimacy with God, something made possible in the present through prayer. Prayer too is a gift of God, not a human achievement. The Spirit enables true communication with God, that is the logic of 8:26–27.

9. There are different views about the translation of the opening of 8:28a. Traditionally the Greek words have been translated as "all things work together for good" (the NRSV follows the King James Version). While some ancient manuscripts have a text that can be translated this way, other versions read "in all things God works for the good," and that is probably a more accurate translation. Paul is not claiming that God directly causes everything that happens, or that in some impersonal way everything will work out for the best. Rather Paul means (on the basis of God's act in vindicating the crucified Christ) that no matter what happens, God works in all things for the good. This may not be clear to spectators, but it is evident to persons of faith (those who love God and are called according to God's restorative purpose for his creation).

10. As noted earlier, the context for interpreting 8:29–30 is not speculative (philosophically or theologically) but practical. When Paul speaks of predestination, he is assuring believers that they participate in God's redemptive plan, one that stretches from eternity to eternity. He is also indicating that this transformative plan includes adoption into God's family, a destiny that involves "glorification," that is, conformity to the image of Christ. Paul's teaching here reminds us that to be Christian means to be "a little Christ," something only possible for those who bear Christ's image.

11. It may seem strange that Paul should place one of his most eloquent passages of comfort and assurance immediately following a discussion of divine foreknowledge and predestination, yet from Paul's perspective, nothing could be more appropriate. God's foreknowing and predestining us in Christ is the way God saves us. The way God demonstrates he is on our side is through the gift of his Son. If God was willing to grant us Christ, is there anything he would withhold from us? The remainder of the passage clearly shows the answer to be a resounding No!

12. Verses 35–38 use a series of questions to arrive at one conclusion: the only powers or persons that can accuse or condemn us—God or Christ—are in fact the very ones who protect us. Paul ends the chapter as he began: "There is therefore now no condemnation for those who are in Christ Jesus" (8:1). Paul gives the reason for this astonishing confidence in verses 38–39: No dimension of reality, natural or

supernatural, has the power to frustrate God's care and love for us (see also 5:1–8). Other powers might affect our lives in temporary ways, but only God affects our final destiny. There, laid bare, is the basis of Christian confidence: the surety of grace.

Essay 8: Understanding Paul's View of "Inaugurated" Eschatology

In the broadest sense of the term, "eschatology" is "the study of final things or end-time events." The "end" in question may refer to an individual's death and afterlife, which scholars call "personal eschatology," or to events that mark the closing of history, called "cosmic eschatology." A characteristic Christian belief, inherited from the Hebrew scriptures (Old Testament), is that time is linear, not cyclical, meaning that history has a beginning and will one day come to an end. Such historical perspective, combined with Jewish monotheism, gave birth to eschatology, an outlook that views history as purposeful and therefore as moving toward a climactic resolution or restoration, at which time everything would be made right. First-century Jewish eschatology claimed that God would soon act within history to vindicate his people and to establish permanent justice and peace. This belief included the great promises articulated by biblical prophets, notably Isaiah, Jeremiah, and Ezekiel. The writings of the post-exilic prophets spoke of a restoration still to be realized, a liberation they described as a new exodus.

Despite the biblical emphasis on the future, there is a clear sense in the New Testament that with the coming of Jesus Christ, all of God's covenant promises to Israel are being fulfilled: "For in (Christ Jesus) every one of God's promises is a 'Yes'" (2 Cor. 1:20). And that's what is meant by "inaugurated" eschatology; it speaks of final things as being here now. God's dream for the world, God's new way of living and thinking, called the kingdom of God, is possible in the present, even though that final life in all its fullness has not yet arrived. There is a tension throughout the New Testament between "the already" and "the not yet," meaning that God's long-awaited eschatological transformation of reality, including judgment of evil and reward of faith (eternal life), is underway in the present, initiated by Jesus' coming into the world.

In keeping with this understanding, Jesus of Nazareth likely viewed his mission as prophetic, announcing, like John the Baptist before him, God's coming kingdom. But Jesus, it seems, went beyond John's role, embodying in his person and his ministry the presence of that kingdom. For Jesus, the all-encompassing rule of God was near, which, when it came in its fullness, would restore Israel's role as "light to the nations" and challenge evil in all its manifestations, political, social, and economic. The coming kingdom of God was not a new sort of religion, a new moral code, or a new soteriology (a doctrine about how one might go to heaven after death). Nor was it a new sociological analysis, critique, or agenda. It was about Israel's story reaching its climax, about Israel's history moving toward its decisive moment.[1]

E. P. Sanders, in his classic text *Jesus and Judaism*, maintains that before the outbreak of the War of the Jews against Rome in AD 66, "common Judaism" held the following hopes for the future: the restoration of the tribes of Israel; the conversion, destruction, or subjugation of the Gentiles; the renewal of Jerusalem, including a new or rebuilt temple; and the purification of God's people and their worship.[2] Whatever one makes of his idea of a common Judaism, surely the beliefs Sanders highlights were widespread among Jesus' contemporaries, as was apocalyptic eschatology in general. According to Sanders, Jesus was an apocalyptic prophet standing in the tradition of Jewish restoration theology. He shared the beliefs common in Judaism, together with this prevailing understanding of Israel's story and hope. Having established the essential Jewishness of Jesus on this topic, Sanders finds primitive Christianity to be a movement in continuity with Jesus' hopes and expectations: "The most certain fact of all is that early Christianity was an eschatological movement."[3]

Biblical support for that contention can be found in the well-known fact that, with the exception of Philemon, 2 John, and 3 John (all three of which are brief and nearly devoid of theology), apocalyptic eschatology appears in all first-century Christian documents. First Thessalonians, the earliest extant Christian writing, is full of apocalyptic expectation. The New Testament is saturated with the belief that God is "making all things new" (Rev. 21:5). Despite a future component, such hope is radically this-worldly and now-oriented.

In recent years a distinction has been drawn between the term "eschatological" and "apocalyptic." While earlier scholarship tended to treat the terms interchangeably, the latter term is now being used to refer to a particular type of literature, found within sections of Judaism during the

---

1. Borg and Wright, *Meaning of Jesus*, 31-35.
2. Sanders, *Jesus and Judaism*, 279-303.
3. Sanders, "Jesus: His Religious Type," 6.

period extending from about two hundred years before Christ to about two hundred years after his coming. This literature, filled with symbolic numbers and figures, viewed the world pessimistically; its authors regarded the secular world and its political oppression as a sign of cosmic evil, which only divine intervention could defeat. The term "apocalyptic" also refers to the perspective and worldview espoused in that literature. Apocalyptic writings generally focus on the expectation of God's imminent intervention in the affairs of the world, in which God's people will be delivered and their enemies destroyed, with the present world-order being overthrown and replaced with a restored creation.

Paul's writings, clearly eschatological in nature, contain various apocalyptic themes. At several points, Paul emphasizes that the coming of Christ inaugurates a new era or "age." Although this new age, which Paul designates a "new creation" (2 Cor. 5:17), has yet to be fulfilled, its presence can already be experienced. For this reason, Paul can refer to the "end of the ages" in Christ (1 Cor. 10:11). Yet he disagrees with opponents at Corinth who taught that the final age was fully present. For Paul, the ultimate transformation of the world is yet to come, but may be confidently awaited (Rom. 8:18–25).

There is no doubt that Paul viewed the resurrection of Jesus as an eschatological event, which affirmed that the "new age" really had been inaugurated. Paul clearly saw Jesus' death and resurrection as events that enabled believers to live in the knowledge that death—a dominant feature of the "present age"—had been overcome. Paul anticipates the future coming of Jesus Christ in judgment at the end of time, confirming the new life of believers and their triumph over sin and death. Yet according to Paul's eschatological perspective, belief in Christ, mediated by the sacrament of baptism, enables believers to enter into present union with him in his dying and rising again (Rom 6:3–8). Those who are baptized into Christ are united "in Christ," and with Christ in the one mystical body of Christ (1 Cor. 10:17; 12:13; Rom. 12:5; Gal. 3:28). Since in this body dying and rising with Christ have taken place, in relation to the law Christians are counted as dead, over whom the law has no more authority (Rom. 7:4–6). They have ceased to live "in the flesh" (Rom. 7:5) or to walk "according to the flesh" (Rom. 8:4–5, 12–13). Their flesh, with its passions and lusts, has been destroyed, as though they had been crucified with Christ (Gal. 5:24).

If in their outward bearing they still appear natural, yet the animating power in them is no longer of a natural but of a supernatural character. That animating power is the Spirit of God, which is also the power that lives in Christ (Rom. 8:9-11). Since the power of Christ's resurrected state of existence is also theirs, they are a new creation (2 Cor. 5:17; Gal. 2:20), that is to say, they are already creatures of the new world. This is no mere individualistic experience for Christians, however, but a corporate one, for through the sacraments a special union of Christians is formed, the eschatological community of the messianic kingdom of God. When Paul speaks of being "in Christ" and of the church as the "body of Christ," he has in mind two further concepts, adoption into the family of God (Rom. 8:14-17; Gal. 3:26-27) and the kingdom of God (Rom. 14:17; see 1 Thess. 2:12; 1 Cor. 4:20; 15:50). Inasmuch as believers have died and risen again with Christ and possess the Spirit, they are already partakers of the kingdom of God. The church, this "communion of saints," is itself an eschatological entity.

The Old Testament analogies to baptism and the Eucharist that Paul cites in 1 Corinthians 10:1-6 are interesting. The passing of the Israelites under the cloud and their crossing of the Red Sea are described as a baptism "into Moses." The eating of manna and the drinking of the water from the rock are the counterparts of the eating and drinking of the Eucharist (notice that Paul views the water-providing rock, which follows them in the wilderness, to be Christ; 1 Cor. 10:4). Paul here raises to the rank of sacrament experiences undergone by the whole nation, which neither the participants nor anyone else subsequently had regarded as sacramental. Like the Israelites aided to the attainment of the Promised Land by saving acts of God, these events are prototypes of baptism and the Eucharist, by which God's new covenant community, "on whom the ends of the ages have come" (1 Cor. 10:11), is consecrated to the attainment of the Messianic kingdom. The results, however, are not guaranteed. As ungodly acts kept many Israelites from attaining the Promised Land, so too the effect of baptism and the Eucharist can be annulled by ungodly conduct (1 Cor. 10:5-11).

A major theme of Paul's eschatology is the coming of the Holy Spirit, viewed as confirmation that the new age had dawned in Christ. One of the most significant aspects of Paul's eschatological perspective is his interpretation of the gift of the Spirit to believers as a "guarantee" or "pledge" of their future hope (2 Cor. 1:22; 5:5), as the first fruits of God's promise to renew all things (Rom. 8:23). The nature and implications of the Spirit's presence and operation in the lives of believers are clearly set forth in Romans 8:

- The Spirit imparts life (8:6, 10). To be "in the Spirit" (8:9) is to be "in Christ" (8:1), meaning that one now is a fellow-member of all others who are similarly incorporated into Christ (12:5).
- The Spirit bestows freedom (8:2; cf. 6:18, 22). "Spirit and "flesh" wage perpetual warfare with one another. Whereas "flesh" would enslave us to the "law of sin and death," the Spirit assures us eventual victory. The Spirit's role in this struggle illustrates the principle concisely stated in 2 Corinthians 3:17: "where the Spirit of the Lord is, there is freedom."
- The Spirit makes us children of God (8:15), and adoption brings inheritance: "if children, then heirs, heirs of God and joint heirs with Christ" (8:17).
- The Spirit intercedes for us (8:26–27). Such intercession is intimate, powerful, and produces results, because it comes from within believers, whom the Spirit indwells.
- The Spirit fulfills God's promise to make all things new (8:23). According to the prophet Joel, the outpouring of the Spirit of God would be a sign of the approaching "day of the Lord" (Joel 2:28–32). This prophecy was quoted by Peter when the Spirit descended upon the disciples on the Day of Pentecost (Acts 2:16). The present interval "between the ages" is in a peculiar sense the age of the Spirit. In this age the Spirit makes effective in believers what Christ has accomplished for them, communicating to them the power of the living and exalted Lord while also enabling them to live in the present enjoyment of the glory yet to be revealed (Rom. 8:28–30).

Romans 8 offers a celebratory description of present Christian existence, rooted in God's past action in Jesus Christ, assured of God's future action for Christ's people and for the whole world, and sustained in the present by the Spirit. This is the moment when what God did for Jesus at Easter, God will do not only for those who are in Christ but for the whole created order. This passage also completes Paul's message about God's covenant righteousness. The covenant had been established to make things right; in Romans, we see on a large scale how this is to happen. Through the Abrahamic promise, God has been faithful to the whole creation. Paul was convinced that the *eschaton* (the final event), God's goal for the world, had begun in Christ and that it was already under way. Paul's "new creation" language is good news for individuals but also for communities and the world.

If heaven will eventually be on earth, as the book of Revelation indicates (21:2–3), if God's kingdom will one day fully manifest itself on earth, as Matthew indicates (6:10), and if there will be a future resurrection, as 1 Corinthians declares (15:53), then Christians must be concerned not only about heavenly things but also about earthly things—for all creation shall one day be redeemed (Rom. 8:19–20). No one should be more concerned about caring for the earth and matters of global import than Christians, since they are evidently God's concern as well. God not only made creation, God loves all of creation, and is already in the process of redeeming it. It is an impoverished vision of the gospel "that cares for the souls of the unsaved but not their bodies or minds, that cares for heaven but not the conditions on earth, that cares for spiritual things but not also material things."[4]

Optional Group Activity

Divide the participants into five groups to discuss the question: "If all believers have God's Holy Spirit, what are the implications of this indwelling?" Ask Group 1 to explore the implications and merits of the fact that the Spirit imparts life (8:6, 10). Ask Group 2 to explore the implications and merits of the fact that the Spirit bestows freedom (8:2). Ask Group 3 to explore the implications and merits of the fact that the Spirit makes us children of God (8:15–17). Ask Group 4 to explore the implications and merits of the fact that the Spirit intercedes for us (8:26–27). Ask Group 5 to explore the implications and merits of the fact that the Spirit makes all things new (8:23). At the conclusion, reconvene the small groups into one and ask each group to share its insights with the others.

If time allows, give participants time to write down one takeaway (insight) from their reading or group discussion and then to share it with the class.

---

4. Witherington, *John's Wisdom*, 113.

Part II

Grace for All
The Unity of Jews and Christians
(Romans 9:1—11:36)

As a Christian Jew, Paul had originally hoped that a unified community of non-Christian Jews and Christian Jews would be the future of Judaism. God would create that unity from the Jews as well as the Gentiles (Rom. 9:24) because there is no distinction between Jew and Gentile (10:12). But by the late 50s, when he wrote to the Romans, Paul knew that something had gone seriously wrong with that expected unity. It was not happening and already looked like it would not happen. Hence his anguished cry in 9:2–3: "I wish that I myself were accursed and cut off from Christ for the sake of my own people, my kindred according to the flesh." For Paul, this was not just a human problem to be solved, but a divine "mystery" (11:25) to be pondered. In this segment of Romans, Paul's focus is on God, and how or why God has permitted this disunity.

Romans is written, let us recall, not simply as a way for Paul to present his theological credentials to the Roman church, but to help sort out problems there. Paul wants to use the Roman church as a base of operations in the Western Mediterranean, much as he had used Antioch as a base in the East. The problem that Paul foresaw in Rome was the mirror-image of that which he had met in Antioch. There, the church's inner circle consisted of Jewish Christians eager to convert Gentiles to Jewish Christianity. In Rome Paul foresaw the danger of a largely Gentile church so relishing its status as the true people of God that it was consigning ethnic Jews to second-class citizenship within the church.

PART II—GRACE FOR ALL

What does Paul need to say to the Roman church at this stage of its life? The answer must be set against a historical backdrop. First, Rome had a long history of anti-Jewish sentiment. Gentile Christians in Rome, especially during the period when Jews had been expelled from the capital after riots in the late 40s, might have found it easy to accommodate to these popular attitudes. Although Christianity had begun among the Jews, God might now have rejected them, something Christians could do as well. Second, the return of considerable numbers of Jews to Rome after Claudius's death in AD 54 possibly had a significant impact on the small, young church in Rome. Assuming that the Roman church consisted of a handful of house churches, its total membership numbering no more than several dozen, it must have seemed threatening for thousands of Jews suddenly to reappear in the capital, for the synagogues to be full again. It would be very easy for the church to be threatened by this sudden Jewish incursion and to regard them as the enemy. Third, by the late 50s there was increasing political tension in Galilee and Judea, and any Gentile Christians in Rome would be eager to distance themselves from any sense of complicity with the impending revolt.

Paul, anxious about these possibilities, wishes to argue for two things: total equality of Jew and Gentile within the church, and a mission to Gentiles. From this perspective, we can see that Paul's retelling of Israel's story in 9:6—10:21 is itself designed not only to suggest a new way of reading Israel's own history but also quietly to undermine the attitudes of Rome. Paul's way of construing Jewish history makes it impossible to dismiss unbelieving Jews as forever outside God's ongoing plan.

Romans is the letter in which he plants this goal of the mission and unity of the church in the firmest possible theological soil, the exposition of the righteousness of God, by which is meant essentially God's covenant faithfulness to Abraham, promises of a worldwide family characterized by faith, in and through whom the evil of the world would be undone. With this in mind, Romans 9–11 functions as the climax of Paul's theological argument and brings into focus the letter's practical aim.

Session Nine

Grace in History

Summary: Romans 9–10 continues Paul's theological argument regarding God's faithfulness and brings it to its practical conclusion. This unit brings into sharp relief a question that has been in the background of Romans all along: the persistent unbelief of Israel, God's chosen people. Chapters 9–10 examine Israel's rejection of God's plan through the law and in Christ and God's response. The discussion addresses profound issues of theodicy, the character and purpose of God, election, and the trustworthiness of scripture. This section builds on previous discussions regarding God's impartiality and faithfulness and the role of Abraham and the law in God's plan of salvation. The purpose is not primarily about human responsibility or Israel's unbelief, but the ways in which, through Christ and Christian witness, Israel is transformed from an ethnic people into a worldwide family. The closing essay addresses the theme of God's righteousness, arguing that divine justice is restorative rather than punitive.

Assignment: Read Session 9 of *Grace Revealed* and Romans 9:1—10:21. Complete the following task, writing the answer in your journal. [Be prepared to share your views with others in the class.] In 3:1 Paul asked whether there is any advantage to being a Jew. Having answered in the affirmative, he offers a list of seven in 9:4–5, noting benefits already mentioned in chapters 1–8. The final advantage is also the most important, the coming of the Messiah from Israel. Make a list of these benefits, defining each one, and identify passages in Romans where Paul mentions or discusses these topics.

PART II—GRACE FOR ALL

Key Verse(s): Romans 9:16; 10:4

Central Theme: The justice of God's dealing with Israel and the world

Technical Words and Concepts: universalism, predeterminism, "incarnation" theology, Christology/Christological, election, theocentric, theodicy, remnant, stumbling stone, midrash, covenant justice

Learning Objectives

In this session participants will examine:

1. The place of Romans 9–11 in Paul's overall argument
2. Paul's Christology
3. The equality of Jews and Gentiles within God's plan of salvation
4. The justice of God's principle of selection (of God's covenant promise to Abraham's posterity)
5. The nature of Israel's "unbelief"
6. How Christ fulfills God's law
7. The distinction between predestination and predeterminism, and how God's elective activity is ultimately motivated by grace

Outline to Romans 9:1—10:21

I. Grace for All 9:1—11:36
   A. Grace in History 9:1—11:36
      1. Israel's Rejection 9:1—11:10
         a. God's Election of Israel 9:1–18
         b. God's Wrath and Mercy 9:19–29
         c. God's Impartiality and Faithfulness 9:30—10:21

Romans 9:1—10:21: Flow of the Argument

The main thrust of Romans 9–11 is the faithfulness of God to Jew and Gentile alike, and their coming together in Christ. The purpose of election depends upon the call of God, not on anything humans do (9:6–13). Is this arbitrary or unjust? No, says Paul, and the form of his reply is significant. As usual, he is preoccupied with the loving purpose of God (9:16). Had Paul mentioned that God's plan was to bless all nations and peoples, it would have been clearer that God is not autocratic. Nevertheless, the emphasis upon the merciful goodness of God here is enough to show that Paul's argument supposes a God of grace. This becomes clear when we consider Paul's entire argument. Instead of dwelling on the darker side of reprobation, as in 1:18—3:20, Paul turns to the gracious aim of God in providence (see 9:23-24). At the present, Paul adds, God has a providential purpose in the disobedience of Israel (9:25-26). The disbelief of the majority in Israel has turned to the benefit of the Gentiles. Will Israel's unbelief last forever? No, it is temporary.

The function of chapters 9-11 of Romans is much debated. Is it integral to the argument of the letter or, as the British scholar C. H. Dodd suggested, an old sermon Paul inserted here without relevance to the rest of the letter? Even Paul's goal in this chapter is disputed. Some see the argument pointing toward the ultimate conversion of Jews to faith in Christ as their Messiah, while others argue in favor of a "two-covenant" theology, in which God's covenant with Christ and the church in no sense replaces, but simply parallels, God's continuing covenant with ethnic Israel. Some see this section simply as addressing the problem of Jewish-Gentile relationships within the church, specifically the church in Rome. When Romans 9-11 is taken seriously as part of Paul's letter, this is often combined with the view that Paul envisions either a full-blown universalism (in which all humans will be saved) or at least a Jewish covenant of salvation apart from the Christian gospel. The key passage, the goal of Paul's argument, is 11:25-32. Whatever one's interpretation, Paul's expectation leads to this conclusion: "God's response to universal human disobedience is universal mercy. God even uses Israel's unbelief for the benefit of Gentiles. When God's plan is consummated, all Israel will be saved."

To further understand Paul's argument, let us recall that in Rome Paul foresaw the danger of the largely Gentile church so relishing its status as the true people of God that it could consign Jewish Christians to second-class citizens and ethnic Jews to condemnation. Paul, anxious about these possibilities, wishes to argue two things: total equality of Jew and Gentile within God's saving plan and a mission primarily to Gentiles. This, arguably, had been his policy in the Eastern Empire; it is his intention to follow the same in the West. Romans is the letter in which he plants this goal of the mission and unity of the church in the rich theological soil of the righteousness of God, namely, God's covenant faithfulness to Abraham in which he promised "a worldwide family characterized by faith, in and through whom the evil of the world would be undone."[1]

---

1. Wright, *Climax of the Covenant*, 234.

PART II—GRACE FOR ALL

Within this overall purpose, Romans 9–11 functions as the climax of Paul's theological argument throughout and brings to focus the letter's practical aim. The whole of Romans 1–11, then, is an exposition of how God has been faithful, in Jesus Christ, to the promises made to Abraham. This exposition reaches its climax in the theological and historical survey of chapter 9. The historical segment begins in 9:6–9 with Abraham and works through to the prophets before moving to Christ (10:4) and the mission of the church (10:9–21; 11:13–32). The theology that produces this understanding of mission in chapters 10 and 11 is then, in chapters 12–15, made the basis of the appeal for unity in the church (notice how this understanding points to 15:7–13 as the climax of the entire epistle).

Paul concluded Romans 1–8 with a massive assurance of God's unfailing love and omnipotent grace. Nothing in all creation, Paul assured his readers, can separate them from that loving grace. The glimpses Paul provides into God's glorious future put into sharp relief a question that has been in the background of Paul's entire discussion: the persistent unbelief of Israel, God's chosen people. They have rejected the very Christ who was born from their race and for their redemption, as he was born for the redemption of all humanity. Is not God's plan for creation thwarted by their rejection of that plan? Can God's redemption of all creation be complete without Israel? How much comfort is there in being told that nothing can separate us from God's love when there is apparently something separating the chosen people from God's love? Is their final fate to remain separated from the redemption of humanity? It is to these questions that Paul turns in this segment of his letter.

The argument has three basic parts: 9:6–29; 9:30—10:21; and 11:1–32. The first and third parts address the question whether God's Word or plan have failed: Is God still faithful to Israel? Paul provides a theocentric argument, as the middle part of the argument shows, although the focus can shift to Israel and its failures and future, so that both God and Israel are defended and misconceptions about God's salvation plan are refuted. There are profound issues of theodicy, the character of God, election, and the trustworthiness of scripture involved in this discussion. This section builds on what was said in chapters 1–3 about God's impartiality and faithfulness, in chapter 4 about Abraham, in chapters 5–8 about the law, and in chapter 8 about predestination and the final outcome of God's plan of salvation.

The passion of Paul's words in chapters 9–11 reflects the urgency of the matter as he plans to visit Rome. There must be some semblance of agreement between Jewish and Gentile believers in Rome before he arrives. He is concerned to remove the impediments to such unity here and in the ethical sections that follow. We should not overlook that we are dealing with the diatribe form of discussion here once again. This explains the appearance of an inordinate number of questions, including numerous rhetorical questions, often followed by declarative answers and then by scriptural support. This section of Romans is the most scripture-saturated in the entire letter. In fact, over 30 percent of the scripture citations in the undisputed Pauline letters are in Romans 9–11. Paul needs all the biblical support he can muster in his argument against misperceptions of Jewish Christians by Gentile Christians.

If Paul's driving concern in Romans 9–11 is the failure of the Jews to believe the gospel, the issue has to do not merely with Israel but with God, particularly with God's righteousness (10:4). The question throughout has to do with the character and purpose of God, particularly faithfulness to his promises, and hence the impartial justice of his dealings with Israel and the world. Thus the opening claim in 9:6 concerns the unfailing character of God's word; 9:14 raises the question of whether God is unrighteous; 9:19 the question of why God still finds fault; and 9:19-23 of the rights of the potter over the clay, a question taken from the discussions in Isaiah and Jeremiah of God's covenant relationship with Israel (Isa. 29:16; 45:9; 64:8; Jer. 18:6). After the climactic statement of 10:3-4, the argument of chapter 11 remains focused not merely on the future of the Jews but on the character of God, as 11:22, 29, and 32 bear witness and 11:33-36 celebrate.

Paul is arguing that the events of Israel's rejection of the gospel of Jesus Christ are the paradoxical outworking of God's covenant faithfulness. Only by such a process—Israel's unbelief, the turning to the Gentiles, and the affirmation of ultimate salvation to the Jews—can God be true to the promises to Abraham, promises of a worldwide family. Paul's list of Jewish privileges in 9:4-5 culminate in Jesus, the Messiah not only of the Jews but of the whole world (see also 10:12). As long as the Jews cling to ancestral privilege, they are denying God's intended universal salvation. Behind this picture stands the doctrine of creation, with its implication that the God who made promises to Israel is also the creator of the whole world.

How then is God faithful to the covenant? Did God have two plans? No, there was one plan all along, a plan of grace, not race. God's plan from the beginning worked according to a principle of selection. God never promised Abraham that all of his physical offspring would be within the initial covenant (9:6–13). From the start there is a "double Israel," Israel according to the flesh (Ishmael, Esau) and Israel according to the promise (Isaac, Jacob). In 9:14–18 Paul faces the question of whether this principle of selection, this progressive narrowing down of the "seed" of Abraham, means that God is unjust. Paul moves on in history, declaring that even covenant Israel is rebellious and sinful. At the time of the exodus, specifically in the golden calf incident, Israel as a whole stood condemned, with only Moses pleading to God on her behalf (hence the reference in 9:15). So God's dealings with Israel are just, a justice of the covenant God who furthers the promise despite the failure of his people. This leads to 9:19–29, Paul's version of the Jewish doctrine of God's righteousness. God will judge, but at the moment he is patient. Scripture always envisaged that Israel had failed, not God, and that there would be a process of judgment and mercy, of exile and restoration. Though disobedient Israel, the "vessel of wrath" according to the flesh, had failed in her vocation, God's call of election would continue with faithful Israel, the "vessel of mercy." The point is not that the creator decides arbitrarily to save some and condemn others, but that the creator enters into a new covenant with humanity through Christ. That theme continues in 9:30—10:21.

The passage is not about "human responsibility" as such, nor simply about Israel's unbelief, but about the way in which, through Christ and Christian proclamation, Israel is transformed from being an ethnic people into a worldwide family. Having relied on self-righteousness instead of God's righteousness, Israel had confused grace with race, resulting in an idolatry of national privilege; hence Paul's statement in 10:4: "For Christ is the end of the law so that there may be righteousness for everyone who believes." It is Christ who fulfills the law, Christ who provides the requisite righteousness. The law was a good thing, given deliberately by God for a specific task and a particular period of time. When the task is done and the time is up, the law reaches its goal. The law is not a bad thing to be abolished but rather a good thing whose job is done. Christ is the fulfillment of God's paradoxical purposes for Israel and hence for the world: "He is the climax of the covenant."[2] This leads to the establishment of the Gentile mission (10:14–18) and the demonstration of Jewish obstinacy (10:19–21), the latter closing the section as it began (compare 9:30–31 with 10:20–21).

As we examine this passage in detail, four points should be kept in mind. The first is the fact that Paul is addressing Israel as chosen people,

---

2. Ibid., 241.

not the fate of individuals who may, from time to time, question or distrust God's promise in Christ. The second is a reminder that as we read the rehearsal of Israel's history in chapter 9, we must be mindful that Paul has not abandoned his conviction that God's activity is ultimately motivated by grace. The third point we must note is the distinction between predestination and predeterminism. While predestination sets the final outcome of a process, predeterminism allows no room for free thought. Using as analogy an automobile trip to another city, predestination sets the goal of the journey, without determining the route by which it can be reached. The goal of the journey is set, although the actual route taken may vary depending on choices made. Paul in chapter 9 is speaking of predestination, not predeterminism. The final point concerns Paul's style in Romans. Readers must be cautioned against stopping at a single verse or passage to ponder its density. Each verse and passage must be seen as part of a larger, growing argument. Nowhere is this caution more essential than Romans 9–11. Here, as Paul works through his argument, he poses a series of questions raised by his Gentile mission. No one part is complete by itself. Not until we near the close of chapter 11 is it clear where Paul's thinking has taken him.

Romans 9:5 and Paul's Christology

One of the most debated verses in Romans, indeed in all Paul's letters, is the ending of 9:5 (some translations, such as the NRSV or NIV, note the variant readings in the footnotes). In a passage where Paul mentions the advantages given to the Israelites, he concludes by saying that "from them comes the Messiah, according to the flesh, who is over all, God blessed for ever, Amen." This translation (NRSV) ascribes divinity to Jesus, declaring Christ is "God over all." While this view comes close to "incarnation" theology, as Jesus is portrayed in John's Gospel, many scholars believe such a Christology is "higher" (more advanced and therefore later) than anything found elsewhere in Paul and even in the Synoptic gospels (Matthew, Mark, and Luke). For this reason they translate the passage differently, such as "from them comes the Messiah according to the flesh. God who is over all be blessed for ever, Amen," thereby stating something about Christ and then concluding with a blessing to God. If it is true that Paul here explicitly calls Jesus "God," it would the only place in his letters where he does so.

As recent Christological studies show, a compelling argument can be made that Paul indeed holds to "incarnation" theology, and an examination into neglected passages such as Galatians 4:14 seems to bear this out. In this passage Paul calls Christ an angel, using the construction "but as ... as" to do so. When he uses that grammatical language elsewhere (see 1 Cor. 3:1; 2 Cor. 2:17), he is not contrasting two things but rather is stating that two things are the same. If Paul understand Jesus to be an angel, as is likely, he is not just any angel but probably God's chief angel, known in the Hebrew Bible as "the Angel of the Lord." If that is so, as New Testament specialist Susan Garrett argues,[3] then "virtually everything Paul says about Christ throughout his letters makes perfect sense. As the Angel of the Lord, Christ is a preexistent being who is divine; he can be called God; and he is God's manifestation on earth in human flesh."[4] When we apply this information to the "Christ Hymn," an early hymn or poem cited by Paul in Philippians 2:6–11, things fit beautifully. This is not to say Jesus is the Father, since the Father exalts him. And Jesus is definitely not "equal" with God in his preexistent state, for after his death he is exalted even higher than before his act of obedience, though still not the equal of God (see 1 Cor. 15:28).

When it says in Philippians 2:6 that Jesus was "in the form of God," this does not mean that he was the equal of God the Father; it means he was "Godlike" or divine, like the chief angel (the Angel of the Lord) referred to in the Hebrew scriptures (see Gen. 16:7, 13; 18:1—19:1; Exod. 3:2). As New Testament scholar Charles Gieschen states, this Angel of the Lord is either the "visible manifestation" of God or a distinct figure, separate from God, who is bestowed with God's own authority.[5] If this is what Paul believed about Jesus, that he is the figure who appeared to Hagar, Abraham, and Moses, who is sometimes called "God" in the Hebrew Bible, then that helps to explain the meaning of the final two stanzas of the "Christ Hymn" (Phil. 2:10–11). There we find statements that allude to Isaiah 45:22–23, in a context where the prophet Isaiah states explicitly that it is to God alone that "every knee shall bow and every tongue confess." In the Philippians hymn "Jesus has been granted the status and honor and glory of the One Almighty God himself."[6] If that is Paul's Christology, it is exceedingly "high."

---

3. Garrett, *No Ordinary Angel*, 11. The view that Jesus was the preexistent Angel of the Lord who appeared in the Old Testament was held by early church thinkers such as Justin Martyr (*Dialogue* 56, 127).

4. Ehrman, *How Jesus became God*, 253.

5. Gieschen, *Angelomorphic Christology*, 68; Ehrman, ibid., 57.

6. Ehrman, ibid., 265.

Textual Analysis: Topics to Ponder or Discuss

Romans 9:1–18

1. The tone of the letter shifts dramatically at the beginning of chapter 9, as triumphal rejoicing gives way to lament and sorrow. Who is included among the "us" who cannot be separated from God's love? Reminiscent of Moses's willingness to be cut off for the sake of worshippers of the golden calf (Exod. 32:31–32), Paul offers himself in behalf of fellow Jews.

2. Despite the shift in tone, Romans 9–11 does not introduce a new topic. From the start Paul had expounded his understanding of the gospel for the "Jew first and also the Greek" (1:16). Already in 3:1 he asks whether there is any advantage to being a Jew. Having answered in the affirmative, he offers a longer list in 9:4–5, noting seven benefits already mentioned in chapters 1–8. The final advantage is also the most important, the coming of the Messiah from Israel. Do you agree with Paul that Christ is the most important benefit?

3. The ending of 9:5 presents a problem in translation (those using NRSV or NIV Bibles will see the variant readings in the footnotes). The most important of these are: (a) "From them comes the Messiah, according to the flesh, who is over all, God blessed for ever, Amen." (b) Another reads: "From them comes the Messiah according to the flesh. God who is over all be blessed for ever, Amen." (c) A third reads: "From them comes the Messiah, according to the flesh, who is over all. God be blessed for ever, Amen." In your estimation, how do these versions differ Christologically (in their understanding of Jesus' identity)? Which version best fits the context? Which best fits Paul's view of Christ? [Note: As you answer these questions, keep in mind that Paul is not following the language or viewpoint of later creeds, but presenting an early view of Jesus. The first option ascribes divinity to Jesus. Do we find such a claim elsewhere in Romans? While this view comes close to how Jesus is portrayed in John's Gospel, this Christology does not seem to conform to Paul's view of Christ or to Paul's context (see 1 Cor. 15:28). Though Paul is thinking of Christ, the context is a Jewish formula of thanksgiving and praise to "the God who is over all" and who is the real subject of chapters 9–11.]

4. In 9:6–13 Paul reviews certain aspects of election in the patriarchal story in order to refute the suggestion that God's word has failed (9:6). As Paul reviews God's purposes in the past he recognizes that they operate according to a principle of selection: by choosing one family from the whole human race; by continuing that practice within the chosen family itself (Isaac rather than Ishmael; Jacob rather than Esau); and finally (as he notes in passing in 9:5 and emphatically in 10:4), by choosing one individual to carry God's plan by himself. Even the role of Pharaoh was the result of God's choosing (9:17). As Paul distinguishes the "children of the promise" from the general physical posterity of Abraham, he is not trying to make room for believing Gentiles among Abraham's children, as he does elsewhere. Rather, he is presenting an historical account with which every Jew would agree: the descendants of Abraham through Ishmael (Gen. 25:12–18) and through Esau (Gen. 36:1–8) were not included in "Israel." He clinches his argument in rabbinic fashion with one text from the law and one from the prophets (9:12–13). The reversal in verse 12 contains a subtle implication, namely, that the Jews (the elder) will serve the Gentiles (the younger), hinted at in 9:33 and 10:19 and declared openly in 11:11–12.

5. The quotation in 9:13 from Malachi 1:2–3 needs to be examined carefully. What did Malachi mean when he stated that God loved Jacob and hated Esau? As we have seen, election does not mean individuals, groups, or nations can sit back and take it easy. It does not mean that one is inherently superior. But it does heighten the expectation: "to whom much has been given, much will be required" (Luke 12:48). Paul's quotation from Malachi presents a new problem, upon which Paul reflects in 9:14–24. One may soften the language by noting that Hebrew has no comparative adverbs; there are Old Testament texts in which "to hate" simply means "to love less," but this still raises the issue of injustice or favoritism on God's part. Two points help answer this accusation. The story of the birth of the twins has to do with God's choice of nations through which the divine purpose in history is accomplished, not the selection of individuals for salvation or damnation. Also, "love" and "hate" in the prophetic idiom have nothing to do with affection and hostility, but mean simply "choose" and "not choose" (see Luke 14:26; in Deuteronomy 5:9 "hate" means "not choose," that is, "reject").

6. In 9:14–18 Paul's shift to Moses and Pharaoh introduces a new dimension, that God's election is not arbitrary, but a matter of asserting power and presence in human affairs to fulfill his purpose for history—a purpose resisted by Pharaoh.

7. One of the striking things here is that Paul offers no critical remarks. His point is not to criticize individual Israelites or to identify the limits of Abraham's family, but to insist that it is God who elects and who does so according to divine purposes, which are neither arbitrary nor capricious, but merciful and benevolent. Verse 16 reinforces verse 11.

Romans 9:19–29

8. This discussion leads to Paul's analogy of the potter and the clay, an issue taken from the discussions in Isaiah and Jeremiah of God's covenant relationship with Israel (Isa. 29:16; 45:9; 64:8; Jer. 18:6). The first point Paul makes in speaking of God as creator is that God has no equal and no standard to which he "must" or "should" conform (9:19–20). This point must be established, but it is the presupposition, not the conclusion of Paul's message. It is easy to take offense at a picture of an impersonal, unfeeling God, particularly when the association is made with the "objects of wrath made for destruction." Yet the point of the analogy is not the power of the potter to fashion a vessel, but the right (9:21) of the potter to determine the use of the vessel. Neither rigid determination nor arbitrary whim, but creative and purposive divine freedom lie at the heart of Paul's understanding of election.

9. The second point Paul stresses in this passage is that the sovereign creator is a God of mercy. Grace cannot be exacted or compelled, or it is no longer grace. Verses 22–24 introduce a hypothetical point: "What if God . . ." In fact, the God revealed in Christ has not arbitrarily chosen some and rejected others, but has "endured with much patience . . . in order to make known the riches of his glory for the objects of mercy" (9:22–23). The syntax of 9:22–23 is exceedingly difficult, but these verses appear to be an elaboration on verse 21. God has indeed acted with mercy and with wrath, but God's actions have as their goal a glorious mercy, both for Jews and for Gentiles (9:24). One way to translate "objects of mercy" in 9:24 is "objects through whom God brings his mercy to others." God's final goal all along, Paul argues, involved an expanded chosen people. Paul's stance here is not

PART II—GRACE FOR ALL

that of an impartial spectator but of a Christian confessing that God has in fact chosen and called Jews and Gentiles alike to be his people.

10. This section of the argument (9:25–29) concludes with citations from Hosea and Isaiah, supporting in reverse order what Paul has just said about Jews and non-Jews. In Hosea God is portrayed as the husband who takes back his underserving wife (Israel) after her repeated unfaithfulness. Originally directed to sinful Israel, Paul understands this text to point to the inclusion of Jews and Gentiles in the one people of God. The text from Isaiah (actually from a variety of prophetic passages) returns to God's reliability in the election of "true Israel." "Remnant" in 9:27, like "survivors" (literally "seed") in 9:29, refers to the authentic line of descent from Abraham described positively in 9:6–13. Paul's point here is that from the beginning, only a part of Israel (a "remnant") should be included in God's new people. Since the origin of Israel, as well as its continuation, was a matter of God's choice and not of genetic heritage, no one, least of all the Israelites, should be surprised if God continues to constitute a chosen people by his own act of choice. [Note: The word "only" in 9:27 is added by the translator of the NRSV and does not appear in the original Greek. Chapter 11 will suggest that there is a remnant, but this remnant is not the only object of God's salvation.]

Romans 9:30—10:21

11. In the previous section Paul discussed the status of Israel as chosen people, a topic he treated earlier in his letter (3:1–8). In this section Paul expands on another topic he treated earlier, namely, the purpose of the law (3:31—4:22). If the law God gave to Israel as his chosen people did not prevent Israel from rejecting Christ, what can we say about Israel's relationship to that law or, perhaps more importantly, about the purpose of that law? And what can we say about the relationship of the law and Christ? Are they opposed to one another?

12. In this section Paul draws out the implications of his startling conclusion that "chosen people" now include more than physical descendants of Abraham. The upshot of that conclusion is that the Gentiles, who were originally excluded from the chosen people, nevertheless are the ones who have accepted relationship with God based on trust, whereas the Israelites, possessing the law that was intended to uphold that relationship, had not achieved the same trust, which was the

purpose of the law. The reason? The Israelites thought the law pointed to the contribution they had to make to that relationship with God ("as if it were based on works," 9:32) and hence lost the point of the law, which was to engender trust in the God who had chosen them. Having substituted the means (godliness) for the end (trust), the inevitable outcome was that when Christ came as the one who personified the call contained in the law to trust in God, the chosen people rejected him. That which was the cornerstone of election—trust in God—became instead a stumbling stone (9:30). Faith (trust), it seems, was a requirement all along.

13. Paul's citation in 9:33 combines portions of Isaiah 28:16 and 8:14. The assurance given to those who trust in God had been laid down as a foundation stone in Zion, but it became a rock of stumbling, as God said he would himself become to those who refuse his message, and Israel has stumbled on that rock (Rom. 9:32). This is Paul's own people, and the reason for his anguish in (9:2-3). On the basis of Psalm 118:32, Christianity after Paul developed a complex mosaic of "stone" passages to apply to Christ (1 Pet. 2:6-8; Matt. 21:42; Mark 12:10; Luke 20:17; Acts 4:11; Eph. 2:20; see also Luke 2:34), so Paul's later readers have assumed that the stone of 9:33 refers to Christ. Some Christian interpreters argue that the stone refers to the gospel. What does Paul have in mind here? (Notice that Paul cites the second line of the quotation in 10:11). However one takes the citation in 9:33, this verse counts as one of the most remarkable of Paul's Old Testament quotations because of what it attributes to God: placing in the midst of his people a base of security that is at the same time an obstacle over which they will stumble (see Paul's use of the figure of the stumbling block in 1 Cor. 1:21-24).

14. Recalling 9:1-5, chapter 10 begins with a prayer for the salvation of Israel, reiterating that Israel has a zeal for God, but it is not enlightened. Paul is ascribing to Israel the same attitude that he too had before coming to faith in Christ (see Gal. 1:13-14; Phil. 3:6).

15. Tragically, Israel's rejection did not occur because she was not religious enough, but because she was overly religious. In setting out to merit God's grace, Israel ignored grace and shifted the area of trust from God's goodness to their own goodness. That is the point of 10:1-3. What the law intended—a trustful relationship with God—it

was unable to produce. It was not until Christ came that sin's power was broken, and the law was freed from that power. That is why Christ is both the fulfillment of the intended role of the law (the proper relationship of creature and creator) and the end of its primary function in that relationship. Paul means both when he says: "Christ is the end of the law" (10:4). Christ is the goal for which the law was established, namely trust in God (see 3:31), but also the end of the law as the primary means of a relationship with God.

16. Paul demonstrates how Christ is the goal of the law in 10:6–13. Verse 5 indicates that Christ is the end of the law in the matter of righteousness (right standing with God), which depends on divine faithfulness rather than on human effort. Because Christ, not the law, is now the basis for trusting God, Christ is the end of the law as the means of salvation.

17. Verses 6–10 contain Paul's midrash (Paul is here employing a Hebrew mode of interpreting scripture) of Deuteronomy 30:14. The point is that righteousness is not a matter of human searching or striving. One does not need to be transported in a vision to heaven to find Christ, or make a subterranean journey, as is sometimes described in apocalyptic literature, to bring him up from the dead. The Word, both written and incarnate, is near at hand. In verses 9–10, trusting God totally ("with the heart") and acknowledging such trust through public confession ("with your lips") are what Christ as fulfiller of the law brings about. Seeing the guiding hand of God in the events of Jesus is what the Christian faith is all about. Above all, God's trustworthiness is demonstrated in Jesus' rising from the dead. Note that the emphasis in verse 9b is on God raising Christ from the dead, not on the event of resurrection as such. Jesus' resurrection is important because it shows God can be trusted even to overcome death. Trusting in that God from the heart is what leads to right standing with God.

18. In 10:11 Paul sums up his argument with a verse from the Hebrew scriptures. [Note: Remember that Jews regarded scripture broadly as God's law.] If the religious function of the old covenant has been ended by Christ, as Paul declares, then Christians might well wonder why Paul continues to quote it. The answer becomes plain if we understand scripture in the light of Christ. His coming makes clear the true purpose of the law (see 2 Cor. 3:12–16, where Paul says exactly

that). Viewed from that perspective, the law (the entirety of the Hebrew Bible) is embraced as a vehicle that enhances our understanding of the covenantal trust in God to which we are summoned in Christ.

19. The use of the term "Lord" in 10:9–13 can be confusing. The confession in verse 9 joins two elementary Christian creeds to indicate that salvation is the result of true confession coupled with true believing. The confession is parallel to the one in 1 Corinthians 12:3, which suggests that Paul is using a set formula his audience will recognize. As in many of Paul's quotations from the Old Testament, "Lord" stands for the name of God in 10:12–13 and does not refer separately to Christ. But this fusing of the text from Deuteronomy 30 with Paul's own message about the "faith that we proclaim" in 10:8b shows his perception of complete continuity and consistency between the God of Israel and the preaching of what God has done in Christ (10:17). In verse 12 Paul reiterates God's impartiality, a theme enunciated earlier in the letter. In Paul's mind there is no distinction between Jews and Gentiles because there is one Lord over all.

20. In 10:13 the verb "saved" appears in the future tense. Joel 2:32 is quoted, and the emphasis is on "all." All who call on this Lord will be saved. Paul is here countering any notion that God has plans to save only a few or desires to bless only a few. Paul's emphasis is on the wideness of God's mercy, not the narrowness of the elect. Beginning at 10:14 we have a sequence of events required for someone to be saved. [Note: This passage says nothing about God's predetermined decrees of election. The emphasis is on the necessity of preaching and of response. Paul amplifies the problem in 10:18–19 to include Gentiles.] The quotation of Deuteronomy 32:21 in verse 19 and Isaiah 65:1–2 in verses 20 and 21 provides the basis for Paul's analysis in chapter 11 of the case regarding Israel. Can it be that Israel did not hear or understand? The Old Testament text from Psalm 19:4 in verse 18 indicates that Israel did hear. The quotation from Deuteronomy, probably in reference to the golden calf incident, is intended to goad the Israelites and show them God's ongoing faithfulness (this striking motif is resumed in 11:11, 14). The third scriptural citation in 10:20 serves a double purpose, to show God's mercy to the undeserving Gentiles who are presently included in God's people, and also to those Jews who are presently excluded. This, however, is not Paul's final word on God's plan for history, as becomes clear immediately at the beginning of chapter 11.

PART II—GRACE FOR ALL

Essay 9: Understanding Paul's View of Divine Righteousness

The phrase "righteousness of God," crucial to Paul's theology and central in Romans, has been the subject of intense scholarly debate. The debate is between those who view the concept as a reference to a quality of God (God's own righteousness) or as denoting a status that humans have from God (a righteousness given to humans). In this essay we will argue for the first option. That is not to say that there is no such thing as a righteous status held by believers, for there is (this topic is discussed in essay 3), but that this is not what Paul means by the phrase "the righteousness of God."

The expression is found eight times in Romans (1:17; 3:5, 21, 22, 25, 26; and 10:3 twice), only once in the other Pauline letters (2 Cor. 5:21; its use in Phil. 3:9 is different) and three times in the rest of the New Testament. The noun "righteousness" is characteristic of Romans, where it is used thirty-three times. It is striking that Paul does not explain the phrase, but begins by announcing that the "righteousness of God" has been revealed (1:17).

To properly understand this concept, an understanding of the Old Testament is indispensable. Paul assumes his readers were well-grounded in this scripture and so constantly used its categories and wording to make his points. Righteousness language (the noun *dikaiosyne*, the adjective *dikaios* [righteous] and the verb *dikaioo* [to make righteous or to justify)[7] was common in normal Greek, but its significance for the New Testament is based on the use of these words to translate Hebrew words *zedeq* or *zedaqah*. In the Old Testament, when "righteousness" is used of God, it can have three distinct (though interrelated) meanings.

- It can denote God's justice, as in Psalm 50:6: "The heavens declare his righteousness, for God himself is judge." God is absolutely just and impartial, fairly determining the rights and wrongs of individuals and situations.

---

[7]. "Righteousness" and its related terms "right, righteous, to be (make or declare) righteous" can also be translated "justification, justice, just, or justify," from the Latin *justitia*. English translations employ "righteousness" terms about three times as often as "justification" words, but both must be considered in grasping what is a single biblical concept. The interrelatedness of the two concepts is seen in Romans 3:21–24: "The righteousness of God has been disclosed . . . they are now justified."

- It can denote God's covenant faithfulness, specifically, God's faithfulness to the promise that through Abraham all the families (nations) of the world would be blessed (see Gen. 12:3; Rom. 4:16, 17; Gal. 3:6–9, 14). Through this covenant God promises not only to bless Israel but also, thereby, to renew creation. The prophecy of Isaiah, particularly chapters 40–55, exerted an enormous influence on Paul and the New Testament. The final flourish of Isaiah 55 cannot be overlooked, especially in connection with Romans 8.
- It can denote God's saving activity (see Isa. 51:5–8, noting the parallelism between deliverance [*zedeq* or *zedaqah*] and salvation):

    v. 5: I will bring near my *deliverance*//my *salvation* has gone out;

    v. 6: my *salvation* will be forever//my *deliverance* will never be ended;

    v. 8: my *deliverance* will be forever//my *salvation* to all generations.[8]

    Righteousness, however, is not the same thing as salvation; God's righteousness is the reason why God saves Israel.

In describing the dealings of God with humanity prior to the coming of Christ, Paul resorts to the term "righteousness," a concept that connotes restorative rather than punitive justice: "righteousness" is "the power of God for salvation to everyone who has faith, to the Jew first and also to the Greek" (Rom. 1:16). In the Old Testament righteousness frequently denotes the active grace by which God restores the people of Israel or vindicates their cause, granting them victory or success. When they were wronged by foes, they had the right to appeal to God for deliverance. In championing their interests against threats and accusations, God became their justifier (Isa. 51:5). As the people were penitent and loyal, God provided them with gracious care and protection.

In Romans, Paul is dealing with a different situation, and he takes the old term "righteousness" and extends its meaning. The problem of sin has come to the fore, and it is no longer a question of people needing vindication, but of humanity requiring reconciliation to God. The two parties are God and sinful humans. God's saving power (or righteousness) is needed by those who are wrong, not wronged. Humans are, Paul says, enemies of

---

8. Note the variety of English translations for the Hebrew root *zdk* here: "righteousness" (NIV); "justice" (NAB); "triumph" (Jewish Tanakh Translation).

God, alienated and estranged, who cannot count upon God's protecting favor or loyalty to their interests.

Why did Paul use this Greek term *dikaiosyne*, inadequately rendered "justice" or "righteousness"? He took a classical term that provided him several advantages; it had an adjective and a verb to correspond; he could use it not only of God's free action and moral concern but of God's relationship with human individuals. Also—and particularly important in his literary context—the term was suggested by Habakkuk 2:4, a great prophetic passage about faith: "the one who is righteous (*dikaios*, i.e., the person who is in right relation to God) will live by faith" (1:17). In the background lies also Paul's awareness of what Isaiah's Suffering Servant (understood as a prophecy regarding Jesus as Messiah) was appointed to do, to "make many righteous" (5:19) by being wounded for their transgressions (Isa. 53:5). In the Old Testament God is indeed righteous in punishing wrongdoing, but more often in vindicating his people. The latter was not understood as an obligation on the part of God to Israel so much as the manifestation of God's grace.

We are left, then, with two closely related senses that have to do with God's covenant faithfulness, both as a quality in God and as an active power that expresses that faithfulness to accomplish what the covenant always promised: to deal with evil, to save his people, and to do so justly, with impartiality. Since, for Paul, God is the creator, always active within his world, we should expect to find God's attributes and actions belonging extremely closely together.

But this covenant loyalty, this covenant justice, is not purely a matter of saving activity. It requires justice upon covenant-breaking Israel, and only then merciful rescue of penitent Israel. That is why the gospel contains within itself, as Paul insists in Romans 2:16, the message of future judgment as well as the news of salvation. What God's righteousness never becomes, in the Jewish background which Paul richly sums up, is an attribute that is passed on to his people. Nor does Paul treat it this way. What we find, rather, is that Paul utilizes Old Testament themes that cluster around the question of God's faithfulness to Israel, to Abraham, and to the world. How the covenant is fulfilled, and who will be God's covenant people when this occurs, is precisely what Romans 9–11 is about, not an appendix to the letter but its proper climax.

Optional Group Activity

Divide the participants into three groups to discuss the meaning of the expression "righteousness of God." Ask Group 1 to evaluate righteousness as God's justice. Ask Group 2 to evaluate righteousness as God's covenant faithfulness. Ask Group 3 to evaluate righteousness as God's saving activity. Ask each group to include in their deliberations whether God's justice is primarily punitive or restorative. At the conclusion, reconvene the small groups into one and ask each group to share its insights with the others.

If time allows, give participants time to write down one takeaway (insight) from their reading or group discussion and then to share it with the class.

Session Ten

Grace for All

Summary: Romans 11 heightens Paul's discussion of grace, demonstrating God's plan of salvation for Jews and Gentiles. The persistent unbelief of Israel, God's chosen people, forces the question of whether their unbelief has thwarted God's plan for the redemption of creation through Christ. Paul replies that God still intends to save ethnic Jews. He returns to the theme of a righteous remnant to illustrate the gracious mystery of God's ways in human history. The lapse of the large majority within Israel serves a providential purpose, the inclusion of Gentiles in God's plan of salvation. Paul notes, ingeniously, that in admitting Gentiles as covenant people, God meant to provoke unbelieving Jews to a godly envy. In the future God will replace the Jews to their former position, since "the gifts and the calling of God are irrevocable" (11:29). Using the analogy of the olive tree, Paul argues that God's plan progresses through three stages: from choosing Israel (the holy root), to hardening Israel (some branches are cut off) in order to save the Gentiles (engrafted shoots), and then to saving Gentiles in order finally to save Israel. Paul calls God's plan in saving Jews and Gentiles a "mystery" (11:25), meaning it is not obvious to human reason or capable of being understood empirically. Paul views the rejection of Israel as a means to a blissful end, exhibiting the full sweep of God's merciful grace, which is God's true design for the world (11:32). The closing essay examines the concept of election biblically and theologically.

Assignment: Read Session 10 of *Grace Revealed* and Romans 11:1–36. Answer the following questions, writing the answers in your journal. [Be prepared to share your views with others in the class.] Romans 11:26 is one of the most controversial passage in Paul's writings. The dispute concerns the meaning of the phrase "all Israel will be saved." Who are the recipients of God's gracious election? The reference can mean (1) Jews and Gentiles in Christ (for the entire church as the spiritual "Israel" see Gal. 6:16), (2) all the elect of Israel, (3) ethnic Israel (all Jews), (4) all Jews alive at the end of history, (5) all Jews who place their trust in Jesus as Messiah, or, by implication, (6) all human beings (the full number of Gentiles and of Jews). On the basis of your reading of Romans, which of these options best represents Paul's hope for the future? Why? Which of these best represents your own view? Why? [Note: In your response, keep in mind your definition of "salvation," whether in the narrower sense of destiny in heaven or hell or in the broader sense of covenant relationship with God.]

Key Verse(s): Romans 11:26–32

Central Theme: God's plan for history culminates in restorative justice

Technical Words and Concepts: mystery, hardening of Israel, fullness of Gentiles, supersessionism, analogy of the olive tree, "all Israel," double predestination

Learning Objectives

In this session participants will examine:

1. Paul's understanding of a righteous remnant
2. The role of Israel's hardening in God's plan
3. Paul's analogy of the olive tree
4. The meaning of the phrase "all Israel will be saved" in 11:26
5. God's ultimate plan of salvation for Jews and Gentiles

Outline to Romans 11:1–36

I. Grace in History 9:1—11:36
   A. Israel's Rejection 9:1—11:10
      1. A Remnant Continues 11:1–10
   B. Gentile Acceptance 11:11–24
   C. Israel's Acceptance 11:25–36

PART II—GRACE FOR ALL

Romans 11:1–36: Flow of the Argument

Two concerns dominate Romans 9–11: the question of unbelieving Israel and the question of God's faithfulness. The two, of course, are intimately connected. Paul's heartbreaking grief in 9:1–3 speaks eloquently of the first, and his opening denial in 9:6 addresses his second concern. And when we turn to the end of the section and find the salvation of Israel guaranteed by God's gifts, call, and overall purpose (11:26–32), we can be sure we have correctly identified the double theme. The line of argument in these chapters is this:

God is free to do as God pleases (chapter 9);

Israel is responsible for rejecting God's grace (chapter 10);

Israel will eventually be saved (chapter 11).

Romans 9 and 10 address the persistent unbelief of Israel, God's chosen people, a question that has been in the background the whole time. They have rejected the very person who was born from their race and for their redemption, as he was born for the redemption of all humanity. Has God's plan for the redemption of all creation through Christ been thwarted by their rejection of that plan?

The main thrust of Paul's argument is to arrive at the questions of 11:1 and 11:11 on firm theological ground. Paul's aim throughout chapter 11 is to argue that God still intends to save ethnic Jews. Paul is himself an example of the fact that Jews can still be saved (11:1–6); he is part of the "remnant" (9:27; 11:5), chosen by God so that the "purpose of election might continue" (9:11). Paul does not say that Roman Gentile Christians should engage in evangelism among their unbelieving Jewish neighbors. But he declares that part of the point of his own Gentile mission is to make unbelieving Jews jealous of seeing their privileges now shared by non-Jews, and so to bring them to faith at last (11:14).

Paul's reference to a remnant chosen by grace in 11:1–6 is fresh proof that he is not thinking of personal salvation but of the collective functions of those selected by God to carry on his purpose. The remnant was selected to spread the faith and further the cause of God on earth. Paul adopts the category of "the remnant" to illustrate the gracious mystery of God's ways in human history. The goal of the remnant is to regenerate the inert mass in due time.

Thus far Paul has been arguing along the characteristic view of grace, but in chapter 11 he advances to a position that is the real difficulty in the entire argument, a peak so precipitous that few dare follow: that the mere fact of a remnant being chosen within Israel (9:5–6; 11:1–6) indicates that God has a future for the whole people in the course of providence. This exceptional deliverance comes in 11:11–12. Here Paul explains that this lapse of the large majority cannot be final. He explains, ingeniously, that Israel will become jealous of the Gentiles enjoying what was once their position of favor. In fact, Paul ascribes this to a providential purpose. In admitting Gentiles as covenant people, God meant to provoke the unbelieving Jews to a godly envy. To this argument he adds another, based on racial solidarity. The mere fact that a minority of Jews already believe the gospel proves that the eventual transformation has begun. God has only made a beginning with Israel; as the root of the nation (patriarchs like Abraham) is holy, that is, in fellowship with God, the branches of the tree will follow (11:15–16): "They are beloved, for the sake of their ancestors" (11:28; see 9:5). One day God is sure to replace the Jews in their former position, since "the gifts and the calling of God are irrevocable" (11:29). It is a mystery, Paul declares, but one he infers from the changeless purpose of God: "to be merciful to all" (11:32).

Paul's message, as his theology, should not be separated from the basic concern that shaped his thinking: the relation between Jews and Gentiles and their role in God's plan. That plan, expounded in Romans, Paul calls a "mystery" (11:25), meaning it is not obvious to human reason or capable of being understood empirically. Rather, God's plan is discernable through specific events, such as the choosing (election) of Abraham and the life and death of Jesus—these become key to understanding God's purpose for creation. But not even these events are open to rational deduction. Only the final consummation of God's plan will make absolutely clear what the clues have been. Yet a God whose plan is grace for all will not leave his creatures without knowledge of that plan, and Paul's function in Romans is to make clear that knowledge. God's plan of grace, surprisingly, includes the hardening of Israel.

Various explanations for Israel's rejection of Christ can be given: (1) Israel's election was only temporary, until the coming of Christ; (2) Israel's election was never valid, and their claims to a special relationship to God were self-serving; and (3) Israel rejected Christ, so in the end God rejected them. While each view is plausible, all are wrong. As Paul explains, the reason for Israel's rejection of Christ is—grace! Grace for Gentiles, and finally grace for Israel as well. God has consigned "all in disobedience so that he may be merciful to all" (11:32). God's plan, says Paul, progresses from God choosing Israel (election), to God's hardening Israel in order to save Gentiles, and then to saving Gentiles in order finally to save Israel.

Recall the hardening of Pharaoh (9:17–18), which served the purposes of God's gracious plan; recall the hardening of vessels of wrath for the purpose of showing mercy (9:22–24); recall the hardening of Israel, done for the purposes of God's mercy to that very Israel (11:15–16). Consider the total rebellion of all creation, done for the purpose of the mercy to be shown to that creation (11:32). That is the mystery of which Paul speaks.

Israel's hardening, then, is temporary and serves the purposes of grace. Because that is so, because God can use even rebellion and disobedience in his plan of mercy on all, we may have utter confidence in God's plan. Nothing, not even the rejection of God's Son by God's people, could affect God's purposes of grace. It is that assurance that Paul sings forth in the close of this unit (11:33–36). What a glorious God! That God's response to disobedience is mercy is the theme that runs throughout Israel's prophetic literature and is summed up in a passage like Isaiah 59, where a list of human shortcomings is climaxed by a declaration of God's unending covenant faithfulness, or Jeremiah 31:31–37, where the climax of God's judgment against Israel is a new covenant that cannot be broken as was the covenant of former times. It is not by chance that Paul quotes from these passages in Romans 11:26–27.

As we learn in chapter 11, God has not yet spoken a final word to Israel, for all Israel will be saved before the end comes. Paul views the rejection of Israel as a strange means to a blissful end, exhibiting the full sweep of merciful grace, which is God's true design for the world (11:32). On this hopeful note he ends the discussion. The argument of Romans 9–11 begins with a cry of anguish, but it ends in a cry of ecstasy. The close of the passage is as impressive as its poignant opening.

Textual Analysis: Topics to Ponder or Discuss

Romans 11:1–10

1. At issue in chapter 9, as in 11:1, is the fairness of God. If God fashions creatures according to his will, showing mercy to some and hardening

others, why does God act that way? We have learned that all things work together in accordance with God's plan (8:28). We have also learned that Israel has rejected God's mercy in his Son. Does that mean that God has rejected Israel? Paul uses two examples to arrive at his conclusion: himself (if God had rejected Israel, then Paul could never have been called as an apostle) and Elijah (who concluded from the events of his day that God surely had rejected his people). Elijah was wrong, for God had preserved a remnant even in Elijah's faithless age, and, Paul affirms, God has preserved a remnant in Paul's time as well (11:5). Paul's point in 11:1–6 is clear: God is in control, and that is good news. Because what motivates God is grace. Our only hope for survival is if God deals with us in grace. Those who would have it another way thereby seal their own fate. Yet God will not have it so. God is merciful, and God's mercy will prevail. That is the gist of the entire chapter.

2. A nagging issue persists: Israel is hardened to the gospel. If God is in control, it is he who has hardened them. Indeed, this is affirmed by Israel's scripture: God has dimmed their eyes and closed their ears. Is it not a contradiction of terms to describe God's election this way? If so, what purpose does election serve? Was Israel chosen only to serve as a negative example to the Gentiles (see 2:24)? Does the hardening of Israel lead to condemnation? "Have they," as Paul frames it, "stumbled so as to fall" (11:11)?

3. Paul's support of the temporary hardening of Israel in God's plan comes from Israel's scripture (see Luke 24:44): the Law (Deut. 29:4), the Prophets (Isa. 29:10), and the Psalms (Ps. 69:22–23). Here as elsewhere, the quotations do not agree exactly with the English translations of the original Hebrew texts because Paul customarily used the Septuagint, the Greek translation used by Hellenistic Jews and early Christians.

Romans 11:11–24

4. The sovereign God, who does not directly cause everything that happens but who works in everything for good (8:28), is able to bring good out of the present situation, when most Jews have rejected Christian faith. The point Paul is making in 11:11–12 is that even the hardening of Israel serves the purposes of mercy. And it serves the purposes of mercy not only for Gentiles but for Israel as well. When

Israel sees the mercy they have rejected become real in the Gentiles, the new chosen people who confess the lordship of Christ, they will become envious of that grace and return to become a part of that new chosen people. Verses 11–12 are key to Paul's argument and essential for rightly discerning the meaning of 11:26a. Here Paul expands upon 11:6, emphasizing that God's final purpose in election is redemptive. But where does that leave Israel? If Israel's stumbling benefits the Gentiles, what good does that do Israel? Paul hints at the answer by speaking of Israel's "full inclusion" (The NRSV translation introduces a bias, as the Greek word *plēroma* means "fullness," "full strength," "full number," "completion," or "complete number") in God's redemptive purpose. What we find implied in Paul's discussion in 9:14–21 we find expressed here: God's actions are motivated by mercy. [Note: The same Greek word (*plēroma*) is used of Gentiles in 11:25.]

5. In 11:13 Paul turns to the Gentile Christians at Rome. Again we are reminded that Paul has not been writing an abstract essay on Jewish-Christian relations, but is writing a letter to a particular church in a particular situation. Gentile Christians have become the majority in the Roman church and Paul sees his Gentile mission as a step in God's plan finally to include Jews and Gentiles in the one redeemed people of God.

6. When Paul speaks of "reconciliation of the world" and of "life from the dead" in 11:15, he is using eschatological language to describe God's act on behalf of humanity. He does not see the one renewed people of God as an ordinary occurrence in human history, but as an aspect of the eschatological events by which God will consummate history (to understand Paul's eschatological terminology, we must keep in mind the driving force of his vision of the restoration of creation in 8:18–39). Paul expected the *eschaton* in the near future, viewing his mission to the Gentiles as part of God's preparation for the triumphal end of history.

7. On "first fruits" in 11:16, see 8:23 and 1 Corinthians 15:20. The present nucleus of Jewish Christians is the pledge that all humanity will finally be included in God's reconciling plan for history. The holiness of the root (faithful Israel) points to the holiness of the whole vine (the entire people of God, composed of Jewish and Gentile believers). As the "remnant" is the pledge of the future redemption of "all

Israel" (11:26), so the fledgling Roman congregation (comprised of Jewish and Gentile believers) is the pledge of the future acceptance of all people by God (11:32).

8. The analogy of the olive tree in 11:17-24 reinforces points Paul has made throughout Romans. First, the primacy of grace. It is clear that in this tree, all branches have been engrafted by grace. This is true of the wild branches (Gentiles) but also of the natural branches (Israel) broken off by their rejection of trust (in God and in Christ). If the natural branches are regrafted, it is on the same status as the Gentiles, that is, by grace alone. This leads to the second point, that the tree is an analogy of history rather than of doctrine. Here one is susceptible to the error of supersessionism, the doctrine that the church has replaced Israel in God's plan. Rather the reverse has happened, that Israel continues through history as the people of God and that Gentiles who come to faith in Jesus are engrafted into God's remnant tree, while Jews who reject Christ are temporarily excluded. Third, to speak of grace is also to speak of human responsibility. Grace may be free, but it is not to be presumed upon, is not to lead to arrogance, and above all it is not cheap. The God of grace remains the Lord of creation, a fact one forgets at one's peril. God can remove engrafted branches as he did natural branches. The God who is gracious in election can also be severe against those who play loose with his grace (11:22; see also 6:1, 15). Grace, to be effective, demands the response of trust. To presume upon God's kindness is dangerous (2:4). Grace is not permission to do as one pleases. Such permission, as Paul discussed in 1:24-28, is not a manifestation of God's grace but of God's wrath. Rather, "grace is the summons to respond in trust to the God of grace and to shape one's life by the structures of that grace."[1] The response is important, but the priority belongs to grace.

Romans 11:25-36

9. With verse 25 Paul moves toward his conclusion, which he terms a "mystery," a term with apocalyptic connotation (see Dan. 2:18-18, 27-30; 1 Cor. 15:51). The term does not refer to something difficult to understand, but rather to something concealed that can only be known by revelation. The mystery is not about Israel's "partial hardening" (11:25), since this has been Paul's argument since 11:8, nor of

---

1. Achtemeier, *Romans*, 184.

the salvation of the Gentiles prior to the salvation of Israel, but of the inseparable connection in God's plan between Israel's unbelief and the faith of the Gentiles.[2] Verse 26 begins with an adverb (*houtōs*), meaning "thus," "so," or "in this manner." The mystery of which Paul speaks pertains not to an order of events but rather to the manner and method of God's plan. Here Paul summarizes the argument he has been making in this chapter: God has accomplished the hardening of "part" of Israel (the "rest" of 11:7) while the "full number" (*plēroma*) of Gentiles come in, and then "all Israel will be saved" (11:26). He finds this mystery anticipated in the words of Isaiah 59:20–21 and 27:9 (though in altered form). The original reference of Isaiah 59:20 may have been to God as deliverer, though there is evidence that later Jews viewed it as referring to the Messiah, and it is likely that this is how Paul understood the reference. Paul is rejecting at every point a rigid determinism that divides humanity into two groups, namely, the "insiders" and the "outsiders," the "saved" and the "damned." While "part" of Israel is currently at enmity with God, Israel remains God's beloved.

10. The meaning of "Israel" here is debated. Building on the logic of 4:16, some view the term as a reference to the Christian church, including Jewish and Gentile believers, where Abraham is said to be the father of believing Gentiles as well as believing Jews. However, it is unlikely that "Israel" in verse 26 means something different than in verse 25, where it surely does not refer to Gentiles. In Romans Paul never equates the church explicitly with Israel. It seems clear that when he says "all Israel" will be saved, he has in mind ethnic Israel (that is, all Jews).

11. Some interpreters find in verses such as 10:13, 11:14 and 11:22 grounds for limiting the number of the saved in 11:26 to professing Christians, primarily Jewish Christians. They also state that Paul would have set limits on the meaning of "all Israel," noting that where this expression occurs in Old Testament passages (see 1 Sam. 7:5; 25:1; 1 Kgs. 12:1; 2 Chron. 12:1; and Dan. 9:11), "all" does not mean literally every single Israelite. Such argumentation, however, focuses on future judgment and distracts from Paul's central concern, living faithfully in the present. When Paul stresses faith in Christ for salvation, the focus is on the present. And when Paul speaks of God's future judgment, the

---

2. Beker, *Paul the Apostle*, 334.

reference is to judgment according to deeds (see 2:6–11, 14–16, and 29), not to possible damnation. Such judgment, however, is ultimately restorative, not punitive, for according to Paul, nothing can exclude one from God's love (8:31–39). [For an examination of the views of Augustine, Calvin, and Karl Barth on election, predestination, and salvation, see essay 10 below.]

12. When Paul speaks of Israel's salvation, he is not envisioning a mass conversion of Israel but an act of God foretold in scripture. The expression "all Israel" is not a designation for the Jewish-Christian church, yet it is not separable from Israel's process of coming to faith and from the jealousy that the Gentiles provoke in the present time (Rom. 11:13, 23). Paul's view of Israel's destiny is dissimilar from that portrayed in Ephesians, where Israel is absorbed in the one church of Jews and Gentiles and hence ceases to exist as a separate entity (Eph. 2:11–22). Jewish Christianity does not simply displace the Jewish people and does not represent their fullness; rather, Jewish Christians symbolize God's continuing faithfulness to Israel. Paul envisions a special destiny for Israel, including entrance into God's eschatological kingdom, unique in time and in manner. The promise of Israel's future reconciliation represents God's covenant faithfulness to Israel, faithfulness both historical and eschatological.

13. Two verses provide the theological character of Paul's argument. First, God's faithfulness to Israel rests on election, on the fact that "the gifts and calling of God are irrevocable" (11:29). Second, the salvation of all is dependent on grace (11:20–32). For both Jews and Gentiles have "sinned and fall short of the glory of God" (3:23). What disobedience does, grace undoes.

14. Romans 9–11 ends as it began, with a doxology (see 9:5; 11:33–36), composed in part from Old Testament citations. God remains beyond human manipulation, yet faithful obedience and hope depend on God who is faithful. All creation joins Paul in praise of this God, unsearchable in justice and inscrutable in mercy.

Essay 10: Understanding Paul's View of Election

Election, the idea of being "called" or chosen by God, is an essential biblical motif, indispensable to Israel's identity and to Christian self-understanding.

PART II—GRACE FOR ALL

Election means that God takes the initiative in establishing the covenant relationship. God enters the historical situation in an act of self-giving (disclosure of the divine name) and in acts of benevolence toward a people in distress (see Exod. 3:1–17). Israel does not first choose God, but rather is chosen by God.

The underlying significance of the patriarchal stories in Genesis is not so much the stories of the patriarchs but the story of Israel's self-understanding. At the time this material was put into writing, the main question was not, "Who are Abraham, Isaac, Jacob, and Joseph?" but "Who is Israel?" Israel was grappling with her identity, her self-understanding as a people called by God. The theological answer was found in the doctrine of election.

What does election mean? The biblical answer is given in the portrayal of Abraham, Isaac, and Jacob, patriarchs whose lives were characterized by the following traits:

- They *lived by faith in God*. In Abraham, Israel understands that they have been called into existence by God himself, that they had been created by God's initiative and preserved by God's grace.

- They were *called to be a servant people*. Election does not mean that one people is chosen because they are better than others, but rather that they are called to spread God's grace. In Abraham, God brings one person of faith into existence in order that God's blessing might be extended to all humanity. This is the Bible's stress on election, that when God calls a people, they are called to service, and the rest of the Old Testament, and then the gospels and epistles, show what it means to be a servant people. The Bible makes it clear that Israel's calling is part of God's healing intention for the world (the biblical word for healing, health, wholeness, and goodness is "salvation," similar in meaning to the Hebrew word *shalom*). In the Bible, the election of a people becomes the basis for good news, what the New Testament calls "gospel."

- They were *called to pilgrimage*, namely, to a life of mobility, movement, and change. Biblical faith is a calling faith, a calling to be on the way, to be moving in God's direction, to be pioneers of faith. So Abraham is the ancestor of a pilgrim people, and his story and that of the patriarchs is the story of God on the move with his people.

In Romans 9–11 the problem of election comes to the fore. Paul has concluded the second major section of his letter (chapters 5–8) with a massive reassurance of God's unfailing love and omnipotent grace. Nothing in all creation, Paul assures his readers, can separate them from that loving grace, since it is the Lord of that creation who is the author of such grace. Where the reality of that grace, incarnate in Christ and present in his Spirit, is recognized and allowed to work, there the redemptive power of that grace is already transforming the community of the faithful. Within that community the future redemption of God's total creation has become visible in anticipatory form. Foreknowledge . . . predestination . . . election (Rom. 8:29-30): no doubt Paul emphasizes these ideas to reassure Christians of their secure standing in God's purpose (Rom. 8:31-39). But what of Israel, the chosen people of God (Rom. 9:4; 11:2)?

Paul's glimpse of the future puts into sharp relief a question that has been in the background the whole time, the persistent unbelief of Israel, God's chosen people. They have rejected the very person who was born from their race and for their redemption, as he was born for the redemption of all humanity. Has God's plan for the redemption of all creation through Christ been thwarted by their rejection of that plan?

The normal view, found in the synoptic tradition, is either that the Gentiles who believe join the patriarchs, while the Jews are left out (Matt. 8:11-12), or that the privileges of the Jews have ceased, owing to their rejection of Christ (Mark 12:1-9). Paul's earlier writings suggest that he shared this opinion: "God's wrath has overtaken them at last" (1 Thess. 2:16). But in Romans 9–11 Paul adopts another point of view. In this difficult passage Paul is thinking aloud, addressing questions and doubts that troubled him throughout his ministry. In one sense he is arguing against himself, that is, against ideas forced upon him by the facts of life. Having finished his mission in the eastern Mediterranean region, he can see that the majority of Jews have rejected Christ. But he is also writing to Gentile Christians at Rome, both to dispel ideas that his gospel of freedom meant relaxing the ethical and religious value of the law, and also to counter an air of superiority toward the Jewish people, based on the perception that because Gentiles were now the majority in the church, the Jews had been displaced from the purpose of God. All through Romans this double protest appears: against discarding the law, and the danger of self-righteousness.

In Romans 11 Paul reaches the climax of the discussion he began in the first chapter. The story of human rebellion, in which Jews and Gentiles alike shared; the new beginning with Abraham and his descendants; the redemption in Christ now possible for all who trust God; the creation of a new people through whom the good news of God's redemptive action is to be spread abroad—this story of election finds its culmination in Romans 11. Fittingly enough, since the story of the rescue of God's creation began with Israel, it will also conclude with them.

Romans 11 also displays Paul's understanding of the reasons for, and the outcome of, Israel's rejection of Christ as God's messianic gift of grace. The reason is twofold: to create space in God's plan for the inclusion of the Gentiles and also, surprisingly, to create space in that plan for Israel herself. Paul's conclusion in Romans 11 is in keeping with the tone of the letter, indeed with the tone of his theology: Israel's failure, as humanity's, has a silver lining—the redemption of creation. Human weakness is such that unless God has grace upon all, no human being could be saved.

Grace, Election, and Predestination in Augustine, Calvin, and Karl Barth

The traditional view of predestination, as articulated by Augustine, Calvin, and other representatives of orthodoxy, claims that humanity is contaminated by sin and unable to break from its grasp. Only grace can set humans free. Yet grace is not bestowed universally; it is only granted to some individuals. As a result, only the elect will be saved; the rest will perish. Predestination involves the recognition that God withholds the means of salvation from those who are not elected. Later followers of Augustine taught a doctrine of "double predestination," whereby God allocates some to eternal life and the rest to eternal condemnation, solely on the basis of divine will, without any reference to their merits or demerits.

Building on the contributions of Augustine and Calvin, the twentieth-century theologian Karl Barth used a unique Christological approach to arrive at a startling conclusion. For Barth, predestination refers not to the election of select humans for preferential treatment but rather to God's election of Jesus Christ to serve as mediator between humanity and deity. Barth's starting point is with God's free and sovereign decision to enter into fellowship with all humanity. By electing Christ for the redemption of humanity, it is Christ who is rejected, not humanity. The cross, representing God's judgment upon sin, is God's "No" to humanity. However, this "No" does not result in the exclusion and rejection of humanity, for God's "No" to sin is borne by Christ, who died for all. In Christ, then, we find

God's judgment *and* God's redemption, God's "No" to sin and God's "Yes" to grace. Because Christ is the sole elected individual, his mediatorial role leads to God's final word to humanity, which remains "Yes." Barth's doctrine of predestination, pointing to universal restoration and the salvation of all humanity, eliminates condemnation of humanity. The only one who is predestined to condemnation is Jesus Christ, who from all eternity willed to represent humanity. Barth's perspective is rejected by many Christians, particularly evangelicals and fundamentalists, who consider his methodology and conclusions to compromise the traditional Christian doctrines of human nature, sin, and grace.

Optional Group Activity

Divide the participants into three groups to discuss the question of election (chosen for what?). Ask each group to consider one question, answering the question both theoretically and practically (through personal examples), searching the patriarchal stories in Genesis 12–50 for guidance. Ask Group 1 to address the question: What does it mean to live by faith? Ask Group 2 to address the question: What does it mean to be a servant people? As Group 3 to address the question: What does it mean to live a life of pilgrimage? At the conclusion, reconvene the small groups into one and ask each group to share its insights with the others.

If time allows, give participants time to write down one takeaway (insight) from their reading or group discussion and then to share it with the class.

Part III

All from Grace
The Unity of Jewish Christians and Gentile Christians (Romans 12:1—15:13)

IN HIS LETTER TO the Romans, Paul has been emphasizing the coming together of different cultures in obedience to the same Lord. Romans 12:1—15:13 provides coherent arguments that center on issues that detracted or were likely to detract from the unity or stability of the Roman Christian community. Paul wishes to see the gospel fully realized in Rome, which involves Christian Jews and Gentiles not merely getting along with each other but actually forming a unified people of God. The aim of chapters 1–11 was to produce a situation where the audience understood that Jews and Gentiles are on equal footing in grace. All stand under the mercy of God and have need of it. The aim of chapters 9–11 was to counter anti-Semitic feelings or attitudes of Roman Gentile superiority, which were hindering the possibility of a unified body of Christians, Jewish and Gentile, in Rome. Paul made clear there that God had not given up on Israel, nor had God's promises to Jews failed. In chapters 12–15 Paul attempts to bring harmony to the church's life, to its members' relationship with the community, the state, and the neighbor in Christ.

As Paul writes this letter, recall that Claudius had recently died (in AD 54) and that Nero was the new emperor. Nero was only sixteen in 54, and so required advisors who would serve in a sense as guardians. His moral advisor was Seneca, the Stoic philosopher, and it is due largely to his tutelage and guidance that the first five years of Nero's reign were stable. Nero

PART III—ALL FROM GRACE

allowed the Senate more power than had Claudius. He also immediately allowed Jews to return to Rome on his accession, which was about four years before Paul wrote Romans. Until 59, there was relative peace and calm, especially in Rome, and there was much hope that the emperor would continue along the positive track he was following. He had, after all, promised such at his accession. That event was carefully structured, with Seneca giving a series of speeches meant to establish the tone of Nero's reign as just and restrained. These speeches are of significance for what Paul will say about Roman officials in Romans 13:1–7.

At such a time the poet Calpurnius Siculus wrote hopefully to the Romans: "Amid untroubled peace, the Golden Age springs to a second birth . . . while he (Nero), a very God, shall rule the nations."[1] It was also a time when Paul could tell the Romans: "Do not be conformed to this world, but be transformed by the renewing of your minds" (Rom. 12:2). Such transformation, he admonishes, depends on living "peaceably with all" (Rom. 12:8), a context undermined less than a decade later by the ruthless Nero, who unleashed a devastating persecution of Christians in Rome following the great fire of AD 64, which destroyed or severely damaged two-thirds of Rome, finally stopped after a week of urban terror. Nero, himself blamed for having ordered the fire, substituted Christians as culprits. The Roman historian Tacitus, writing early in the second century AD, tells of Nero's scapegoat persecution of those "whom the crowd styled Christians. . . . First, then, the confessed members of the sect were arrested; next, on their disclosures vast numbers were convicted, not so much on the count of arson as for hatred of the human race. And derision accompanied their end; they were covered with wild beasts' skins and torn to death by dogs; or they were fastened on crosses, and, when daylight failed, were burned to serve as lamps by night."[2]

What strikes us immediately about Romans 12:1—15:13 are Paul's admonitions not only to external peace but especially to internal peace: "Live in harmony with one another," he says in 12:16 and 15:5. Harmony is required, it would seem, because God has granted them divergences within Christian faith or differences of Christian faith. In other words, Paul's exhortation does not presuppose unity without diversity, but rather diversity within unity. The closing chapters of Romans address the unique situation that required such a lengthy plea for peaceful unity.

1. *Eclogue* 1.42.46.
2. *Annals* 15.44.2, 4.

Session Eleven

Grace and the Community

Summary: The discussion in Romans 12–13 shifts from theological issues to practical instruction on life in the Christian community, particularly on the impact the gospel makes on relationships. Paul does not simply exhort believers to higher moral standards, but rather presents guidelines that promote unity within the church. The appeal is not to humanistic effort but to God's faithfulness and love, defined by the death and resurrection of Christ. This call for faithful response is rooted in Paul's eschatological perspective that Christians are living out of the resources of the age to come. As citizens of God's new kingdom, believers are called to live in conformity not with values of the old age but with values of the emerging new age. Paul's ethical admonitions provide examples of God's structuring grace as it bears on the neighbor, the governing authorities, and other segments of human society. The believers' fundamental response to God's gracious lordship is to allow themselves to be shaped totally by that lordship, rather than by the lordship operating in secular society. The closing essay examines the variety of spiritual gifts believers receive from God to promote the church's unity and wellbeing.

Assignment: Read Session 11 of *Grace Revealed*, Romans 12–13, and 1 Corinthians 12–14. Answer the following questions, writing the answers in your journal. [Be prepared to share your views with others in the class.] One of the topics addressed in this week's reading is "spiritual gifts." Is this a topic with which you are familiar? Can you name a spiritual gift you see in yourself? (this can include gifts not found in these passages). Is there a gift you desire that you do not currently have or use? Can you think of how you might acquire or put this gift into practice? How are spiritual gifts useful for building the church as a whole?

Key Verse(s): Romans 12:1–2, 21; 13:10

Central Theme: Transforming to God's lordship rather than conforming to the world's lordship

Technical Words and Concepts: "living" sacrifice, ecclesiology, spiritual gifts, love (*agapē*), church-state relations, charismatic, *pneuma*, *charis*, fruit of the Spirit, *charismata*, *diakonia*

Learning Objectives

In this session participants will examine:

1. Paul's understanding of the lordship of God and of the transformation it accomplishes in one's life
2. Paul's understanding of the term "love" and how this understanding applies to everyday life, particularly in situations of conflict
3. The eschatological nature of Paul's teaching in Romans 12:1–2 and 13:8–14
4. Paul's view of the role of secular government
5. Guidelines for determining when and how to oppose government policies
6. The nature of spiritual gifts and their use in upbuilding communities of faith

Outline to Romans 12:1—13:14

I. Grace in Society 12:1—15:13

   A. Grace and the Community 12:1–21

      1. Living Within the Dawning Age to Come: Foundational Statement 12:1–2

      2. Appeal for Unity and Love 12:3–13

      3. Responsibility toward Outsiders 12:14–21

   B. Grace and the State 13:1–14

      1. Responsibility toward Authorities 13:1–7

      2. Appeal for Unity and Love 13:8–10

      3. Living Within the Dawning Age to Come 13:11–14

Romans 12:1—13:14: Flow of the Argument

Chapters 12:1—15:13 subdivide into two segments of nearly identical length: 12:1—13:14 and 14:1—15:13, the first part being more general and the second more specific. The broader concerns seem to be unrelated to specific problems in the community, whereas the second unit addresses examples occasioned by the major issue that called forth the writing of Romans, the coexistence of Jews and Gentiles in one religious fellowship (Paul does not use the word "church" in Romans until chapter 16). Chapters 1–11 have served to shape the identity of the house churches in Rome and to mold believers' understanding of themselves as Christian people. Readers have been encouraged to think of themselves as people who belong to the new age inaugurated by God, redeemed by grace and freed from the controlling power of sin.

At 12:1 the content and tone of Romans shift dramatically, from profound theological issues to practical instruction for the Christian community. In chapters 12–16 key words and themes from chapters 1–11 are absent, particularly the "righteousness/justice" terminology. As we might expect, "faith" continues as an important theme (12:3, 6; 14:1–2, 23–24), though its meaning appears different from its usage in chapters 3–4 and 10. Despite these differences, we should avoid making sharp distinction between Paul's "theology" and his "ethics." For Paul, faithful thinking and faithful living belong together. Paul's theology is always ethical, and his ethics are always theological, even if some of his letters divide into sections to invite such labeling. The function of chapters 13–16, though primarily exhortatory, is not, however, to inspire "religious" behavior or to supply a moral dimension to life. The Jewish and Greco-Roman worlds of Paul's day were full of both. Rather, what Paul's audience needs are guidelines that promote unity to religious life and integrity to morality, appealing not to humanistic effort but to God's faithfulness and love, defined by the death and resurrection of Christ. Paul's "indicative," rooted in the gospel, provides the context and the challenge for his "imperative." His call for faithful response is addressed to individuals living in the confluence of God's "already" and "not yet" kingdom, in conformity not with values of the old age but with values of the emerging new age. Paul's ecclesiology (his doctrine of what it means to be the church of Jesus Christ) is closely related to his eschatology.

Romans 12:1–2 provides the foundation for what it means to be a citizen of God's new kingdom. This passage draws explicitly on the Jewish eschatological view that world history divides into two ages, the "present age" and the "age to come," but it reframes that Jewish perspective by insisting that the two now overlap and that Christians belong in the latter. Paul is not, therefore, exhorting Christians to do better what other people have tried to do. It is, rather, that the new day has begun to dawn, and that those who belong to Christ must live in its light rather than in the darkness of the present world. This view indicates how Paul's argument in Romans 12 and 13 is constructed. Taken together, this unit forms a chiasm. A chiastic structure, as noted earlier, is an X- or V-shaped pattern found in the literature of Paul's time, in which clauses, verses, or units are related to one other through a reversal of structure in order to make a larger point. If the pattern consists of six scenes, as here, the focus may be on the inner (the third and fourth, C and C') or the outer scenes (A or A'). The main development of chapters 12–13, viewed chiastically, appears thus:

> A. 12:1–2 living within the dawning age to come
> > B. 12:3–13 appeal for unity and love
> > > C. 12:14–21 responsibility toward outsiders
> > > C'. 13:1–7 responsibility toward authorities
> > B'. 13:8–10 appeal for unity and love
> A'. 13:11–14 living within the dawning age to come

As 12:1–2 shares a common theme with 13:11–14, so 12:3–13 has much in common with 13:8–10. In between is 12:14—13:7, parenthetical but hardly incidental to the surrounding themes. Seen in this light, 13:1–7 need not be regarded as an outlier in Paul's teaching but as relating to the preceding passage, which deals with avoiding vengeance.

If Paul's "theological" story was and is the story of God's grace toward his rebellious creatures, the results of that story continue to be a matter of grace. The very fact that Paul can include ethical admonitions in his letter is a further demonstration of that grace. It is Paul's conviction that only when the power of sin has been broken, only when God's grace has triumphed over sin and evil, can ethical admonition serve any function other than the increase of sin. Paul's ethical admonitions, therefore, display a further reality, in addition to the victory of God's grace over human rebellion. They show that grace is not an excuse for permissiveness, in which "anything goes." Such permissiveness, as Paul made clear in 1:24–32, is not a manifestation of God's care but of his wrath. Grace is the opposite of permissiveness.

Grace brings with itself the power to restructure our lives in ways appropriate for life under the lordship of God. The ethical admonitions of chapters 12–15 provide examples of the structuring effects of grace as they bear on a variety of circles in human society. The fundamental response to the gracious lordship of God displayed in Christ is to allow oneself to be shaped totally by that new lordship, rather than by the lordship that operates in "this world" (12:1–2). Beginning with the Christian community (12:3–13), Paul moves to the wider society (12:14–21) and then to the state (13:1–7) and the neighbor (13:8–14).

Textual Analysis: Topics to Ponder or Discuss

Romans 12:1–21

1. Romans 12:1–2 is the key to Romans 12–15. First, it links Paul's exhortation about daily living with what he has written earlier. Paul's appeal to "the mercies of God" refers to the theme of the previous eleven chapters—grace! These verses then outline the essence of our response to God's grace, a response that will be the theme for the rest of Paul's letter. At the heart of this response is transformation, and this should occur within believers as a result of the new mindset they have received. The Christian is no longer self-serving but delights in God's law (7:22). Yet believers must still present their bodies to God as instruments of righteousness (see 6:13). Here we see the reversal of the situation described in chapter 1: once we were rebels, our bodies given over to disobedience (1:18–32), but now that God has renewed our minds through his Spirit, we are to give ourselves back to God. [Note: The word "body" in 12:1 refers to one's entire being, including one's thoughts and impulses, as under one's discretion for allegiance and action (see 6:12–13, 19).]

2. The imperatives in 12:1–2 are not an abstract ethic addressed to individuals, but a word to individuals as part of a community that discerns the divine will. The context is also eschatological. Readers are urged not to be conformed to this "world" [literally "this age"; the Greek word is *aiōn* (age), not *kosmos* (world)] but to be transformed to a reordered life. Its significant manifestation will be a renewed "mind," meaning one regains the lost capacity to "discern" God's will (see 1:11). The gift of discernment, one of the church's spiritual gifts (see 1

PART III—ALL FROM GRACE

Cor. 12:10), enables the community to distinguish the important from the trivial, the genuine from the imitation, and thus good from evil. Christian decision-making is part of one's worship of God. [Note: The world asks for our allegiance by squeezing us into its mold, sometimes blatantly, sometimes subtly. Currently, the media is one of the world's most powerful instruments for conformity. Can you think of other ways the world squeezes you into its mold? What about the communities of which you are a part? Can you help to change patterns of conformity at your school, family, workplace, gym, or athletic team? As you gain the wisdom of spiritual discernment, how might this change your shopping, eating, and entertainment patterns and priorities?]

3. Paul's admonition to believers in 12:1 about presenting their bodies as "living sacrifices" reminds us of the importance of metaphorical language in the Bible. The mercies of God call for reordered lives that represent a "living sacrifice." Such transformation is declared "spiritual worship." Paul declares that dedication of the entire self to God serves as the authentic worship appropriate to a reordered human life.

4. In 12:3–21 Paul indicates that the greatest impact the gospel has upon our lives is in challenging and changing our relationships. In 12:3–8 Paul shows how we must start with a sober view of ourselves, as individual members of God's people. One of our greatest temptations is to boast about ourselves. There is no room for pride in the believer, and for this Paul gives two clear reasons: (a) Christians are to regard themselves in accordance with the "measure of faith" that God has given them (12:3), and (b) individual Christians are part of a greater whole. Our spiritual life is a gift from God, not something we have earned or achieved on our own. When we see ourselves in the light of the gospel, from the perspective of God's mercy, we understand that we are chosen by grace and that all boasting must end. Using the analogy of the body, whereby each part has a different function to be used for the benefit of the whole, Paul indicates that in the church each person has a gift to be used for the whole of the church. If we understand that this is our calling, to live interdependently, we will remain humble and not succumb to superiority or to its psychological twin, inferiority. Just as we are to give ourselves fully to God (12:1), so we are to give ourselves fully to one another. [Note: It is helpful to compare this passage with 1 Corinthians 12:4–31, especially verses 4–11. Paul's Corinthian congregations had demonstrated the destructive effects of competitive

GRACE AND THE COMMUNITY

individuals on the harmony of the whole. Note that these lists contain no ordered ranking, for the common denominator is God's grace. In Romans, unlike 1 Corinthians, Paul deliberately avoids connecting these gifts with the Spirit; cf. 1 Corinthians 12:11. Can you think why Paul's emphasis changes in Romans?]

5. That Paul's list of gifts in 12:6-8 overlaps but does not exactly conform to the list in 1 Corinthians 12 shows that Paul does not have a firm inventory of specific gifts but is concerned with their origin and function. They represent that "measure of faith" that God gives each believer to live the Christian life and strengthen the life of the church for its mission (prophecy, ministry, teaching, exhortation, giving, leadership, benevolence). The implication is that every Christian has been given a gift, not that some have a spiritual gift and others do not. The difference consists in the fact that not all have received the same gift. This means that while not every Christian will have the gift of preaching, teaching, social action, or of caring for the needs of others, every Christian does have some gift. We also learn that these gifts do not belong solely to the individual, but rather to the whole of the church. While there is diversity of gifts, there are no negligible gifts, no gifts of God the Christian community can afford to ignore. Like election, gifts are an extension of God's grace; if we neglect them, we may lose them. [Note: Paul's emphasis is on interdependence and mutual responsibility, so we should never get stuck in debates about their meaning or become polarized over them. It is interesting that we have here no mention of the more "spectacular" gifts such as tongues or interpretation of tongues. Why make something practical controversial, or why introduce something controversial to an otherwise irenic context?]

6. Having addressed individual Christians, Paul gives instructions to the community as a whole. The remainder of the passage (12:9-21) comprises over twenty brief instructions, most of them without elaboration, regarding how Christians should relate to one another and to society as a whole. As in 1 Corinthians 13:1-3, Paul here considers love to be the supreme gift, the common ground for all Christian behavior. Verses 9-10 look ahead to 13:8-10. It is clear in Paul's writings and throughout the New Testament that love centers not on emotion but on action.

7. When grace structures a community, its display in life is unity, best expressed under the rubric of "love" (12:9–13). Such unity cannot be reduced to uniformity, however. Paul here considers love to be the supreme gift of the Spirit, not as a human emotion or an abstract ethical principle. Christian love (*agapē*) is made specific in terms of the self-sacrifice of Christ, "who loved me and gave himself for me" (Gal. 2:20). The Greek text of verse 9 does not contain the imperative supplied by most English translations at its beginning. Paul may well have intended this to be a statement about the nature of love, rather than advice concerning it. In that case Paul simply declares, "love is not hypocritical," and then draws implications from that fact. Those implications are what Paul then states in 12:9–13; they all demonstrate unhypocritical love in action. These short injunctions are arranged in no obvious pattern but seem linked by key terms or catchwords. Verses 9–13 appear to be focused on relationships within the community and verses 14–21 on external relationships, but even this distinction is questionable. We notice here echoes and reminiscences of identifiable traditions (words of Jesus in 12:14 [Matt. 5:44], 17 and 21 [Matt. 5:39], and of Jewish wisdom traditions in 12:15 [Sir. 7:34], 16 [Prov. 3:7], 17 [Prov. 3:4], and 20 [Prov. 25:21–22]). This helps interpret the difficult saying in 12:20 about heaping "burning coals on their heads." The coals represent the burning shame and remorse the offending party feels, which lead to repentance. [Note: Paul is not here providing a list of laws, but rather giving examples of the way grace structures the activities of Christians in their common life with one another.]

8. We learn in 12:19 that revenge is not an option for Christians, because to take revenge into one's own hands is to encroach on God's territory. Here is an instance where the Christian ethic clashes with the values of a secular culture that admires avengers who strike back. The key to gracious living under circumstances of insult and slander is found in 12:18: "so far as it depends on you, live peaceably with all."

9. The entire passage represents the lifestyle of those shaped by the power of grace (good) rather than by the reality of this world (evil). Note how Paul summarizes that idea in 12:21: "do not be overcome by evil, but overcome evil with good."

Romans 13:1-7

10. This passage has caused the church much grief over the years and it needs to be examined with great care. Is the Christian under obligation to support whatever policies the governing authorities may deem appropriate, whether these policies are for the good of the people or simply for the purpose of perpetuating those in power? Is Paul placing on Christians the obligation to obey all edicts of whatever government happens to hold civil power over them? That is the interpretation many German Christians gave to Adolf Hitler under the Third Reich and some British and Dutch in South Africa gave under apartheid rule. Because the passage has no parallel in the undisputed Pauline letters (although see 1 Tim. 2:1-2 and 1 Pet. 2:13-14), some scholars have suggested that it was added to Paul's original letter to Rome. However, there is no early copy of the letter without these verses, so that should not be our solution. It is more important that we recognize the window of opportunity created by Nero's first years of reign, a time of peace and stability in Rome.

11. Because taxation plays an important role in this discussion (see 13:6-7), it may be that the specific situation that prompts this discussion lies in that reference. Roman taxation could be abusive, and the emperor Nero sought in AD 58 (around the time of the writing of this letter) to address widespread abuses in the system. This situation could well mean that Paul hopes to discourage Roman Christians from withholding taxes and thereby putting themselves at risk for punishment (see in this context Jesus' words about what one must render to Caesar and what one must render to God; Mark 12:13-17).

12. In this context, the passage should not be used as a comprehensive theoretical treatment of "the state." Paul is not writing an essay on church and state or general instructions for all times and places, but a letter to a specific situation. That Christians would one day themselves exercise such authority is simply not envisaged. The passage should also be read in the context of Paul's earlier plea "not to be conformed to this present age" (12:2). This passage, in opposing chaotic civil life, establishes the principle that social order has behind it the authority and purpose of God. While the passage sets limits on the freedom of individuals, it also relativizes governing authority. A government that claims for itself total and absolute devotion ceases in that moment to be

an agent of divine order, or a divine servant. It has become instead an idolatrous opponent of God (see 12:19). Governments that claim for themselves divine prerogatives are no longer the kind of governments of which Paul speaks in this chapter. The early Christian reaction to that kind of government can be seen in Revelation 17:1—18:24. Furthermore, Paul describes governments as agents of good, dedicated to promote civil good and punish evil. When a government reverses those roles and begins to reward evil and punish people who do good, or when a government uses excessive force or cruelty as a form of punishment, it wouldn't be the kind of government about which Paul here speaks. Obedience to civil authority is a Christian duty, but it is to be exercised within the framework of the Christian's ultimate commitment of obedience to God.

13. A fundamental problem remains: How does one decide at what point a government has passed from the ranks of God's servants to the ranks of his opponents? On that matter the passage gives no specific advice. There are limits to civil authority, a fact made clear in these verses. In the final analysis, these verses indicate that there is no dimension of life that is beyond God's concern or beyond God's lordship.

14. As we contemplate matters of church and state, we must keep in mind that the situation has changed dramatically since Paul wrote. We no longer live under the Roman Empire, when "subjection" or "rebellion" are the only political options. The modern reader can hear Paul's instruction as a call for responsible participation in government, both by informed voting and by serving in office. Other options are equally available to Christians who act otherwise "because of conscience" (13:5).

Romans 13:8–14

15. Paul's language about fulfilling the law may seem surprising, given that much of what he has said about the law in earlier chapters is negative. By defining certain patterns of behavior as sinful and by inability to help people to accomplish what law demands (see 7:7–10), the law gives sin its power. And yet Paul persist in declaring that the "law is holy, and the commandment is holy, just, and good" (7:12). And 8:4 anticipates that the "just requirement of the law" is fulfilled by those who walk in the Spirit of God. In 13:8–10 that "just requirement" takes on specificity. When Paul states that love is the fulfilling of the law" (13:10), such love does not condone all behavior, but works

actively for another's good: it is this kind of love that fulfills the law, as verse 9 makes clear.

16. Paul concludes his initial discussion of the Christian life by returning in 13:11–14 to the note of eschatological urgency with which he began (12:1–2). The list in verses 13 and 14 is not limited to nocturnal activities; it simply mentions things to avoid. Paul's injunction to "put on the Lord Jesus Christ" (13:14) is an admonition to "be who we are," little Christs. The Christian's clothing is the "armor of light," a reference to the transformed believer who no longer lives in darkness but in the light of the dawning age.

17. The metaphors of wakefulness (13:11), light and day (13:12–13), and of new clothing ("armor"; 13:12) are common ways of depicting the radical transformation expected from those who are members of the Christian community. This change reflects that "salvation" is at hand. In this context "salvation" appears to be a reference to the return of Jesus, which Paul discusses more fully in 1 Thessalonians 4:13–18 and 1 Corinthians 15:12–58.

Essay 11: Understanding Paul's View of Spiritual Gifts

Having addressed the meaning of his gospel of transformation in Romans 5–8, Paul encapsulates that message in 12:1–2: "I appeal to you therefore, brothers and sisters, by the mercies of God, to present your bodies as a living sacrifice, holy and acceptable to God, which is your spiritual worship. Do not be conformed to this world, but be transformed by the renewing of your minds, so that you may discern what is the will of God—what is good and acceptable and perfect." In 12:3—15:13 Paul unpacks some of the specific components of that transformation. He begins in 12:3–8 by reminding us that we live our transformed existence in community.

Central to community life is an understanding of ourselves in line with gifts God has given us. When we contemplate the topic of spiritual gifts, we often think of unusual behavior such as "speaking in tongues," faith healing, and other charismatic activity, particularly as manifested in Pentecostal denominations. Charismatic activity, however, characterized the early church. The Spirit was viewed as the "organizing principle" of the church's life, and everyone participated in church worship. Spiritual gifts were admired in Paul's churches and widely manifest in his time. What

PART III—ALL FROM GRACE

prompted Paul's teaching about "spiritual gifts" in Romans was not their legitimacy but their misuse. Because Paul is concerned with unity in his churches, he introduces the topic with a call to Christian humility, an important manifestation of the transformation that should characterize the believer. Perhaps Paul is especially concerned that believers not take an overly individualistic approach to spirituality. He wants believers to recognize that transformation of character is demonstrated in relationships with one another.

Paul uses various Greek terms to convey the idea that life in Christ is empowered by the Holy Spirit, often *pneumatika* (think of the English word "pneumatic," a reference to air or spirit), which emphasizes the spiritual origin of the gifts (*pneuma* means spirit; see 1 Cor. 14:1), and also *charismata* (think of the English word "charismatic," a reference to spiritual power or extraordinary personality), which emphasizes that gifts are bestowed as an act of divine grace (*charis* means "grace"; see Rom. 12:6). In distinction from "the fruit of the Spirit," which all Christians are to manifest without variation (Gal. 5:22–23), the gifts of the Spirit are understood to vary from one believer to another (Rom. 12:6; 1 Cor. 12:4–11; see also 1 Pet. 4:10). In the letters of undisputed Pauline authorship, there are four separate listings of spiritual gifts: Romans 12:6–8; 1 Corinthians 12:8–10; 12:28; and 12:29–30. Since no lists are identical, they are suggestive rather than definitive.

Paul's premise is that God gives to every believer a spiritual ability to perform for the common good, to encourage and build up the church, which he calls the body of Christ. While Paul's letter was addressed to the Romans, with its diverse constituency of Jewish and Gentile Christians, Paul's letter today speaks to the diversity within local churches as well as the ecumenical nature of the church universal. As the body has many members, each with different functions, so the church is diverse, ethnically, socially, culturally, sexually, linguistically, theologically, and geographically. Paul celebrates this diversity as evidence of the Spirit at work. If all Christians are guided by the Spirit, he reasons, and if it is God's will that harmony and peace should be the hallmarks of the church (1 Cor. 14:33), then God will not only equip Christians for different ministries, but will also give others the grace to recognize and accept such Spirit-led leadership where it emerges.

In Romans 12: 6–8 Paul lists seven gifts: prophecy, ministry, teaching, exhortation, generosity, leadership, and compassion; in 1 Corinthians

12:8–10 he mentions nine: wisdom, knowledge, faith, healing, working miracles, prophecy, discernment of spirits, speaking in tongues (known as glossolalia), and interpretation of tongues. These *charismata*, called "sign gifts," are granted to individuals for the common good.

The *charismata* can be divided into three groups:

- Declarative gifts (power of speaking). Gifts of communication include prophecy, the ability to distinguish between true and false prophecy, speaking in tongues, and the ability to interpret speaking in tongues.
- Dynamic gifts (power of doing). Gifts of practical ministry include faith (the precondition for miracles), healing, and miracles.
- Discerning gifts (power of knowing). Pedagogical gifts include wisdom and knowledge.

The gift of apostleship, ranked first in 1 Corinthians 12:28, is active in all three ways: in the ministry of the word, in pastoral care, and in the working of miracles.

Another list, called *diakonia* (think of the English word "deacon," which refers to an ecclesiastical office) appears in 1 Corinthians 12:28: apostles, prophets, teachers, workers of miracles, healers, assistants, leaders, speakers in tongues. Known as "support" or "service gifts," *diakonia* are granted to individuals for church ministry. Following the biblical (and Reformation) principle of the priesthood of believers, all Christians should consider themselves ministers of Christ, identifying and exercising their spiritual giftedness, thereby presenting themselves as "living sacrifices, holy and acceptable to God, which is our spiritual worship" (see Rom. 12:1). The bottom line is this: every Christian ought to consider his/her *charismata* as a *diakonia*, as a ministry of service to others.

The simple imagery Paul uses in speaking of spiritual gifts introduces four decisive aspects of Paul's thinking on the church and its members:

- All members are indispensable
- All members are different
- All members are equal
- All members are responsible

Responding to disruptions caused by speaking in tongues in his Corinthian congregation, Paul builds up prophecy (see 1 Cor. 14), with its functions of edification, exhortation, and comfort, as preferable to the others, because it is intelligible and beneficial to all. As in the teaching of Jesus (see Mark 12:28–34 and John 13:31–35), Paul puts love for God and others at the heart of his "new covenant ethics." Therefore, he concludes his discussion on spiritual gifts, both in 1 Corinthians 12–14 and in Romans 12, with an exhortation to love, which he calls "a still more excellent way" (1 Cor. 12:31; see 1 Cor. 13:1–13 and Rom. 12:9–10; 13:8–10), for those who love embody the character of God. In referring to "love," Paul is using the Greek word *agapē*, a reference to the sacrificial love displayed by Christ on the cross.

If "sacrifice" means "to make things sacred," such love is the means God has chosen for the transformation of the world and its inhabitants. Paul calls believers everywhere to this ministry of love (our "spiritual worship"), working out their salvation with fear and trembling. But then he adds, as he must: "for it is God who is at work in you" (Phil. 2:12–13). God's transforming revolution begins with you, and with me. That's the good news of Paul's gospel. And it is good news because it requires grace, without which no spiritual gift is sure.

Optional Group Activity

Divide the participants into four groups to discuss the topic of church-state relations. Ask each group to begin by describing Paul's view of the role of government and then by summarizing arguments for and against Paul's admonition to "be subject to governing authorities." Then ask them to role-play by representing one position on the political spectrum. Ask Group A to discuss the merits of "allegiance to country, right or wrong." Ask Group B to discuss the merits of "being a good citizen" (adhering to the democratic process of change by ballot). Ask Group C to discuss the merits of "civil protest when necessary." Ask Group D to discuss the merits of "all government is corrupt and the best response is civil disobedience." At the conclusion, reconvene the small groups into one and ask each group to share its insights with the others.

If time allows, give participants time to write down one takeaway (insight) from their reading or group discussion and then to share it with the class.

Session Twelve

Grace and the Neighbor

Summary: In Romans 14:1—15:13 Paul discusses dangers posed to the unity of the church at Rome. He frames his discussion in terms of "weak" and "strong" Christians and warns against setting one's understanding of the Christian life as a norm against which to judge other responses. While it is clear that the conflict is between Jewish and Gentile Christians, this is not to say that the "weak" are Jewish Christians or that the "strong" are Gentile Christians. Paul sees himself as one of the "strong," but he resists attempts by either side to impose its convictions about conduct upon the other. His advice to both groups is to respect one another's convictions, for people are accountable first to God. To tells the "weak" not to go against their conscience and the "strong" not to patronize weaker Christians or parade their freedom before them, thereby offending them or causing them to act against their own conscience. While Paul addresses convictions about eating, drinking, and observance of special days in this passage, what he says can be expanded to other forms of conduct. Like Paul, modern Christians should not view the "weak" as theologically deficient or the "strong" as theologically correct. Paul's terminology refers rather to degrees of freedom in matters of conduct. In this regard Paul's point is clear: Christians must follow the dictates of their own conscience. While there are limits to Christian behavior, there is also freedom in matters of conduct. However, with freedom comes responsibility and accountability. The model for Christian conduct is always Christ. The concluding essay addresses Paul's alternate vision of how life on earth can and should be.

PART III—ALL FROM GRACE

Assignment: Read Session 12 of *Grace Revealed* and Romans 14:1—15:13. Answer the following questions, writing the answers in your journal. [Be prepared to share your views with others in the class.] If you attend church regularly, identify areas of disagreement between groups in the congregation that are divisive (these can range from political, social, and economic views to practical matters such as consumption of alcohol, entertainment, sexual lifestyle, and religious customs and practices). Why are these divisive? Where do you draw the line between practices that are allowable, questionable, or forbidden? What changes in attitude and behavior might you adopt to promote greater unity in your family or church?

Key Verse(s): Romans 14:13, 19

Central Theme: Celebrating Christian freedom in the "grey areas" of life

Technical Words and Concepts: "weak" Christians, "strong" Christians, Sabbath regulations, early Jesus movement, Pax Romana

Learning Objectives
In this session participants will examine:

1. Disputes over food and special days in the Roman church
2. Paul's use of "weak" and "strong" to depict matters of conscience
3. Paul's advice both to the "weak" and the "strong"
4. The relevance of Paul's teaching to contemporary issues and situations where Christians disagree about acceptable faith and practice

Outline to Romans 14:1—15:13
I. Grace in Society 12:1—15:13
   A. Grace and the Neighbor 14:1—15:13
      1. Upholding the Weak 14:1-12
      2. Setting a Good Example 14:13-23
      3. Serving One Another 15:1-13

Romans 14:1—15:13: Flow of the Argument

We conclude our study of Romans by examining the second half of Paul's ethical instructions. Once again Paul turns to specific issues that inspired the letter, specifically the dangers posed to the unity within the Christian community by different conceptions of the proper response to the gospel of Christ. He frames his discussion in terms of the "weak" (traditionalists?) and the "strong" (progressives?) and warns against setting one's own understanding of the proper response to the gospel as the norm against which to judge other responses. Paul considers himself one of the "strong," who, he argues, should follow the example of Christ in pleasing neighbors rather than themselves (15:1–6).

Paul does not take sides on who is more correct, the "weak" or the "strong." He is intent rather on meeting the threat to Christian unity posed by attempts of either side to make its convictions about conduct the sole means of response. His advice to both groups is the same: Respect the convictions of the other group. Paul feels there is room within the Christian community for differing ways of responding to the gospel with respect to customs and behavior and warns that any attempt to impose uniformity in those matters will threaten the very unity whose preservation is sought.

While Paul addresses the problem of convictions about eating and drinking and observance of special days in this passage, what he says can be expanded to cover other forms of conduct as well. Paul's appeal to scripture to support his teaching resurfaces in this section (see 14:11; 15:3; 15:9–12), and his references to Christ multiply. These tendencies signal to the reader the importance he places on these topics. We know from his other letters that Paul was deeply concerned with the unity of the church. He was troubled by factions and divisions, particularly within the Corinthian churches, and was regularly opposed by traveling evangelists who attacked his gospel and sought to undermine his ministry. There was also tension and disagreement with believers in the mother church at Jerusalem. The dissension was caused by attitudes within Judaism and by differences between Jews and Gentiles.

Paul is not concerned simply to affirm the truth of the gospel; he wants Roman Christians to obey its imperative and to change their behavior. If the gospel is for Jew and Gentile alike, as he repeatedly stated, then these groups simply had to find a way to coexist in peace and mutual support. Ultimately Paul's efforts to hold these groups together failed. By the second century Gentile churches had split from Jewish-Christian churches, and the Gentile arrogance that Paul had warned against in Romans 11 won out. It is remarkable that nowhere between 14:1 and 15:5 does Paul use the words "Jew" and "Gentile" or "circumcised" and "uncircumcised." These terms reappear in 15:7–13, in the context of scriptural quotations that celebrate the fact that Gentiles are joining the worldwide family of God.

PART III—ALL FROM GRACE

Paul here is addressing Christians; all are to give allegiance to Jesus as Lord, a point he makes pivotal in 14:1–12, and each has a duty to others as brothers and sisters in Christ (14:10, 15). This section is not, as in chapter 11, a way of speaking about how Christians should live alongside non-Christian Jewish neighbors in Rome: these instructions are for believers in the church. While the conflict between "weak" and "strong" is between Jewish and Gentile Christians, this is not to say that "the weak" are Jewish Christians and "the strong" are Gentile Christians. Paul himself is a Jewish Christian who sees himself as one of the "strong"; likewise, as we learn from Galatians, there might be Gentile Christians whom Paul would categorize as "weak" (see Gal. 3:1–5; 4:8–11). Though it is possible that the "weak" included Jewish Christians returning to Rome to find "strong" Gentile Christians in control of the rites and practices of the common life, it is equally possible that there might have been Gentile Christians who were vegetarians (14:2) and who did not drink wine (14:21). While Jews had kosher laws, most were neither vegetarians nor teetotalers. The conflict between "weak" and "strong" is therefore unlikely to have been an argument stereotyping Jewish and Gentile Christians. This might explain why Paul does not mention "Jews" or "Gentiles" until the final summary paragraph.

When Paul speaks of those who are "weak in faith" (14:1), he is not suggesting that they are deficient as people who only accept part of the Christian gospel. Rather they are people whose faith, though real, has not matured to the point where they understand its full implications. Paul knows from practical experience that people cannot be hurried on matters of faith and that, provided they build on the basic foundation, their relative "strength" or "weakness" should not hinder Christian fellowship. Paul's point is clear: All who trust the same Lord belong together in the same family. There are limits to what is permitted by way of Christian behavior, but there is also freedom, perhaps more freedom in matters of eating and drinking or what is done on Sunday than we are accustomed to think.

Romans 14:1—15:13 divides into three segments. The first (14:1–12) introduces the topic and provides the basic analysis and answer: The weak and the strong are accountable to the same Lord. The second (14:13–23) focuses on mutual respect by both sides. This leads to 15:1–13, which emphasizes the welcoming nature of Christ, whose servant role is the ultimate basis for Christian unity. This final section serves not only as the conclusion of chapters 12–15 but of the letter as a whole.

Textual Analysis: Topics to Ponder or Discuss

Romans 14:1–12

1. The first major argument of the section (14:1–12) hinges on the fact that Jesus is Lord (The word "Lord" occurs no fewer than ten times between verse 4 and verse 11) and on the belief that God raised him from the dead. Yet again we see the interrelationship of theology and ethics for Paul.

2. Despite cultural and behavioral differences among Christians, Paul's emphasis is on welcoming one another in fellowship (the repetition of "welcome" in 15:7 frames the reference). The person who is "weak in faith" (14:1) is not one whose commitment is weak or whose faith is shaky, but rather one who lacks confidence about what is acceptable or permissible (14:2). The "weak" are represented as vegetarians; the "strong" have no religious restrictions on what they may eat (see 14:14: "nothing is unclean in itself"). The prohibitions of the "weak" also include drinking wine (14:21) and the observance of certain days as particularly holy (14:5). As regards scruples (matters of conscience), Paul insists that neither side may judge or question each other's motives because "God has welcomed them" (14:3). Using the analogy of household servants, Paul indicates that Christians are servants of God, and servants should not judge the servants of another (14:4). Whatever their dietary practices, all worship the same Lord. If God is willing to accept those who are "weak" or "strong," who is in a position to condemn God's acceptance?

3. The argument moves forward in 14:5–8. Here Paul extends the application to include how one may act on certain days. Apparently Paul felt the Old Testament Sabbath regulations as well as the pagan holy days had been rendered non-obligatory in Christ (see also 1 Cor. 8:4–13). Those who judge the behavior of fellow Christians are declared wrong on the principle that all sincere Christian behavior is rooted in the lordship of God. It is God's approval, not human approval, that matters. If Christ is Lord of all and has accepted all, Christians of different races, cultures, languages, and customs must find a way to accept each other. The seamless shift between references to God and to Jesus Christ in this passage may or may not be deliberate, but it is

among the features of New Testament writings that gave rise to the church's later Christological formulations.

4. Another reason why it is improper to condemn those who differ in their understanding of appropriate Christian lifestyle rests in the fact that it is God, and not the Christian, who judges in these matters (14:10-12). To set oneself as judge is to encroach upon God's authority. To set oneself and one's preferences as a standard for others in the church is closely allied to self-idolatry. As citizens of God's realm, our own conduct should be enough to keep us occupied.

5. These verses speak of judgment and, as we saw earlier, all will be judged, even faithful Christians (see 2:6; 1 Cor. 3:8-15; 2 Cor. 5:10). With freedom comes responsibility, and Christians ought to take that responsibility seriously. This judgment, however, does not affect one's destiny, for that would contradict everything Paul has said about God's grace to undeserving, sinful creatures. It is a judgment about the quality and responsibility of one's life, emphasizing the need for responsible action. That is the topic to which Paul turns in 14:13-23.

Romans 14:13-23

6. In this section it becomes clear that Paul is among the "strong," and it is equally clear that his admonitions are largely intended for this group rather than for the "weak." In 14:14 Paul establishes the principle that nothing is unclean "in the Lord Jesus," that is, to those who are called to life in the new age inaugurated in Jesus Christ (14:14), but this does not mean one can behave in ways that cause weaker brothers or sisters to act against their conscience (14:13, 15, 20-21). Conceding that food does not defile (14:14, 20; see Mark 7:19), Paul nevertheless claims that it is wrong for one to act contrary to one's scruples. The foundation of right action in every case is a right relationship to God, one based on trust, for whatever does not proceed from faith ("conviction") is sin (14:22-23; on wavering faith, see James 1:6-8). The reference to sin in verse 23 should not be taken as a definitive statement about the nature of sin. In this context it simply means that those who violate their conscience have crossed a line that affects their relationship to God.

Romans 15:1–13

7. Paul's comment about "not pleasing ourselves" in 15:1 is not advice about rejecting our own happiness. The command to love the neighbor as oneself (13:9) always presupposes love for oneself. The command here is to those who are "strong," that they not insist on their own freedom to the detriment of their fellow Christians. Those who are "strong" (secure in their actions) have an obligation not simply to accept the standards of the less strong but to support them (15:1; see Gal. 6:2). The ultimate model for strength is that of Christ (15:6), who "did not regard equality with God as something to be exploited, but emptied himself, taking the form of a slave" (Phil. 2:6-7). That is the Christ Paul's readers are to "put on" (Rom. 13:14).

8. Paul's quotation from Psalm 69:9 in 15:3 is a classic text about the suffering of Israel in general and the righteous one in particular. Paul quoted from this Psalm in 11:9-10 and now does so to indicate that he finds here the pattern of Jesus' own life for our instruction (15:4). Paul concludes his appeal with a prayer for the harmony of the community "in accordance with Christ Jesus" (15:5).

9. In 15:7-13, a passage reminiscent of chapters 9-11, the occasion for friction between Jew and Gentile vanishes before the vision of God's enduring covenant faithfulness to Abraham, thereby fulfilling the promise of a worldwide family embraced by God. Once again, the vision is grounded in God's defining act in Christ (15:8-9), whose entire life was an act of "service," first to the Jews and then to the Gentiles, as a demonstration of grace (see 1:4-6, 16-17). In this section Paul quotes numerous passages to show that God always intended to bring nations of the world into equal fellowship with his chosen people Israel. He starts with the Psalms (18:49), then the Law (Deut. 32: 43), then returns to the Psalms (117:1) before concluding with the Prophets (Isa. 11:10). That this "power of God" that leads to salvation for everyone who relies on him should continue to fill and enrich the lives of his readers is the substance of the petition with which Paul brings the body of his letter to a close. May the God of this hope "fill you with all joy and peace, so that you may abound in hope by the power of the Holy Spirit" (15:13).

PART III—ALL FROM GRACE

Essay 12: Equality: Paul's Vision for Life on Earth

To comprehend Paul, we must understand his Jewishness. He was passionately Jewish; his life and thought, both before and after he became a follower of Jesus, were shaped by Jewish scripture and practice. Paul thought of himself as Jewish throughout his life, not as having converted to a new religion. Without this understanding of Paul's Jewish context, much in his letters is misunderstood.

Paul is second only to Jesus as the most important person in the origins of Christianity. According to the New Testament, Paul was chiefly responsible for expanding the early Jesus movement to include Gentiles (non-Jews) as well as Jews. The result over time was a new religion, even though Paul (like Jesus) saw himself working within Judaism. Neither intended that a new religion would emerge. The same can be said of Peter, John, and other early followers of Jesus. They would not have seen themselves as Christians (for that term was not yet in use) but rather as Jews who had found the Messiah.

Scholars generally use the phrase "early Jesus movement" to speak of the followers of Jesus in the first decades after his death. The use of this phrase recognizes that calling them "Christians," as if they had joined or established a new religion distinct from Judaism, is anachronistic. According to the book of Acts, the believers in Jesus were known as followers of "the Way," the way of Jesus. [Despite the anachronism, readers should note that *Grace Revealed* often calls early followers of Jesus "Christians," "Jewish Christians," or "Gentile Christians."]

The first person we know who aggressively called himself "a Christian" to distinguish himself from "a Jew" was the Syrian Ignatius of Antioch. Converted perhaps around 80 or 90 AD, Ignatius traveled through Asia Minor, writing letters to various churches. After declaring himself a Christian before a Roman magistrate, he was sentenced to the death of a martyr, torn apart by wild animals in the Roman Coliseum around the year 110. Roman magistrates may have been the first to coin the term "Christian," around the year 112, when a governor in Asia Minor named Pliny ordered the arrest of some people whom he called "Christians." Despite the reference in the book of Acts that Jesus' followers "were first called Christians at Antioch" in Syria (Acts 11:26), this reference was probably not written earlier than 85 to 90 AD, by an author who displayed a clear bias to present the Christian movement in as positive a manner as possible and as a unified movement.

To comprehend Paul, we must also understand the importance of the Roman Empire in his day. Paul, his fellow believers, and all who joined his churches, lived under Roman rule, a rule legitimated by an imperial theology that proclaimed the emperor to be the Son of God, Lord, Savior of the World, and the one who promised peace on earth. Such theology was initiated and maintained through military victory and by imperial order. Paul's proclamation of Jesus as Son of God, Lord, Savior, and bringer of peace and justice directly countered Roman imperial theology. For Paul, God as known in Jesus was Lord, and the emperor was not. In this respect, Paul's proclamation that "Jesus is Lord" was highly treasonous. It is not surprising that Paul, like Jesus, was eventually executed by Rome.

Though the meaning of some passages in Romans remains uncertain, the import of Paul's message, remarkably consistent with the message of Jesus, is clear. Like Jesus, Paul "challenged the normalcy of civilization, then and now, with an alternate vision of how life on earth can and should be."[1] In the mid- to late-50s, Paul opened his final letter with a salutation to the Roman Christians: "Grace to you and peace from God our Father and the Lord Jesus Christ" (Rom. 1:7). "Grace and peace": each of Paul's seven authentic letters begins with that greeting. Furthermore, in all of his letters except Philemon, the final farewell mentions "peace." Despite its friendly and pleasant ring, the phrase is used strategically by Paul and, like the phrase "Jesus is Lord," contains a radical anti-imperial thrust, a distinction between the "peace-of-God-in-Christ" and Rome's Pax Romana, the "peace-of-Rome-in-Caesar." The Roman imperial ideology/theology was based on a specific pattern: first comes religion, next war, then victory, and finally peace. That was the vision of Rome: peace through victory, victory through violence. Paul, offering a great alternative, takes the message of Jesus (peace through trust, victory through transforming love) out from the Jewish homeland and across the Roman Empire.

Paul's vision is based on a principle enunciated in his letter to the Galatians, dubbed "the Magna Charta of Christian Liberty." That principle—that truth sets humanity free—is enunciated in Galatians 3:27–29:

> As many of you as were baptized into Christ have clothed yourselves with Christ.
> *There is no longer Jew or Greek,*
> *there is no longer slave or free,*
> *there is no longer male and female;*

---

1. Borg and Crossan, *First Paul*, 19.

for all of you are one in Christ Jesus. And if you belong to Christ, then you are Abraham's offspring, heirs according to the promise.

Paul's statement must be read fully and contextually The central triad cannot be loosened from its framing statements (containing "into" and "with Christ" and "in" and "to Christ"). Quoted without those frames, the passage might be read correctly as denying the validity of slavery, but also incorrectly as denying the validity of the difference between women and men and the ongoing validity of Judaism as a religion separate from Christianity.

Paul's call to equality is repeated in 1 Corinthians 12:13—and again notice the frames:

> For in the one Spirit we were all baptized into one body
> —Jews and Greeks, slaves or free—
> and we were all made to drink of one Spirit.

For Paul, life "in Christ" or life "in the Spirit" represents a transformed Christian life committed to the justice of equality. From where does this vision of equality derive? Recall that "grace and peace" in all the greetings of Paul's seven authentic letters comes from "God the Father." Is Paul using bad theology, or dated theology, when he speaks of God as "Father"? To ask that question is to miss the point. Paul is contrasting two models, the Roman model of "emperor," "warrior," and "king" with the householder or homemaker model, the only other model available. What makes a good or a bad householder? "For Paul, God is the good householder, who establishes a just, fair, and equal distribution of rights and responsibilities, of duties and privileges. Are all children well fed, clothed, and sheltered? Does everyone have enough? For Paul, the Householder of the earth-house, the Homemaker of the world-home, is God, and all people are God's dependents and God's children. God as Householder is the One who has responsibility and charge for the home's extended family."[2]

For Paul, the justice of equality is primarily about God and indirectly about us. Paul is not thinking about democracy, social justice, or human rights, but about the honor and glory of God revealed in how Christ lived and died and how that reality should be reflected in a just world. That is precisely the subject of Romans: God's passionate desire to heal a broken world, to end injustice founded on violence, and to bring about a unified and peaceful earth. Our task today, as followers of Christ, is to take Paul's

2. Ibid., 114.

vision and by thought and action join with others of like mind in applying its transforming power to the issues of our day: injustice, poverty, violence, racism, sexism, militarism, materialism, and the like.

Optional Group Activity

Divide the participants into two groups to role-play how your church or study group can be more open to diversity and more welcoming to strangers. One group will represent the "weak" and the other the "strong" within your church or study group. Ask Group 1 (the "weak") to read Romans 14:1–12 and then to discuss what they believe, how they feel about Paul's advice, and what to do about it. In light of Romans 14:13, ask the group to suggest some examples of "stumbling-blocks." Ask Group 2 (the "strong") to read Romans 14:13—15:2 and then to discuss what they believe, how they feel about Paul's advice, and what to do about it. In light of Romans 14:13, ask the group to suggest some examples of "stumbling-blocks." At the conclusion, reconvene the small groups into one and ask each group to share its insights with the others. Then ask participants to brainstorm on how your church or group can be more welcoming of people from socially and culturally diverse backgrounds, following Paul's instruction in Romans 15:7.

If time allows, give participants time to write down one takeaway (insight) from their reading or group discussion and then to share it with the class.

Appendix A

A Chronology of Biblical Events

Patriarchal Period	1850–1700 BC
The Exodus from Egypt	c. 1250
Period of the Judges	1200–1025
United Kingdom (David and Solomon)	1025–926
Northern Kingdom (Israel)	926–722
Southern Kingdom (Judah)	926–586
Babylonian Exile	686–538
Maccabean Revolt	167–142
Roman Conquest of Jerusalem (Pompey)	63
Assassination of Julius Caesar	44
Rule by Herod the Great	37–4
Emperor Augustus (Octavian)	30 BC–AD 14
Birth of Jesus	c. 6–4 BC
Rule by Herod Antipas	4 BC–AD 39
Judea Becomes a Roman Province	AD 6
Birth of Paul	c. AD 8
Emperor Tiberius	14–37
Paul Studies in Jerusalem; Becomes a Pharisee	c. 20–30
Pontius Pilate (procurator)	26–36
Crucifixion of Jesus	c. 30

APPENDIX A

Paul Persecutes Followers of Jesus	c. 30–33
Conversion of Paul	c. 33
Paul in Arabia, Damascus, and Jerusalem	33–36
Paul Preaches in Tarsus and Surrounding Region	c. 36–44
Emperor Caligula	37–41
Emperor Claudius	41–54
Paul Teaches in Antioch	44–46
Paul Visits Jerusalem with Barnabas and Titus	46
Paul's First Missionary Journey	47–48
Jerusalem Council	49
Paul's Second Missionary Journey	49–53
Paul Writes 1 Thessalonians	
Paul's Third Missionary Journey (3-year stay at Ephesus)	53–58
Paul Writes Galatians, Philippians, Philemon, 1 and 2 Corinthians	
Paul Writes Romans	57 or 58
Emperor Nero	54–68
Paul Arrested in Jerusalem	58
Paul Imprisoned at Caesarea	58–60
Paul's Voyage to Rome	60–61
Paul Under House Arrest in Rome	61–64
Paul's Martyrdom under Nero	64
Revolt of Jews Against Rome	66–70
Gospel of Mark Written	c. 69–70
Fall of Jerusalem	70
Deutero-Pauline Epistles Written [Colossians, Ephesians, and 2 Thessalonians]	c. 80–100
Pastoral and General Epistles Written [1 and 2 Timothy, Titus; Hebrews, James, 1 Peter, 1, 2, and 3 John]	c. 80–100
Gospel of Matthew Written	c. 80

A CHRONOLOGY OF BIBLICAL EVENTS

Gospel of Luke Written	c. 85
Book of Acts Written	c. 85–90
Gospel of John Written	c. 95
Book of Revelation Written	c. 96
Books of Jude and Second Peter Written	c. 98–120

Appendix B

Guidelines for Leading a Bible Study

Note About Participants

PEOPLE WHO CHOOSE TO attend a Bible study do so for a wide variety of motives and bring with them varied levels of readiness and ability. When individuals are invited to attend a group Bible study, they should be made aware from the beginning that this is not a study where the leader does all the work of preparation and presentation. Every participant is expected to have read the appropriate material in *Grace Revealed* and to complete the assignment from Romans prior to each session.

Given the busy schedules most people have, there may be times when persons come to a session with minimum preparation. You should not compromise the expectation of adequate preparation, because the experience for the whole group will suffer if the reading is not taken seriously. In such situations, encourage persons who have not read the material or done the homework assignments not to participate in the discussion until others have had a chance. Also, when working in small groups, try to ensure that those who are not prepared are distributed among the groups rather than grouped together.

Some participants will have had a lot of experience with studying the Bible, while for others this may be their first experience with Bible study. It is important for each person to feel that he or she belongs to the group.

GUIDELINES FOR LEADING A BIBLE STUDY

Encourage both experienced and inexperienced participants to be mindful and appreciative of each other.

One way to ensure full participation is to ask participants to keep a journal, to write in it regularly, and to bring it to each session. The journal will be used to record the weekly homework assignment as well as to take notes on their reading and on class interaction. In addition to a journal, participants should bring to class a Bible as well as a copy of *Grace Revealed*.

Planning a Session

While *Grace Revealed* provides resources for each session, it is important to prepare your own session plan appropriate for your group. This study is designed to be completed in twelve sessions, each *60 to 75 minutes in length*. Each session follows a fourfold pattern:

1. *Opening*, 5 minutes (a time of prayer and scripture reading, run by the leader or by someone appointed in advance; the leader may ask if there are any prayer requests).

2. *Overview*, 15 to 30 minutes (this can be in the form of a presentation by the leader or in a group discussion on the topic of the homework assignment).

3. *General or small-group discussion*, 20 to 30 minutes (depending on the size of the class, the leader may divide the class into groups of threes or fours to discuss one or more topics from the passage; see also the "Optional Group Activities" found at the end of each chapter).

4. *Closing*, 5 to 15 minutes (run by the leader or by someone appointed in advance). This may include a report and general discussion on the small-group activity, a time of reflection (see "Takeaway" statement below), or a comment by the leader and a closing prayer.

If sessions last *45 to 60 minutes*, the recommended time allotments and activities should be adjusted accordingly.

The Session Plans in this Leader's Guide include:

1. *Reading Assignment*. This assignment should be mentioned to participants in advance of class, at least one week beforehand.

2. *Homework Assignment*. This assignment should be mentioned in advance of class, at least one week beforehand. Participants (students)

are asked to answer the specific question(s) or task, writing their answer in their journal, and to be prepared to share their views with others during class time. [Note: Leaders need to decide in advance whether they want to include the results of these assignments in class. They may be used as part of the opening exercises to get discussion started.]

3. *Central Theme.* This theme represents a succinct statement that summarizes one or more key concepts from the assigned segment from Romans; leaders and participants are encouraged to construct a statement of their own that encapsulates for them the unit's central teaching.

4. *Outline.* The outline is provided to help readers and leader to discern the main points and sub points of the unit from Romans.

5. *Learning Objectives.* These statements presenting the learning objectives indicate what the leader will help the participants to accomplish as a result of their study. When leading adults, it is appropriate to share session objectives with the members of the group at the beginning of each class. The selection of activities is then guided by the objectives considered most important. The statements of learning objectives can also be used as a basis for evaluating whether or not the participants have learned what was intended.

6. *Key Verse(s).* Each session of this study identifies a key verse(s) from each passage. Individual readers and Bible study leaders are encouraged to add or substitute their own choices.

7. *Technical Words and Concepts.* This list of key terms is included to help leaders and participants develop their intellectual and theological vocabulary. Leaders are encouraged to introduce these terms in their presentation and in class discussion when appropriate.

8. *Flow of the Argument.* This section provides an overview of the assigned unit from Romans.

9. *Textual Analysis.* This section provides detailed commentary on specific verses and passages within the assigned unit. Some questions helpful for group discussion are embedded in this section.

10. *Questions to Ponder.* A list of questions is found at the end of sessions 1 and 2 of *Grace Revealed*. Questions also appear in the "Textual Analysis" segments and may be used for individual study, during general

GUIDELINES FOR LEADING A BIBLE STUDY

discussion, or in small groups. The leader (or leaders of the small groups) should become familiar with these questions in advance and choose those they deem most appropriate. Leaders (and participants) are encouraged to add their own questions to this list.

11. *Optional Group Activities.* At the discretion of the leader or leaders and as time allows, this optional activity, found at the end of sessions 3–12, can be substituted for questions addressed by the breakaway (small group) sessions. If time allows, reconvene the class and ask each group to share its insights with the others.

12. *Takeaway* (5 to 8 minutes). During this (optional) segment, usually part of the closing, ask participants to identify and record in their journal their takeaway (key insight) from that week's reading or from their group discussion (give the class 3 minutes of silence and 5 minutes to share).

13. *Looking Ahead.* In order to work effectively during the next session, specific homework assignment needs to be given to participants and small group leaders. Make sure everyone knows in advance what their responsibilities are for the coming week. [*Important Note*: Your job as leader includes deciding whether you will make a presentation during class or devote the majority of class time to large- and small-group discussion. For each session, identify or select questions for discussion. You might plan to take a few minutes at the start of class to provide a list of discussion questions to the participants, asking them to add any questions of their own to the list. Decide whether you might start class with a discussion of the homework assignment. You will also need to decide in advance whether you wish to include the "Optional Group Activity" or whether you will substitute a discussion of the homework assignment at this time. During class, remember to pace yourself. Time constraints will require flexibility on your part, including the need to delete or modify questions and activities you have selected. It is better to do a few things well than to try to include more activities than time will allow.]

14. *Fellowship.* Depending on the setting, the session may close with a time of fellowship and refreshments. If the leader/host so chooses, a time of fellowship may precede the session.

APPENDIX B

Types of Discussion Leaders

There are many factors that contribute to the effective, productive working of a group. What follows is an attempt to summarize several important considerations about effective group leadership. There are numerous types of leaders. Which kind do you wish to be:

1. An *autocratic leader* is one who assumes all the responsibility for the group, and who is primarily concerned about accomplishing a task. There are times when such an approach is necessary, but this study of the Bible will be most successful when the leader does not do all the work for the group.
2. The *laissez-faire leader* is one who sits back, enjoys what is happening, and lets the group go its own way. It is important at times not to be too agenda-conscious, but this study of the Bible assumes that the leader is actively engaged in guiding the group's process.
3. The *democratic leader* functions in a partnership style. This approach to the study of the Bible will be most effective when led by persons who seek to involve others in sharing their questions, insights, and affirmations.

Leaders of this study are encouraged to keep the following guidelines in mind:

- Adults are responsible for their own learning;
- Adults learn best when they can participate directly in the process of their own learning;
- Learning is reinforced best when adults have opportunities to practice skills and to express ideas in their own words.
- Learning occurs within an environment of trusting relationships.

Therefore, the activities should represent a cooperative, collaborative, non-threatening style of learning.

Leadership and Group Dynamics

Because participants will have questions, opinions, and insights about many aspects of the study of the Bible, *leaders need to keep the group focused on the topic or task*, knowing when to let the discussion proceed with its own momentum and when to direct the discussion back to the topic. It is not uncommon in a group to have one person who is both well informed and quite verbal do most of the talking. Others in the group may be intimidated or discouraged or have little desire to talk. Such a circumstance is not healthy for the long-term life of the group. *When one person dominates the discussion,* the leader may need to be direct and speak with that participant privately or else interject by inviting others to speak by saying, "What do others of you think about . . ." or "Let's share as many ideas as we can about . . ." If leaders encourage members of the group to think and speak for themselves so that there is a lot of interaction, there will be times *when people offer a contradictory point of view* to that of the author or of the group. When disagreements occur, you can accept what persons say without agreeing with them. You can encourage them to clarify what they mean or to provide evidence for their position. It is not necessary to defend the author or even an accepted view from scripture. However, it is important that you and the others in the class have read carefully and worked hard to understand the text.

A basic premise of this study is that the leader is a learner among other learners. It is not necessary for leaders to be fully knowledgeable in all subjects of the study. It is much more important to know where to turn for the needed information (such as a Study Bible, a Bible handbook, a Bible dictionary, a theological text, or an appropriate Bible commentary). In such cases, the following resources are recommended:

- Study Bibles: *The Harper Collins Study Bible, The New Oxford Annotated Study Bible,* and *The New Interpreters Study Bible;* The *Eerdmans Dictionary of the Bible.*

- One Volume Bible Commentaries: *HarperCollins Bible Commentary, The New Jerome Biblical Commentary, The New Interpreter's Bible Commentary.*

- Bible Dictionaries: *HarperCollins Bible Dictionary;* the *Anchor Bible Dictionary,* or the *New Interpreter's Dictionary of the Bible.*

How will you respond when you don't know the answer to a question? There is nothing more frustrating to a group than a leader who tries to bluff his or her way through a topic or a question. At such times it is helpful to encourage the group to work toward its own understanding and to be willing to admit that you don't know something.

APPENDIX B

If leaders desire to involve persons in serious interaction with one another and with the subject of the session, they need to ask effective questions. Questions may be one of the most valuable resources available to the leader as well as to the participants. Generally speaking, there seem to be three different types or levels of questions: (a) *information questions*, which presume right answers; (b) *interpretation questions*, which require participants to think about, analyze, explore, and evaluate a subject, and (c) *personalized questions*, whereby leaders encourage participants to apply the subject to themselves in a personal way that helps them to express their own identity.

When you lead, try to use all three types, but be intentional about making room for the latter. Questions at this level are essential if persons are to grow in their faith and life commitments. In using questions of a personal nature we must be careful to avoid embarrassing participants by getting too personal or putting them "on the spot."

When preparing to lead a discussion that utilizes a variety of questions, the following guidelines will be helpful to keep in mind.

1. Ask questions that are open-ended, analytical, or probing, rather that questions with only one right answer or implying a "yes" or "no" response.
2. Ask only one question at a time; more than one question is confusing and lacks focus.
3. Present questions to the whole group, rather than putting one person "on the spot."
4. Provide feedback after a person responds, so participants know they have been heard;
5. After asking a question, give participants time to think.
6. Use an inquiry style rather than an interrogative style; some examples are "what are your thoughts about . . . ? "why do you suppose . . ." who do you think will . . . ? "what is the possibility of . . . ? or "what are some reasons . . . ?" Inquiry conveys to the group that you are interested in what they think and say, whereas interrogation puts persons on the defensive and inhibits creativity.
7. Encourage people to ask their own questions, and let them know you value them and their perspective, whether you agree with it or not.

GUIDELINES FOR LEADING A BIBLE STUDY

In order for effective group process to develop, there are simple yet significant things you can do as leader:

- Know the participants' names and speak inclusively so that everyone feels free to participate and share of themselves with one another.
- Arrange the room so that persons are in a circle or square, preferably seated at tables so they do not have to juggle Bibles, books, and cups on their laps.
- Make sure that the group adheres to the class time and try not to make a habit of going past the allotted time.
- Be sure the meeting space is comfortable with regard to heat, lighting, and seating.
- Always make room for mystery and uncertainty. There is nothing that destroys Bible studies more than threatening attitudes, condescending language, or a competitive environment where there are winners and losers. The losers may not return and eventually only one or two people will show up, blaming others for failure.
- In order to build a community of trust and a place for participants to share their experiences with God, leaders should remind the group that what is shared in class should be kept confidential.
- Acknowledge the presence and influence of the Holy Spirit at all times, and in all relations and situations, allow the gifts of the Spirit full sway (see Galatians 5:22–23: love, joy, peace, patience, kindness, goodness, faithfulness, gentleness, and self-control); without God's Spirit, our efforts are vain.

Appendix C

The Essentials
Twelve Takeaways from Our Study of Romans

STUDENTS IN MY CLASSES on Romans are often asked to keep a journal, noting insights and questions from readings and class discussion. They are asked to prioritize twelve key ideas learned during the term. These are my takeaways:

1. The Bible contains the perceptions and misperceptions of two faith communities: ancient Israel and early Christianity. Modern Christians are encouraged to utilize the historical-metaphorical approach to scripture rather than the literal-factual-absolute interpretation, understanding biblical and theological terms in their ancient historical context before applying them to current issues and concerns.

2. Romans is a letter, not a doctrinal treatise. In Romans Paul is primarily concerned with relations between Jews and Gentiles, not theology or doctrine. Even Paul's doctrine of justification by faith has its context in his reflection on the relation between Jews and Gentiles and not within the questions of free will or of how individuals are saved (see Rom. 1:16–17; 3:28–29).

3. In his ministry Paul's evangelistic focus was on the conversion of Gentiles, not Jews.

4. The starting point for understanding God's relation to the cosmos is "original blessing," not "original sin."

5. For Paul, sin and salvation are relational, this-worldly concepts. These concepts are primarily about nations and peoples—about covenant relationship—not about individuals going to heaven or hell (in Romans there is no mention of people going to heaven or to hell). The biblical emphasis on sin and salvation is always relational and the focus primarily this-worldly.

6. The centrality of grace in Romans; "all for grace, grace for all, all from grace"—election, disobedience, predestination, law, wrath, judgment, all is grace. God's plan for creation is restorative, not punitive. God is the Great Physician, bringing healing, peace, and wellbeing through restored covenant relationship. In all things God works for the good: herein is grace revealed.

7. When the Bible speaks of God's righteousness, the primary reference is God's faithfulness to his covenant with Abraham, promising the blessings of reconciliation to Israel and through Israel to all humanity.

8. The biblical emphasis on election is to service, not to privilege or status.

9. Paul's Christology centers around the concept of "inaugurated" eschatology; Christ came to inaugurate God's kingdom and reveal God's love and plan for humanity.

10. Paul views the cross, not primarily as a means of torture and execution, but as a revelation of God's love and passion for the world.

11. The biblical emphasis on faith is not so much on belief in Christ but on faithfulness and trust; faith is primarily relational, not doctrinal.

12. Though Paul views the Mosaic law as holy, just, and good (Rom. 7:12), Christians are no longer under law but under grace (Rom. 6:14). Paul speaks of the Mosaic law as having a temporary, tutorial, first-half-of-life role for Christians, and not a final or definitive role.

Bibliography

Achtemeier, Paul J. *Romans*. Interpretation: A Bible Commentary for Teaching and Preaching. Louisville: John Knox, 1985.
Barrett, C. K. *A Commentary on the Epistle to the Romans*. Harper New Testament Commentaries. New York: Harper & Row, 1957.
Barth, Karl. *The Epistle to the Romans*. 6th ed. Translated by Edwyn C. Hoskyns. London: Oxford University Press, 1933.
Beker, J. Christiaan. *Paul's Apocalyptic Gospel*. Philadelphia: Fortress, 1982.
———. *Paul the Apostle: The Triumph of God in Life and Thought*. Minneapolis: Fortress, 1980.
———. *The Triumph of God: The Essence of Paul's Thought*. Minneapolis: Fortress, 1990.
Borg, Marcus J. *The Heart of Christianity*. New York: HarperSanFrancisco, 2004.
———. *Reading the Bible Again for the First Time*. New York: HarperSanFrancisco, 2001.
———. *Speaking Christian*. New York: HarperOne, 2011.
Borg, Marcus J. and John Dominic Crossan. *The First Paul*. New York: HarperOne, 2009.
Borg, Marcus J. and N. T. Wright. *The Meaning of Jesus: Two Visions*. New York: HarperSanFrancisco, 2000.
Brown, Raymond E. *An Introduction to the New Testament*. New York. Doubleday, 1997.
Brown, Raymond E, Joseph A. Fitzmyer, and Roland E. Murphy. *The New Jerome Biblical Commentary*. Upper Saddle River, NJ: Prentice Hall, 1990.
Bruce, F. F. *The Epistle of Paul to the Romans*. Tyndale New Testament Commentaries. Grand Rapids, MI: Eerdmans, 1963.
———. *Paul, Apostle of the Heart Set Free*. Grand Rapids: Eerdmans, 1991.
Caird, G. B. and L. D. Hurst. *New Testament Theology*. Oxford: Clarendon, 1994.
Cranfield, C. E. B. *Romans: A Shorter Commentary*. Grand Rapids, MI: Eerdmans, 1985.
Dodd, C. H. *The Epistle of Paul to the Romans*. New York: Harper & Row, 1932.
Drane, John. *Introducing the New Testament*. Revised and Updated. Minneapolis: Fortress, 2001.
Dunn, James D. G. *Romans*. Word Biblical Commentary. Vol 38, 2 vols. Dallas: Word, 1988.
———. *The Theology of Paul the Apostle*. Grand Rapids, MI: Eerdmans, 1998.
Ehrman, Bart D. *How Jesus became God*. New York: HarperOne, 2014.
Fitzmyer, Joseph A. *Romans*. The Anchor Bible, vol. 33. Garden City, NY: Doubleday, 1992.

BIBLIOGRAPHY

Garrett, Susan R. *No Ordinary Angel: Celestial Spirits and Christian Claims About Jesus.* New Haven, CT: Yale University Press, 2008.
Gieschen, Charles A. *Angelomorphic Christology: Antecedents and Early Evidence.* Leiden: E. J. Brill, 1998.
Griffith-Jones, Robin. *The Gospel According to Paul.* New York: HarperSanFrancisco, 2004.
Jewett, Robert. *Romans: A Commentary.* Minneapolis: Fortress, 2007.
Käsemann, Ernst. *Commentary on Romans.* Translated and edited by Geoffrey W. Bromiley. Grand Rapids, MI: Eerdmans, 1980.
McGrath, Alister E. *Christian Theology: An Introduction.* 5th ed. Malden, MA: Wiley-Blackwell, 2011.
Minear, Paul S. *The Obedience of Faith.* Studies in Biblical Theology, vol. 19. London: SCM, 1971.
Moffatt, James. *Grace in the New Testament.* New York: Long & Smith, 1932.
Moo, Douglas J. *The Epistle to the Romans.* The New International Commentary on the New Testament. Grand Rapids, MI: Eerdmans, 1996.
———. *The NIV Application Commentary: Romans.* Grand Rapids, MI: Zondervan, 2000.
Morris, Leon. *The Epistle to the Romans.* Grand Rapids, MI: Eerdmans, 1988.
Nanos, Mark D. *The Mystery of Romans: The Jewish Context of Paul's Letter.* Minneapolis: Fortress, 1996.
Ridderbos, Herman N. *Paul: An Outline of His Theology.* Grand Rapids: MI: Eerdmans, 1975.
Sanders, E. P. "Jesus: His Religious Type." *Reflections* 87 (1992) 4–12.
———. *Paul.* New York: Oxford University Press, 1991.
———. *Paul and Palestinian Judaism.* Philadelphia: Fortress, 1977.
———. *Paul, the Law, and the Jewish People.* Philadelphia: Fortress, 1983.
Schweitzer, Albert. *The Mysticism of Paul the Apostle.* New York: Seabury, 1968 [1930].
Spong, John Shelby. *Re-Claiming the Bible for a Non-Religious World.* New York: HarperOne, 2011.
———. *Rescuing the Bible from Fundamentalism.* New York: HarperSanFrancisco, 1991.
Stendahl, Krister. *Final Account: Paul's Letter to the Romans.* Minneapolis: Augsburg Fortress, 1995.
———. *Paul Among Jews and Gentiles.* Philadelphia: Fortress, 1976.
Stewart, James S. *A Man in Christ: The Vital Elements of St. Paul's Religion.* New York: Harper & Row, 1963 (1935).
Stott, John. *Romans: God's Good News for the World.* Downers Grove, IL: InterVarsity, 1994.
Williams, Patricia A. *Doing without Adam and Eve: Sociobiology and Original Sin.* Minneapolis: Fortress, 2001.
Witherington III, Ben. *John's Wisdom: A Commentary on the Fourth Gospel.* Louisville: Westminster John Knox, 1995.
Witherington III, Ben with Darlene Hyatt. *Paul's Letter to the Romans: A Socio-Rhetorical Commentary.* Grand Rapids, MI: Eerdmans, 2004.
Wright, N. T. *The Climax of the Covenant: Christ and the Law in Pauline Theology.* Minneapolis: Fortress, 1993.
———. *Paul for Everyone: Romans.* 2 vols. Louisville: Westminster John Knox, 2004.
———. *What St. Paul Really Said.* Grand Rapids, MI: Eerdmans, 1997.

Subject and Name Index

Abraham (patriarch), 81, 83, 87–89, 152, 171
   covenant of God with, 6, 45, 74, 84, 144
   election of, 171, 178
   offspring of, 45, 50, 81, 83, 88, 89, 151, 153–54, 158, 159, 160, 176
   role of, 82, 83, 85, 126, 149
Acts, book of
   date of, 17
   reliability of, 17–20
Adam, 94, 122
   Adamic nature, 76, 104, 105
   and Christ, 28, 61, 94, 99, 104
   life in, 28, 94, 99, 105, 121
   sin of, 91, 94, 99–100, 101, 104–6, 138
adoption, 134, 138, 143, 144
agapē, 76, 192, 198
"all Israel," 169, 172, 174–75, 176, 177
Anselm of Canterbury, 107
antinomianism. *See* libertinism
apocalyptic, 141–42, 162, 175
   two-age framework, 114, 140, 142, 188
apostle(s), 44
Apostles Creed, 92
Apostolic Decree, 32
Aquinas, Thomas, 55
atheism, 69
atonement, 85, 109
   substitutionary, 107, 109
autonomy, 71
Augustine (bishop), 8, 9, 11–12

and original sin, 99, 101
and predestination, 180

baptism, 61, 88, 109, 113, 116–17, 142, 143
Barth, Karl, 12, 180–81
boasting, 83, 87, 137, 190
body, 137, 189
Bonhoeffer, Dietrich, 39–40
Borg, Marcus, 31, 108

Calvin, John, 8, 12, 55
   and predestination, 9, 180
charis, 38, 196
charisma(ta), 38, 196, 197
charismatic, x, 132, 195, 196
chiasm, chiastic, 96, 97, 103, 131, 188
Christ. *See* Jesus Christ
"Christ Hymn," 156
Christian life, 95–96, 114, 131, 132, 137, 199, 203, 204, 207–9
   "weak" and "strong" Christians, 199, 200–202, 203, 204, 205, 209
Christology/Christological, x, 4, 49, 203–4, 180–81
   adoptionist (exaltation), 49
   of Paul, 110, 155–56, 203, 223
church, 7, 187
   and state. *See* government (civil authority)
   as body of Christ, 7, 143
   as eschatological community, 143
   in Rome, 44–45, 121, 147–48, 174–75, 179, 183–84, 187

SUBJECT AND NAME INDEX

circumcision, 32, 65, 74, 83, 88
Claudius (emperor), 52, 65, 183
Corinth(ians), 8, 23, 33, 56, 132, 137, 142, 190–91, 197, 201
corporate personality, 93
cosmic transformation, 138
covenant, 153
   two-covenant theology, 151
   with Abraham, 74, 87, 126, 144, 148, 152, 205
   with David, 74
   with Israel, 84
created order, 71
creationism, 102
creation spirituality, 26–27, 145
cross, 28, 85–86, 106–10
Crossan, John, 31
crucifixion, 5

David (king)
   covenant with, 74
Day of Atonement, 85
Day of Pentecost, 132, 144
Day of the Lord, 28, 65, 144
determinism, 4
diakonia, 197
diatribe, 27, 63, 66, 72, 73–74, 86, 114
discipleship, 34, 39
"divided self," 114, 115, 121–23
Dodd, C. H., 151

early Jesus movement, 206
ecclesiology, 29, 187
election, 4, 40, 65, 73, 74, 75, 134–36, 150, 152, 154, 158, 159, 160, 161, 163, 168, 169, 170, 171, 173, 174, 177–81, 191, 223
Ephesus, 51–52
eschatology, eschatological, x, 140, 174, 177, 187, 195
   and apocalyptic, 141–42
   and baptism, 142
   and church, 143
   and Holy Spirit, 143–44
   cosmic, 138, 140, 174
   "inaugurated," 29, 130, 140–45
   individual, 4
eschaton, 144, 174

eternal life, 134
Eucharist, 143
evolution, human, 102
   and original sin, 100–103
expiation, 85–86
Ezekiel (prophet), 126, 133, 140, 172

faith, 48, 53–59, 83, 84, 86–87, 98, 187, 204
   and law, 86
   as belief, 9, 50, 57, 88
   as faithfulness, 57–58
   as trust, 9, 50, 57, 62, 88, 160–61, 204
   as vision, 58
   in Jesus Christ, 84, 123, 124
   obedience of, 50, 118
flesh, 33, 120, 122–23, 125, 133, 137, 142, 144
football analogy, 13–15
foreknowledge, 134, 135
forgiveness, 115
Fox, Matthew, 26
freedom, 4, 28, 32, 45, 88, 95–96, 101, 114, 115, 117–19, 128, 131, 134, 144, 199, 202, 204, 205
   from the law, 118, 119, 179
free will, 135, 136
fundamentalism, 25

Galatians, 83, 123, 202
Garrett, Susan, 156
Gentile Christians
   covenant with, 76
   in Rome, 44–45, 46–47, 179
   offering from, 47
Gentiles, 46, 71–72, 73–74, 147
Gieschen, Charles, 156
gifts, spiritual, 38, 191, 195–98
glory, 96, 131, 133, 144
God
   as creator, 62, 153, 159, 166
   as Father, 208
   as householder, 208
   faithfulness of, 34, 45, 48, 53, 75, 83, 86, 88, 98, 103, 104, 132, 148, 151, 153, 163, 165, 166, 170, 172, 177, 205
   glory of, 35, 97, 127

SUBJECT AND NAME INDEX

grace of, 34, 79, 151, 159, 165, 166, 173, 175, 179, 188
impartiality of, 73, 98, 137, 163, 164, 166
lordship of, 78, 163
love of, 79, 97, 104, 110, 140, 152, 177, 192
plan for Jews and Gentiles, 28, 34, 44, 48, 53, 115, 148, 151, 152, 153, 160, 163, 171, 174
righteousness of, 47, 53, 67, 68, 77, 84, 98, 103, 116, 148, 149, 151, 153, 154, 164–66
wrath of, 68, 70, 76–79, 175, 179, 188
See also covenant, with Abraham
See also Jews, God's plan for
God-fearers, 20, 33, 44
gospel, 45–46, 48, 49, 53, 61
government (civil authority), 193–94, 198
grace (mercy), 34, 37–41, 59, 62, 68, 72, 77, 78, 88, 105, 106, 113, 136, 140, 155, 170, 172, 175, 177, 180, 188, 189, 191, 192, 198, 205
and fear, 97
and supernatural virtues, 103
and trust, 175
and works, 161
and wrath, 77, 78, 79
cheap, 39, 40, 111, 175
cooperative, 55
costly, 39, 40
justification and, 135
law and, 117–19
operative, 55
righteousness and, 116
sin and, 116–17
Greeks, 51, 65

Habakkuk (prophet), 48, 53, 166
hate, 158
historical-metaphorical method, 24–27
Holy Spirit, 51, 61, 111, 125–27, 130, 132–33, 137
and apocalyptic hope, 142, 143
and flesh, 33, 144
and hope, 138
life in the, 131, 137, 208

transformation of sinners by, 34–37, 39
hope, 97, 98, 104, 133, 138, 141
homosexuality, 70–71
Hosea (prophet), 160

idolatry, 35, 69, 71, 78
Ignatius of Antioch, 206
imputation, 55
infusion, 55
Isaiah (prophet), 44, 59, 140, 153, 156, 159, 160, 161, 165, 166, 172
Israel. *See* Jews; "all Israel"

Jeremiah (prophet), 126, 140, 153, 159, 172
Jesus Christ
and end of law, 126, 162
and kingdom of God, 140–41
as Angel of the Lord, 156
as apocalyptic prophet, 141
as God, 155, 156
as Lord, 6, 25, 49–50, 163, 202, 207
as Messiah, 31, 46, 124, 125, 166
as Savior, 25, 91, 207
as Son of God, 6, 25, 46, 49, 125, 136, 207
death of, 97–98
See also cross
deity of, 155–56
faith in, 83, 84
life in, 28, 96, 109, 132–34, 135, 137, 139–40, 142, 208
love of. *See* God, love of
obedience of, 113
second Adam, 105–6
titles of, 6, 25, 46, 49–50, 155–56, 163, 202, 203, 207
Jewish Christians, 67, 127, 174, 176
in Jerusalem, 46–47
in Rome, 44
Jews, 73, 74, 77, 121, 122, 147, 176, 177, 178, 179
advantages of, 74, 75, 124, 155, 157
and Gentiles, 54, 65, 66, 147, 150, 163
God's plan for, 34, 152, 153, 160, 170, 171, 174
in Rome, 44–45

229

SUBJECT AND NAME INDEX

Jews *(cont.)*
  priority of, 53, 61, 157
  unbelief of, 149, 151, 152, 153, 154, 161, 170, 171, 173, 174
Judaizers, 32, 33, 83
judgment, 63, 72, 73–74, 75, 99, 136, 166, 176
Junia, 44, 52
justify, justification, 28, 53–59, 61, 83, 97, 98, 117–19, 123, 135, 136
  and sanctification, 98, 116, 118
  forensic interpretation of, 54–55, 98
Justin Martyr, 156n3

kingdom of God, 134, 140, 143, 145, 177, 187

law, 4, 34, 73, 87, 96, 106, 111, 114, 123–28, 194–95
  and Christ, 160
  and faith, 126
  and grace, 75, 117–19
  and love, 76, 128
  and sin, 61, 75–76, 112, 115, 119–23
  end of, 126, 154
  freedom from, 119
  God's, xi, 122, 137, 162, 189
  moral, 67, 73
  Mosaic, 4, 32, 36, 65, 73, 83, 115, 119
  of Christ, 86, 115
  purpose of, 160, 162–63
legalism, 33, 76, 111, 128
libertinism, 33, 111, 116, 126, 128
love. *See* God, love of
Lord, 163
  See also Jesus Christ, as Lord
Luther, Martin, 8, 12, 54, 55, 83, 128

Malachi (prophet), 158
marriage
  analogy of, 113, 119
McGrath, Alistair, 92
Messiah, 4, 5, 6, 46, 151, 153, 155, 157
midrash, 162
mind, 35
  renewal of, 36, 71, 189
monotheism, 69, 87, 140
Mosaic law. *See* law, Mosaic

mystery, 52–53, 136, 147, 168, 171, 175

natural revelation, 69
Nero, 183, 184

original blessing. *See* creation spirituality
original sin, 26, 27, 99–103, 105

paganism, 69
Pastoral Epistles, 10
Paul (apostle)
  and conversion of Jews, 19–20
  and Gentile converts, 32, 147, 148
  and law, 123–28
  and women, 52
  as apostle, 19
  as missionary, 7–8, 19–20, 170
  as Roman citizen, 18
  as theologian, 7, 8–9, 46, 134, 171, 187, 188–89
  conversion of, 5–7, 18–19
  gospel of, 45–46
  impact of, 7–9
  Jewish background of, 3, 32–33, 206
  letters of, 8–9, 10–11
  persecutor of Christians, 5, 18, 115
  portrait in Acts, 17–20
  upbringing of, 18
Paulinism, 29, 30
Pax Romana, 207
peace, 103
Pharaoh, 158, 159, 172
Pharisees, 3–4, 5
Phoebe, 46, 51, 67
Pliny, 206
pneuma, 132, 196
pneumatika, 196
prayer, 138
predestination, 4, 9, 134–36, 139, 155, 180, 181
predeterminism, 4, 155
pride. *See* boasting
prophecy, 197–98
propitiation, 85–86

reconciliation. *See* salvation
redemption, 85, 152, 180

SUBJECT AND NAME INDEX

relationships, 190
remnant, 160, 170, 171, 173, 174
revelation, natural, 69
revenge, 192
righteous, righteousness, 53–56, 61, 77, 78, 98, 127, 132, 134, 162, 164, 166
    punitive, 63, 68, 149, 165, 223
    restorative, 63, 68, 149, 165, 223
    See also God, righteousness of
Roman Catholicism
    view of justification, 54–56
Roman imperial theology, 207
Romans
    and anthropology, 65
    date of, 11
    importance of, 2, 11–12
    outline of, 15–16
    placement in New Testament, 11
    purpose of, 46–47
    scriptural quotations in, 153, 205
    ways to read, 27–28
        apologetic, 31–34, 66–67, 85
        historical, 30–31
        personal transformation, 34–37
        theological, 28–30
Rome
    and anti-Semitism, 148, 183

sacraments. *See* baptism; Eucharist
sacrifice, 109, 110, 190
Sadducees, 3, 4
saints, 50, 98
salvation, 24, 25, 28, 29, 34, 78, 91–92, 102, 104, 124, 134, 163, 195, 205
    and righteousness, 165
    by grace, 112
    cross and, 106–10
    of Israel, 177
    See also "all Israel"
sanctification, 29, 38, 98
    and justification, 98, 116, 118
Sanders, E. P., 141
Sanhedrin, 3
Satan, 52
scripture, 3–4
    inspiration of, 4

    interpreting, 24–27
        See also historical-metaphorical method
    literal reading of, 25, 26
    reading, 22–23
Septuagint, 48, 71, 173
sexuality, 70–71
Shema, 87
sin, 24, 25, 34, 79, 89–91, 92, 96, 116, 204
    and grace, 116–17
    and law, 119–23
    freedom from, 117
    power of, 62, 113, 118
    universality of, 28, 62, 65, 165–66
    See also original sin
slavery, analogy of, 113, 118
sociobiology, 101
soteriology, x, 4, 29
Spirit. *See* Holy Spirit
spiritual gifts. *See* gifts, spiritual
spiritual transformation, 34–37, 102, 104, 109, 130, 133, 138, 195
state. *See* government (civil authority)
stone (rock) of stumbling, 161
suffering, 104, 130, 138, 205
Suffering Servant, 45, 166
supersessionism, 175

taxation, 193
temple theology, 108
Tertius, 9, 52
Torah. *See* law, Mosaic
transformation. *See* spiritual transformation
Trinitarian, 50, 137
truth, 69
typology, 105

universal salvation, 151, 174, 181

Williams, Patricia, 100, 101
Wisdom of Solomon, 71
Witherington, Ben, 66
"world" (values of this age), 189–90

www.ingramcontent.com/pod-product-compliance
Lightning Source LLC
Chambersburg PA
CBHW051636230426
43669CB00013B/2330